ENDURING TRADITIONS

ENDURING TRADITIONS

THE NATIVE PEOPLES OF NEW ENGLAND

Edited by
Laurie Weinstein

Foreword by
RUSSELL PETERS

BERGIN & GARVEY
Westport, Connecticut · London

Library of Congress Cataloging-in-Publication Data

Enduring traditions : the native peoples of New England / edited by
  Laurie Weinstein ; foreword by Russell Peters.
       p. cm.
    Includes bibliographical references and index.
    ISBN 0–89789–349–2 (alk. paper). — ISBN 0–89789–350–6 (pbk :
  alk. paper)
       1. Indians of North America—New England.   I. Weinstein, Laurie
  Lee.
  E78.N5E47   1994
  974'.00497—dc20   93–40158

British Library Cataloguing in Publication Data is available.

Library of Congress Catalog Card Number: 93–40158
ISBN: 0–89789–349–2
       0–89789–350–6 (pbk.)
First published in 1994

Bergin & Garvey, 88 Post Road West, Westport, CT 06881
An imprint of Greenwood Publishing Group, Inc.

Printed in the United States of America

The paper used in this book complies with the
Permanent Paper Standard issued by the National
Information Standards Organization (Z39.48–1984).

P

A portion of the royalties from the sale of this book will go to the Narragansett
Church and the Institute for American Indian Studies.

In memory of John Menta,
whose scholarship, friendship, and enthusiasm helped to inspire this book

Contents

Foreword

Enduring Traditions: The Native Peoples of New England is a valuable contribution to the understanding of the New England tribes of Indians. As we enter an era when native peoples are beginning to research and write about their people, this book provides a compilation of native New England histories written by anthropologists, art historians, and native peoples.

The anthropologists who have contributed to this book have cut against the grain of the traditional writings. Early cultural histories contributed too much misinformation, which has cluttered our educational system. It is refreshing to see the emergence of native writers and younger anthropologists. These new scholars have been inspired by some of my heroes, such as historian Francis Jennings, who had the courage to buck the tide when he wrote *The Invasion of America* in 1975. When Jennings, an Anglo, questioned the traditional interpretation of American history, he raised a few eyebrows. He was way ahead of the authors who contributed to the debunking of the Columbus myth.

William Simmons and Jack Campisi are two other revisionist writers who have inspired this new scholarship. Bill Simmons's *The Spirit of the New England Tribes* is a delightful book that introduces New England native folklore to the public, Anglos and Indians alike. His work records those stories that native people knew and circulated among themselves for hundreds of years. Furthermore, the book helps to unify the New England tribes through the common expression and experience of myth.

Since ours is an oral tradition, on the verge of a transition to the written word, it is important that native peoples become involved in the translation of our history and folklore. The description of our history and culture must be accurately presented. Bill has encouraged us to unite with the common goal of adding to the knowledge of our tribal cultures and traditions.

My special friend is Jack Campisi, an anthropologist who worked for years with many native tribes and wrote *Mashpee Indians: Tribe on Trial*. As I read the book, tears came to my eyes because here is an Anglo (Italian) who grasped the very essence of the Mashpee psyche and was able to put that essence in writing. Although some might question his objectivity (because of his strong ties to Mashpee), Jack adhered to the strictest literary standards.

This book, *Enduring Traditions,* follows from these revisionist histories. I am pleased to see writings by native people included in this book. Trudie Lamb Richmond is one of a few native anthropologists who is often asked to give her views on New England tribes. She bears a great responsibility as both a native person and a scholar to present her views objectively but with an insider's interpretation. The Great Spirit knows that we have been studied enough to satisfy anyone's curiosity. It will be refreshing to have anthropological studies performed by our own people. Trudie serves as a great role model.

I am encouraged that the Columbus Quincentennial has created an atmosphere for a new look at the history of this country. I foresee more revisionist histories, which will include even more accurate accounts of the colonization and the settlement of this country. After all, the history of our region really started with the encounter between Anglos and the New England tribes. This book can be a part of this new era of scholarship when the history of the New England tribes will become a significant part of the history that is taught in our schools.

This is an exciting period, and *Enduring Traditions* will carry the torch for enlightenment.

—Russell Peters
President, Mashpee Tribal Council

Acknowledgments

I am indebted to many people and institutions for help with this book. First and foremost, I thank Western Connecticut State University and my colleagues for their support and encouragement. In particular I thank Philip Steinkrauss and Ruth Corbett for providing me with a generous grant with which to fund photographs, student labor, travel, and other expenses incurred in the writing of this book. My department chair, Jerry Bannister, and Cathie Reynaga were both encouraging throughout the duration of this enterprise, and they also kindly read portions of the manuscript. Emily Timmel, Nina Setaro, and Diana Rodriguez, students in the anthropology program at Western, assisted me with a lot of my last-minute editing, and they helped me organize the index.

I thank Jack Campisi for sharing his expertise with me on twentieth-century land claims. I wish to thank all the contributors too—Barrie Kavasch, Trudie Lamb Richmond, Russell Peters, Kevin McBride, Ken Feder, Paul Robinson, Ann McMullen, Joan Lester, Delinda Passas, and Anabela Marques—who worked with me to make sure that this book would be an important addition to New England Indian studies. I especially thank Barrie Kavasch, who was always encouraging and lent her ear to me whenever I needed some advice. She also helped put together the section on regional resources.

Finally, there are a few other individuals to whom I offer thanks. Lynn Flint, acquisitions editor for Bergin and Garvey, was patient, kind, and informative whenever I called, and she put a lot of faith in my work. Marie Pelletier, of the Graphics Department at Plimoth Plantation, went on assignment for me to either shoot or reproduce photographs of the Mashpee powwow, and exhibits at Plimoth Plantation. Her last-minute efforts were greatly appreciated. I am especially grateful to several very special people for their love and support: my parents, Helen and Sam Weinstein; Martha Farson; John Foristall; George Gorton; Jim Chichetto; Penny Kessler; and my long-time companion, Kroeber, who sprawled across all the manuscripts each day when I worked, and purred her approval.

Introduction

Laurie Weinstein

I remember as a child going to visit the natural history museums and seeing the Indian mannequins dressed in war bonnets, moccasins, and beaded jewelry. The exhibits seemed eerily quiet, and the mannequins had vacant stares. I wondered where the people were who once wore those costumes. I thought that they had vanished into the pages of history along with antique cars and dinosaurs. It was only much later that I learned that the native peoples were still here.

Regrettably, my memories are not unique. Many white Americans still believe that Indians have either vanished or are living in tepees on the Great Plains. The Indians in New England, they say, could not possibly be real; after all, many of them intermarried with blacks and Portuguese, and these mixed communities are scattered almost invisibly throughout the Northeast. Until recently, the New England Indians were largely overlooked by the pages of history. When they were mentioned, it was either in reference to some major conflict, such as King Philip's War or the French and Indian Wars, or it was in reference to the Pilgrims and the first Thanksgiving. Today, we tend to think of native New Englanders in terms of gambling casinos, land suits against white communities, and federal recognition battles. What our prejudices and gross misunderstandings belie, however, is that native communities have survived the centuries, and they have survived despite land loss, conflict, poverty, discrimination, and all-out war against them.

This book fills in some of the gaps in our knowledge about the native New England people. It tells their stories, and in many cases, in their own voices; several of the authors are native people. All contributors focus on the cultural patterns of New England: the special relationship to the land and its resources, native entrepreneurs and leaders who learned European ways and used them to their own advantage, indigenous communities created in response to European pressures, political strategies that empowered groups to press for land, recognition, and autonomy, and art as both an expression of cultural identities and a preserver of traditions and folklore.

NEW ENGLAND SOCIETIES ON THE EVE OF EUROPEAN CONQUEST

This book covers the native New Englanders who spoke dialects of the Eastern Algonquian language, which is part of a wider linguistic affiliation, the Algonquian language family (Goddard 1978:70). Population estimates for the New England groups, just prior to European contact in the sixteenth century, range from approximately 71,000 to 160,000 people (Bragdon 1990:93) for New England and southeastern New York. This population was not distributed evenly. The northern sections of New England from Maine to Newfoundland had a population density of from 12 to 29 people per 100 square kilometers, whereas the southern sections of New England, from New Hampshire south to Long Island Sound, had a population density of approximately 193 people per 100 square kilometers (Snow 1980:34; Bragdon 1990:93). This uneven population distribution was affected by climate and the ability of groups to practice horticulture. The climate was too severe north of the Saco River in Maine to practice horticulture reliably, so the northern groups were principally hunters, gatherers, and fishermen. Southern groups hunted, gathered, and fished too, and they practiced horticulture. The addition of horticulture afforded them a more constant food base, which allowed for a higher population than in northern New England. Southern New Englanders believed that corn, beans, and squashes were special gifts from the Creator Cautantowwit. He lived in the Southwest and gave the people the "first seeds to grow" (Simmons 1986:41). Prehistoric evidence seems to coincide with this sacred myth, for the earliest cultigens did, in fact, come from the South and West from ancient Mesoamerica (Galinat 1977, 1978; Flannery 1973:288; Ceci 1979). Thus far, the earliest archaeological evidence for corn in New England dates to A.D. 950 from the Selden Island site in Lyme, Connecticut (McBride 1993:personal communication).

Native peoples in both northern and southern New England had broad-spectrum (Flannery 1971:90) economies; that is, a variety of foods were tapped for use. Utilization of a wide range of plants and animals promoted survival in spite of the annual variation of some resources (Flannery 1971:90).

In northern New England, groups wintered in single or extended family bark-and-hide wigwams in order to hunt large game animals, such as moose, bear, and deer (Bragdon 1990:94–95; Kehoe 1992:237). They also fished through the ice. Extended family groups included the mother, father, and children, plus additional relatives, such as uncles, aunts, and grandparents, and adopted children. These extended families may have been organized around patrilocal residence patterns (living with the husband's father); however, this kind of living arrangement may have been influenced by the seventeenth-century European presence, since Europeans were patriarchal and projected this kind of arrangement on the Indians with whom they interacted in the seventeenth century (Kehoe 1992:239). Each spring, the families coalesced into larger settlements to exploit the seasonal abundances, such as the spawning fish of salmon, alewives, herring, and the like. Summertime was berry time; in addition, families gathered a variety of roots, nuts, seeds, and vegetable tubers. They also continued to fish: groups like the Micmacs and Eastern Abenakis with coastal locations exploited shellfish and sea mammals (Bragdon 1990:94–95). Winter travel was facilitated by snowshoes and toboggans, and in the warmer months, the birchbark canoe was used to navigate the many lakes and rivers of the North (Kehoe 1992:238).

The southern New England Indians were principally horticulturalists, but they also practiced hunting, gathering, and fishing. All of these supplemental activities were tuned to the demands of the horticultural cycle: during spring, after the danger of frost had passed, families began to plant their fields. Both men and women might clear and plant. Then men left their families for several days to fish at inland streams and lakes or to gather shellfish at the shore. After the harvest in fall, families moved inland to hunt in "warm winter valleys" (Williams 1973 [1643]:46) and to gather acorns and other nuts. Inland, they built larger bark and mat-lined wigwams to house the matrilocally extended families, which coalesced during the winter months.

New England economies were subsistence oriented, not surplus oriented. All important beliefs about the balance of nature and resource use kept their economies at a subsistence level. Resources were to be fully used and not wasted. When an animal or a plant was taken, an offering was given to the spirit of that resource or to the Creator. Early seventeenth-century colonists observed several "thanksgiving" rites. Plymouth colonist Edward Winslow (1974 [1624]:359) noted that when the Wampanoags "would obtain any great matter, meet together and cry unto him; and so likewise for plenty, victory, etc., sing, dance, feast, give thanks." Similarly, the Narragansett were seen to give the Creator beads, knives, and hatchets. All of these items were thrown into a fire to ascend to the Creator on clouds of smoke (Winslow 1974 [1634]:359).

Reciprocity was tied into the whole complex of both intratribal and intertribal relationships throughout the Northeast, and food was a key item in these relationships, as the founder of Providence, Roger Williams, remarked: "Whomsover commeth in when they are eating, they offer them to eat of that which they have, though but little enough prepar'd for themselves" (Williams 1973 [1643]:16).

Political leadership throughout New England was also based on reciprocity. A leader—called a sachem (the term *sagamore* is also used; however, it is used most often in reference to northern New England leaders)—governed by consent of the people. Individuals could choose to desert their sachem if he or she did not fulfill his or her duties or made unwise decisions. Sachems were expected to give away surplus food to people in need, and people gave their sachems a small portion of all the foods they harvested (Weinstein 1983:73–75).

In both the north and the south, the sachem or sagamore's leadership tended to be passed patrilineally, with the leader being a member of a privileged descent group. Some southern New England sachems were women, and many of them inherited their positions through male links. For example, squaw sachem Weetamoe of the Wampanoags was the daughter of another Wampanoag sachem, as well as the wife of first a Wampanoag and then a Narragansett sachem (Weinstein 1983:79; Speck 1928:99–100; Simmons 1978:193).

Leaders were supported by a cadre of advisers or councilmen and a medicine man, called a shaman or powwow. The powwow was both a religious and a medical practitioner who took care of the sick by using herbal concoctions and rituals, all of which were designed to supplicate the spirits and draw out the sickness. Illness could be the result of a people's failure to honor the spiritual world; perhaps a prayer was not given, or someone did not show proper humility toward nature. All thanksgiving ceremonies were led by the powwows, and leaders even called on powwows to advise them about the best times to go to war.

The material cultures of the native peoples went beyond utilitarian form and included the aesthetic, for in order to appeal to the spiritual world, tools and clothing were often beautifully embellished. A composite tool, like a harpoon, for instance, which might be made from a wooden shaft, deer sinew (used for hafting), and a bone or stone head, included the spiritual powers of all the raw materials: wood, deer, bone, and stone.

Northern New Englanders used birchbark, especially in the manufacture of canoes and storage and cooking containers. Birchbark was even used for clothing; directions and messages were occasionally etched on birchbark raincoats to help the Maliseets and Passamaquoddies find their way in the thick woods (Erickson 1978:128). Southern New Englanders used oak and chestnut for many utensils. They built their heavy canoes by digging out a log and manufactured a variety of ceramic cooking and storage vessels.

Both northern and southern groups excelled in weaving; they used native hemps, basswood, and ash to weave a variety of baskets for cooking and storage, mats for housing, and nets and lines for fishing. Both groups also made use of deer and moose hide for clothing and moccasins, and feathers and fur strips for decoration. Their clothing was practical; it was waterproof and warm for the hard winter months and cool for the summer. A lot of the clothing was converted from winter to summer use by simply detaching the sleeves or leggings. (See Bragdon 1990:94–100 for a brief discussion of material culture. See also McMullen and Handsman 1987 for an in-depth study of basketry and Lester 1987a for information on baskets, regalia, jewelry, and pottery.)

ORGANIZATION OF THIS BOOK

This book is divided into three parts. Each part has a brief introduction that provides background to the chapters that follow. Part I—Native Botanicals and Contact History—examines the foods of native New England and the effects of contact and trade upon the indigenous societies. Barrie Kavasch, a well-known author of books about native botanicals and recipes, provides the lead-in chapter, "Native Foods of the Northeast." Kavasch first discusses the various food and medicinal plants of New England, before highlighting how these botanicals were woven into the fabric of everyday life. She is both a trustee and a research associate at the Institute for American Indian Studies, Washington, Connecticut.

Kevin McBride, in Chapter 2, "The Source and Mother of the Fur Trade: Native-Dutch Relations in Eastern New Netherland," examines the archaeological and ethnohistorical evidence of the Dutch presence in New England. The Dutch introduced the other colonies to the lucrative wampum trade, and wampum became a key currency for the developing fur trade in New England. Dr. McBride is an archaeologist at the University of Connecticut in Storrs and the chief archaeologist for the Mashantucket Pequots.

Part II, Survival Through the Ages, examines the ingenious ways native peoples survived European and then American domination. Some groups founded small, autonomous communities; others chose native leaders as go-betweens between themselves and the white community. Ken Feder, an archaeologist at Central Connecticut State University, begins Part II with an examination of the small Lighthouse Village site, a way-station established by a white woman and her Narragansett husband during the mid-eighteenth century that served as a beacon on the Farmington River Turnpike, linking stagecoach travel from Farmington to Riverton. He is also author of several books on methods and theory in archaeology.

Chapter 4, by Paul Robinson, state archaeologist of Rhode Island, covers the Narragansetts of Rhode Island from the late prehistoric cultural time period up through modern developments within the tribe. He begins by illuminating the archaeological record, which indicates differing subsistence patterns between coastal and interior communities. Interior groups farmed corn, beans, and squash, while the coastal groups fished but did not farm until relatively late in their cultural history. Robinson goes on to examine European contact in the sixteenth and seventeenth centuries, the development of reservations and plantations in the late seventeenth through nineteenth centuries, and the tribal politics of the twentieth century, which enabled the Narragansett to win federal recognition and substantial land claims.

In Chapter 5, on the eighteenth-century Mohegan leader Samson Occom, I illuminate how a charismatic preacher attempted to use Christianity to save a number of indigenous New England societies. Occom was part of an eighteenth-century fundamentalist movement, the Great Awakening. Although this movement was a product of the European and American culture, he recognized the message of salvation as open to all people: Indian, white, and black.

Trudie Lamb Richmond, a Schaghticoke woman and assistant director of public programs at the Institute for American Indian Studies in Washington, Connecticut, discusses Schaghticoke history in Chapter 6, tempered by native insights about cultural survival. She refers to the "uphill struggle" to maintain "threads of continuity" on the small 400-acre reservation in northwestern Connecticut.

Part III concerns current issues facing New England tribes. The chapters examine pan-Indianism in the early twentieth century, federal recognition, and political survival, and art, for both symbolic expression and material profit. Chapter 7 is by Ann McMullen, a Ph.D. candidate in anthropology at Brown University and curator of North American ethnology at the Milwaukee Public Museum. McMullen writes about how the Indian Council of New England grew out of the early twentieth-century pan-Indianism (when Indian tribes from all over the country began to unite to press for political rights), which swept the United States. Her larger focus is to demonstrate how native identities survived through the ages, first by coversion (the "restricted use of identifying symbols to avoid recognition and appear like non-natives"), and then by efforts to make themselves more culturally visible and distinctive.

Next, art historian Joan Lester examines the phenomenon of art made for sale and how the artwork of native peoples ensures both cultural and economic survival. Lester is chief curator at the Boston Children's Museum and a lecturer in American studies at Tufts University. She specializes in New England Indian artwork.

The final chapter in this book, which I wrote with Delinda Passas and Anabela Marques, discusses featherworking in native New England. After examining the seventeenth-century documentary sources for the use of feathers as decorations for clothing, hair, and other items, we turn to the contemporary use of feathers and also stress the spiritual value of feathers in both the old and the new contexts. Passas and Marques collaborated with me in 1990–1991 when they were both seniors in the anthropology program at Western Connecticut State University.

REFERENCES

Bragdon, Kathleen. 1990. "The Northeast Culture Area." In *Native North Americans,* edited by Daniel Boxberger, 91–134. Dubuque, Iowa: Kendall/Hunt.

Ceci, Lynn. 1979. "Maize Cultivation in Coastal NY: Archaeological, Agronomical and Documentary Evidence." *North American Archaeologist* 1:45–74.

Erickson, Vincent. 1978. "Maliseet-Passamaquoddy." In *Northeast,* edited by Bruce Trigger, 123–136. Handbook of North American Indians, vol. 15. Washington, D.C.: Smithsonian.

Flannery, Kent. 1971. "Origins of Ecological Effects of Early Domestication in Iran and the Near East." In *Prehistoric Agriculture,* edited by Stuart Struever, 50–79. Garden City, N.Y.: Natural History Press.

———. 1973. "The Origins of Agriculture." In *Annual Review of Anthropology,* 2:271–310. Palo Alto, Calif.: Annual Review.

Galinat, Walton. 1977. "The Origin of Corn." In *Corn and Corn Improvement,* edited by G. F. Sprague, 1–47. Monograph No. 18. Madison, Wis.: American Society of Agronomy.

———. 1978. "The Inheritance of Some Traits Essential to Maize and Teosinte." In *Maize Breeding and Genetics,* edited by D. Walben, 93–111. New York: John Wiley and Sons.

Goddard, Ives. 1978. "Eastern Algonquian Languages." In *Northeast,* edited by Bruce Trigger, 70–77. Handbook of North American Indians, Vol. 15. Washington, D.C.: Smithsonian.

Kehoe, Alice. 1992. *North American Indians: A Comprehensive Account.* 2d ed. Englewood Cliffs, N.J.: Prentice-Hall.

Lester, Joan. 1987a. *We're Still Here: Art of Indian New England. The Children's Museum Collection.* Boston: Children's Museum.

———. 1987b. "We Didn't Make Fancy Baskets Until We Were Discovered: Fancy Basket Making in Maine." In *A Key into the Language of Woodsplint Baskets,* edited by Ann McMullen and Russell Handsman, 38–59. Washington, Conn.: American Indian Archaeological Institute.

McMullen, Ann, and Handsman, R., eds. 1987. *A Key into the Language of Woodsplint Baskets.* Washington, Conn.: American Indian Archaeological Institute.

Simmons, William. 1978. "Narragansett." In *Northeast,* edited by Bruce Trigger, 190–197. Handbook of North American Indians, Vol. 15. Washington, D.C.: Smithsonian.

———. 1986. *The Spirit of New England Tribes.* Hanover, N.H.: University Press of New England.

Snow, Dean. 1980. *The Archaeology of New England.* New York: Academic Press.

Speck, Frank. 1928. "Territorial Subdivisions and Boundaries of the Wampanoag,

Massachusett and Nauset Indians." *Indian Notes and Monographs*. Museum Series No. 49. New York: Museum of the American Indian, Heye Foundation.

Weinstein, Laurie. 1983. "Indian vs. Colonist: Competition for Land in 17th Century Plymouth Colony." Ph.D. dissertation, Southern Methodist University.

Williams, Roger. 1973 [1643]. *A Key Into the Language of America*, edited with a general introduction, notes and comments by John Teunissen and Evelyn Hinz. Detroit: Wayne State University Press.

Winslow, Edward. 1974 [1624]. "Good News from New England . . ." In *Chronicles of the Pilgrim Fathers of the Colony of Plymouth from 1602–1625*, edited by A. Young, 269–376. Baltimore: Genealogical Press Publications.

Part I

Native Botanicals and Contact History

The fifteenth and sixteenth centuries in New England are known as the contact period, for this was when foreign European visitors began to explore, trade, and then settle the new continent they proclaimed they had "discovered." Contact was initially sporadic. The Portuguese, Spanish, English, and French were looking for shorter trade routes to Asia in order to circumvent the laborious and costly overland routes. Instead of finding new routes, these Europeans discovered the rich fishing banks off Newfoundland. They were followed by more of their countrymen plus Bretons, Basques, and Normans, all of whom established fishing and whaling enterprises in northern New England (Fitzhugh 1988; Brasser 1978). The Dutch entered this new economic arena too with the voyages of Henry Hudson during the early seventeenth century.

All of these early voyages left indelible marks on native peoples: "By the time Gosnold visited the coast of Maine in 1602, natives were wearing large copper breastplates and European costumes including waistcoats, breeches, hose and shoes in sea-fashion style" (Fitzhugh 1988:101). Initial contacts were peaceful; however, misunderstandings quickly arose between the native and foreign peoples, and skirmishes followed.

European economic incentives changed during this age of exploration. The short water route to Asia was not found; however, the Europeans did find new items for trade and profit such as fish and whales, plus furs and wampum.

The fur trade was well under way in New England by the early seven-

Illustration by Karen Keohan. (Not shown: Penobscot in Maine, Nipmuck in Massachusetts, and Paugussett in Connecticut.)

teenth century. Furs were prized by Europeans because fur garments were warm, and "they proclaimed the wealth and status of their owners" (Jennings 1975:97). Beaver fur was especially desirable; the "woollen hairs" of the beaver pelt felted best for hats while the "guard" hairs were best for coats (Jennings 1975:100).

European nations vied for trading prerogatives with Indian nations just as Indian nations vied for trading prerogatives with European nations. The Dutch, who were initially quite aggressive in the trade for furs, discovered that they could make their trade even more lucrative by trading wampum for furs. Wampum, made from the columellas of whelk shells, was one medium of exchange among New England Indians long prior to European contact (Ceci 1990). Isaack de Rasiere introduced wampum to the Plymouth colonists, who, to the Dutchman's horror, quickly began to establish trading posts throughout New England and thereby usurped some of New Netherland's power (see Chapter 2).

The fur and wampum trades disrupted all aspects of native life, particularly in the North. The heightened competition between Indian and European groups affected traditional politics as relationships became based on which groups controlled access to furs and wampum. Further, the most successful sachems became those who could wheel and deal the best. The seasonal subsistence and settlement patterns of the natives were affected as more and more time was spent trapping furs and making wampum and less and less time was devoted to planting, hunting, gathering, and fishing. The competition also led to the near extinction of beaver. By the mid-seventeenth century, southern New England was "trapped out" (Salisbury 1982:56–84, for information about how trade affected native groups). Native material culture changed too with the addition of European trade items such as metal tools and utensils, alcohol, broadcloth, guns, and glass beads.

The Europeans received all-important items in exchange from their Indian neighbors: corn, beans, squash, and medicinal botanicals, which were critical to the survival of the nascent colonies. The native peoples also taught the Europeans the lay of the land: how to navigate the rivers and oceans, where to plant, where to hunt and fish, and how to survive the New England winters. So important were these indigenous "trade items" that the 1620 colony of New Plymouth would not have survived the first year without them, because the imported English grains did not withstand New England's harsh climate.

The era of exploration, trade, and settlement led to another unanticipated outcome: disease. Europeans introduced natives to a variety of germs to which native peoples had no adequate immune responses. Massive plagues swept over New England during the late sixteenth and early seventeenth centuries. Indigenous populations almost wholly disappeared in some areas from smallpox, diphtheria measles, pneumonia, dysentery, influenza, and tuberculosis (Calloway 1990:34–54; Salisbury 1982:105; Weinstein 1983:29–30). Native populations declined on the average by 90 to 100 percent.

This first chapter in this part, by Barrie Kavasch, examines the importance of native botanicals to the New England people. She discusses the scientific aspects of native botanicals and medicinals and how these plants were woven into the fabric of native societies in terms of reciprocity and the maintenance of political, familial, and spiritual ties.

Next, Kevin McBride illuminates Dutch exploration and trade in southern New England. He looks at the earliest Dutch voyages, how the Dutch competed with other European nations in the new economic arena of New England, and the effects of Dutch activities on indigenous populations.

REFERENCES

Brasser, T. J. 1978. "Early Indian European Contact." In *Northeast,* edited by Bruce Trigger. 78–88. Handbook of North American Indians, Vol. 15. Washington, D.C.: Smithsonian.

Calloway, Colin. 1990. *The Western Abenakis of Vermont, 1600–1800*. Norman: University of Oklahoma Press.

Ceci, Lynn. 1990. "Native Wampum as a Peripheral Resource in the 17th Century World System." In *Pequots in Southern New England,* edited by L. Hauptman and J. Wherry, 48–64. Norman: University of Oklahoma Press.

Fitzhugh, William, ed. 1985. *Cultures in Contact: The European Impact on Native Cultural Institutions in Eastern North America AD 1000–1800.* Washington, D.C.: Smithsonian.

Jennings, Frances. 1975. *The Invasion of America: Indians, Colonialism and the Cant of Conquest.* Chapel Hill: University of North Carolina Press.

Salisbury, Neal. 1982. *Manitou and Providence: Indians, Europeans, and the Making of New England, 1500–1643.* New York: Oxford University Press.

Weinstein, Laurie. 1983. "Indian vs. Colonist: Competition for Land in 17th Century Plymouth Colony." Ph.D. dissertation, Dept. of Anthropology, Southern Methodist University, Dallas.

———. 1986. " 'We're Still Living on Our Traditional Homeland': The Wampanoag Legacy in New England." In *Strategies for Survival,* edited by Frank Porder, 85–112. Westport, Conn.: Greenwood Press.

1

Native Foods of New England

Barrie Kavasch

Early native American foods illustrated a certain reciprocity with nature, in which indigenous people continually sought balance. Food has always woven the tenuous threads of life in every region. Food is key to survival, health and wellness, economic and political domination—indeed, balance and success. Looking at the seasonal, regional food ways of the tribal Northeast, we see food as the web of life interweaving native people—their festivals, ceremonies, rites of passage, healing rituals, with special, sacred foods, the ongoing food quest, and ever-changing diets. Patterns of hunting and gathering, fishing, and harvesting delineated early lifeways well before agriculture was embraced in the prehistoric Northeast more than a thousand years ago.

The native tribal Northeast ranged from lush woodlands and meadows, lakes and marshes, streams and bogs, coastal bay areas, to subalpine and alpine regions traveled by native Algonquian peoples, and their ancestors, whose archaeological evidence shows that this region now called New England has been peopled for more than 12,000 years.

We can reconstruct some deeper understanding of native dietary diversity through early food observations, historical anecdotes, and references to various tribes' eating practices, archaeological site evidence, food origination legends and regional folklore, hunting and fishing songs, plant-gathering prayers and rituals, and native place names that hold food affiliations. Yet this is still only a fragmentary picture.

Algonquian Indians in the Northeast had long explored the values of utilizing what was easily available in the wild and taught recurring waves of colonists, who depended upon this knowledge, even after more familiar European foods became available. Early settlers in the Northeast discovered not only new lands but various tribes and bands and confederacies of native peoples, along with new diets of diverse seasonally varied foods.[1] American Indian foods have proved to be one of their most enduring gifts.

BACKGROUND

Paleo-Indians foraged, fished, and hunted the rugged Northeast more than 12,000 years ago, and some created distinctive objects that remain to tell us about their culture. Archaeologists have excavated some of their ancient campsites and their hunting and butchering areas. These mammoth and big game hunters knew very different landscape environments; long, gradual changes in the land, and people's diets and lifeways were continual in the eastern woodlands.

The Archaic cultural time period began almost 8,000 years ago and lasted until about 500 B.C. in this region. Slowly warming temperatures and rising sea levels had reshaped the Northeast into its present form by about 3,000 years ago. Indian peoples hunted moose, elk (wapiti), caribou, black bear, and deer, along with many smaller mammals and birds, and from waters they took fish and shellfish. These Archaic hunters-foragers moved in small bands from seasonal camps along waterways teeming with life. They followed seasonal changes in plant and animal resources and traded with neighboring groups. This period is marked by the expanded use of plants, small animals, and shellfish. Middens (refuse heaps) and food storage pits from Archaic campsites contain ancient food remains of diverse shells, bones, and carbonized seeds, berries, and nuts. Some sites have yielded stone grinding tools, proving that Archaic Indian peoples processed their foods and stored extra quantities for lean times.

Elaborate burials speak of Archaic Indians' respect for ancient spiritual beliefs and human life after death. The Red Paint People, an eastern Archaic people who lived in what is now coastal northern New England and eastern Canada between 3000 B.C. and 500 B.C., were noted for their extensive use of ground red iron ore to cover their burial items. Scholars believe that this culture had sacred beliefs about uses for this native ore. (Red continues to be a sacred color to most American Indian people today.) Food remains at these sites indicate a seasonal coastal diet. The varieties of shellfish included the quahog clam *(Venus mercenaria)*, softshell clam *(Mya arenaria)*, razor clam *(Ensus directus)*, common oyster *(Ostrea virginica)*, bay scallop *(Pecten irradians)*, moonshell *(Polinices heros)*, boatshell *(Crepidula fornicata)*, periwinkle *(Littorina littorea)*, welks *(Busycon sp.)*, mussels *(Mytilus sp.)*, and lobster *(Homerus americanus)*. Shellfish must have been harvested often,

SEA HARVESTS

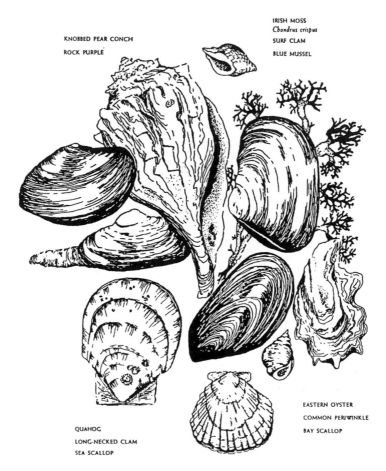

KNOBBED PEAR CONCH

ROCK PURPLE

IRISH MOSS
Chondrus crispus

SURF CLAM

BLUE MUSSEL

EASTERN OYSTER

COMMON PERIWINKLE

BAY SCALLOP

QUAHOG

LONG-NECKED CLAM

SEA SCALLOP

Coastal, bay, and inlet saltwater harvests enriched Algonquian Indian diets with minerals, iodine (especially), and vitamins not known in most terrestrial foods. Sea algae must have been eaten and used in foods and in prehistoric planting fields in similar ways to those documented during early contact and settlement periods. It is unlikely that any storm-tossed, shore-born commodities were overlooked or unexploited, from beached whales, dolphins, skates, and sharks, to the diversity of sea turtles, mollusks, and crustaceans. The only known use of salt in early native diets was through edible sea harvests. (Illustration by Barrie Kavasch. From *Native Harvests: Recipes and Botanicals of the American Indians*. New York: Random House, 1979.)

judging by the numerous and sizable shell middens along the coasts of New England. Obtainable almost all year, these were mineral-rich, predictable resources for prehistoric coastal peoples.

Seasonal migratory runs of fish up rivers and streams in these regions were also rich, dependable resources in prehistoric diets. Native fishermen sought sturgeon *(Acipenser sturio)*, shad *(Alosa sapidissima)*, trout *(Salvelinus* sp.), salmon *(Salmo salar* and sp.), alewives *(Promolobus pseudoharengus)*, yellow perch *(Perca flavescens)*, smelt *(Osmerus mordax)*, striped bass *(Morone saxatilis)*, pike *(Esox lucius)*, pickerel *(Esox americanus)*, bullhead *(Caleichthys felis)*, and eels *(Anguila rostrata)*. Marine fish exploited in early native diets included swordfish *(Xiphias gladius)*, mackerel *(Scomber scombrus)*, bluefish *(Pomatomus saltatrix)*, grouper *(Mycteroperca bonaci)*, haddock *(Melanogammus aeglefinnus)*, halibut *(Hippoglossus hippoglossus)*, and shark *(Carcharodon carcharais)*.

Indian populations steadily increased in the eastern woodlands during the late Archaic and Woodland periods, as native villages grew, centered in the best foraging, fishing, and hunting areas. An abundance of wild resources kept people moving across fertile regions to gather seasonal foods and process them for their expanding diets. Earliest farming began in the southern floodplains more than 1000 years ago with the horticulture of gourds and squashes *(Cucurbita* spp.), beans *(Phaseolus vulgaris)*, corn *(Zea mays)*, Chenopodium species, and sunflowers *(Helianthus annuas)*.[2] Food storage pits, often grass lined, that have been excavated in archaeological sites along the Connecticut River Valley, indicate seasonally rich prehistoric diets:

Wild plant foods provided an important source of nutrition for Connecticut Natives in both historic and prehistoric times. The fact that few of these plant foods have been identified in archaeological sites reflects, in part, the poor preservation of these materials in the acidic soils of New England. In recent years, with the application of rigorous techniques of water separation and flotation, more botanical remains have been extracted from archaeological sites in New England. (Bendremer: 1993:34–35)

Verifying the ethnohistoric records, site remains include black walnut *(Juglans nigra)*, butternut *(Juglans cinera)*, chestnut *(Castanea dentata)*, oak *(Quercus* sp.), chokecherry *(Prunus virginiana)*, American plum *(Prunus americana* and eighteen native species), blueberry *(Vaccinium* sp.), cranberry *(Oxycocus macrocarpus)*, strawberry *(Fragaria vesca americana)*, raspberry *(Rubus* sp.), and Solomon's seal *(Polygonatum* sp.). It is also likely that prehistoric native seasonal diets included groundnut *(Apios americana)*, jerusalem artichoke *(Helianthus tuberosa)*, hawthorns *(Crataegus* sp.—thirty-five native species), shadbush *(Amelanchier* sp.—fifteen native species), holly *(Ilex* sp.—fourteen native species), dogwood *(Cornus* sp.—fifteen native species), sumac *(Rhus* sp.—five native species), black currant *(Ribes americana)*, and red currant *(Ribes rubrum)*.

A large part of late Woodland Indian diets in the Northeast was the white-tailed deer *(Odocoileus virginianus)*, beaver *(Castor canadensis)*, and black bear *(Ursus americanus)*, based on numbers of bone fragments found in many archaeological sites. These were vital food resources in prehistoric times and into historic periods. Along with these, other species identified from sites include moose *(Alces american)*, porcupine *(Erethuzon dorsatum)*, bobcat *(Lynx rufus)*, woodchuck *(Marmota monax)*, skunk *(Mephitis mephitis)*, mink *(Mustela vison)*, raccoon *(Procyon lotor)*, muskrat *(Ondatra zibethica)*, gray squirrel *(Sciurus carolinensis)*, rabbit *(Syvilagus* sp.), red squirrel *(Tamiasciurrus hudsonicus)*, red fox *(Urocyon cinereoargenteus)*, gray fox *(Vulpes fulva)*, wolf *(Canis lupus)*, and Indian dog *(Canis familiaris)*. Also, harbor seal *(Erignathus barbatus)*, Canadian goose *(Branta canadensis)*, black duck *(Anas rubrides)*, and wild turkey *(Meleagris gallopavo)* bones occur in New England prehistoric sites. The Indian dog, now extinct, was the only known domesticated animal, along with the wild turkey, in this region. Subterranean food storage pits excavated at various prehistoric northeastern sites, which were bark or grass lined, indicate increasing awareness and ability to gather food surpluses and put them safely below ground for future needs more than 500 to 1000 years ago.

WILD PLANT FOODS

Indians used hundreds of different native fruits and berries to flavor, color, and cure foods, including wild strawberries, blueberries, cranberries, blackberries, huckleberries, elderberries, and raspberries, along with buffalo-, bear-, goose-, snow-, june-, juniper-, sumac-, spicebush-, catbriar-, viburnum-, sarsaparilla-, and Solomon seal berries, and many others. These were used extensively, either whole, mashed into pastes, pemmicans, butters, or dried like wild raisins. Sometimes they were added to seasonal harvests of mayapples, wild currants, grapes, crabapples, beach plums, wild plums and cherries, rose hips, and numerous other medicinal or high-energy food preparations.

Varieties of carbohydrate-rich nuts that grew throughout the Northeast included acorns, butternuts, black walnuts, beechnuts, chestnuts, hazelnuts, hickory nuts, and many more. By shelling, pounding, and mashing nuts, Indians created butters, creams, meal/flour, gruels, and oils, which were widely used foods and flavorings long before (and after) dairy products were introduced. By roasting or boiling certain nuts, additional foods, flavorings, salves, ointments, and vinegars were created. Tapping and sapping many of the deciduous hardwood trees and nut trees, along with and after the sugaring of maples each year, yielded numerous other flavorful syrups, sugars, and vinegars. Indians sweetened foods and medicines with maple,

Numerous wild plant foods were extensively exploited (all plant parts) for medicines, astringents, dentifrices, beverages, seasonings, fumigants, kinnikinniks, and special ceremonial needs. These five perennials represent a small sample of the abundant woodland native resources with noted uses in the tribal Northeast. (Illustration by Barrie Kavasch, 1986.)

walnut, birch, and corn syrups and sugars, assorted starchy, sweet wild tubers, and wild honey. Fermented soups and natural vinegars flavored many foods and helped to make them more digestible. Countless wilderness beverages and medicinal formulas were developed for early health needs and treatments and probably were used much as our preventative medicines and some health foods are used today. Sassafras, sarsaparilla, and birch beers evolved into classic root beers, tonics, medicinal teas, and "snake oil" medicines, as well as valuable medicinal formulas of earlier fame during the past five centuries. Before formalized medicine, countless individuals (Indian and non-Indian) sought and depended on the curative knowledge of American Indian medicine people. The bark, twigs, and berries of feverbush, spicebush, black alder, sweet fern, slippery elm, wild black cherry, black cherry, black birch, and wild coffee were brewed into strong teas to reduce fevers, swellings, and abscesses and to treat sore throats, coughs, and a constellation of other human ills. Some became early lozenges and cough drops.

Seasonings, condiments, and herbs were essential to help preserve and make foods more palatable. Some seasonings acted as catalysts for other flavors and modified each other and more-bitter foods and medicines. American Indians originated countless unique plant uses and cultivated many wild foods as managed wild resources. Selected freshwater and saltwater algaes, lichens, mosses, liverworts, horsetails, and ferns were notable preservatives and flavoring agents, as well as medicinal salves, and they were useful in diverse medicinal formulas. Regionally, Indians gathered and used cattail pollen; countless wild mushrooms; sweet fern; numerous wild mints; wild onions, garlic, leeks, and mustards; native gingerroot and ginseng root; ground inner tree bark; and selected leaves of many shrubs and trees to season their foods. Amaranth, pumpkin, squash, sunflower seeds, and wild rice were added as flavorings to special foods or roasted and eaten alone or in special mixes for their concentrated energy. Wild mushrooms were sought year round for foods and medicines, with diverse, unique applications in each category. Some tribes held these ephemeral earthy offerings in such high esteem that they were artistically rendered in striking ways. We continue to ponder their special applications.

Wild foods birthed native cultures in the Northeast and provided the economic framework of our expanding new nation. A mushrooming landed gentry largely displaced the various land-reliant cultures of Algonquian Indians, whose self-sufficiency had depended on seasonal, regional foods gained through close associations, respect, and understanding of their natural world. Individual native economies developed over broad territorial regions, which embraced villages, hunting camps (and in some tribes sugaring camps and agricultural fields), seasonal fishing and shellfishing locations, different hunting regions, and diverse environments for gathering important food and medicinal, ceremonial, and technological material. Foods and medicines were developed to fit tribal needs for sustenance, pleasure, social gatherings, and trade, as well as for ceremonial, ritual, and religious observances.

CYCLES

Centuries ago life was more fully integrated with nature, fueled by native animism, the belief that everything has a spirit and must be respected. Animism infused the food quest and the foods eaten or taken for medication with greater energy and meaning. Food ensured survival and was also a required offering through important cycles or renewal beliefs. Respect for life was the key to much of native thought and survival. Corn was the life sustainer to many horticultural tribes and deer and beaver to many eastern woodland tribes.

Plants of the Northeast have excited people's interests for centuries. Native sources of healing and general well-being developed through diverse environmental wisdoms. Native plants provided foods, medicines, beverages, seasonings, preservatives, dyes, poisons, fumigants, and symbolism, as well as substances for technological, magicoreligious, and ceremonial needs.

The native seasonal flow was punctuated with periodic celebrations of thanksgiving. Harvest ceremonies recognized the abundance of tree saps, syrups, and sugars. Certain harvesttimes were so influential in the annual Indian cycle of life that their closest moon was generally named for the honored food: the Maple Moon of late winter, the Strawberry Moon of late spring, the Green Corn Moon of midsummer, and the Wild Rice Moon and Sweet Grass Moon of autumn, followed by the Harvest and Hunter moons. Most Indian tribes were strikingly different from each other, and so to some extent were their foods, medicines, formulas, and ceremonies. Still, many common bonds existed. Much of traditional life was influenced by the lands they hunted, gathered, or gardened on. Mother Earth was—and is—sacred. Many tribal people found it impossible to leave or sell their original homelands, a fact European settlers found to be the antithesis of their thinking.

HORTICULTURE: THE THREE SISTERS AND BEYOND

Corn, first called maize, originally grew wild in Central America and was domesticated, archaeological evidence reveals, more than 7,000 years ago by prehistoric horticultural peoples in what is now highland Mexico. During the following millennia, corn planting, hybridization, and trading spread along pre-Columbian trade routes through much of the Americas, often accompanied by diverse varieties of beans, squashes, melons, gourds, pumpkins, and other members of the great Cucurbit family of vegetables. Corn was subsequently hybridized in every color and most varieties that we know today, long before European settlement began in the Americas. Major varieties of corn included pop, pod, flint, dent, and flour. Early explorers and settlers detailed vast fields of Indian corn, each field growing a different color of corn—yellow, red, blue, black, flesh colored, and speckled corn, each with its own special purpose, meaning, and unique properties. Certain colors had strong religious and ceremonial importance and could be eaten only on special occasions. Beyond this, all plant parts were known to have special uses in foods and medicines and for utilitarian and ceremonial appli-

WILD LETTUCE	WHITE FLOWER GOURD	INDIAN CORN	SQUASH
Lactuca canadensis	*Lagenaria leucantha*	*Zea mays*	*Cucurbita maxima*
	PUMPKIN		WILD ONION
	Cucurbita pepo		*Allium cernuum*

Numerous groups of cultivated and horticultured foods, along with seasonal wild harvests, enriched native diets. Algonquian Indians undoubtedly watched and managed various wild stands and econiches of wild alliums, ferns, milkweeds, marsh plants, and (especially) prodigious seed-bearing plants like knotweed *(Polygonuym erectum)*, goosefoot *(Chenopodium berlandieri)*, maygrass *(Phalarus caroliniana)*, curly dock *(Rumex crispus)*, wild cucumber *(Echinocystis lobata)*, star cucumber *(Sicyos angulatus)*, groundnut *(Apios americana)*, sunflowers *(Helianthus annus,* and spp.), and much more. The concepts of plant domestication must have emerged early from these regional relationships between family and village needs, and the wild resources surrounding them. (Illustration by Barrie Kavasch. From *Native Harvests: Recipes and Botanicals of the American Indians*. New York: Random House, 1979.)

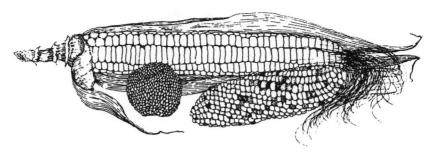

Illustration by Barrie Kavasch.

cations. Games, dolls, masks, and musical instruments were also created from various parts of the corn plants.

Gourds, squash, and pumpkins are believed to be the earliest plants cultivated by prehistoric peoples in the Western Hemisphere over 8,000 years ago. Earliest evidence for beans is about 4,000 years ago, originating in the highland Andes of what is now Ecuador, Peru, and Colombia, along with hundreds of varieties of potatoes, tomatoes, peppers (the great Nightshade family, which also includes tobacco and eggplant), and peanuts. Carried along prehistoric footpaths and trade routes, these early cultigens were being dispersed throughout the Americas thousands of years ago. Yet not all tribes would become farmers.

Numerous varieties of beans and squashes figured among the impressive native American Indian horticultural achievements. These complementary vegetables were often grown together in Indian fields, along with corn, and became the widely respected native triad known as the Three Sisters. These early crops were as perfect together in the field soil as they were in the meal. Countless variations of succotash, corn soups and chowders, breads, and baked, stuffed pumpkins and squashes were developed from colorful native food preparations. With experimental ingenuity, these sophisticated early cultures domesticated and hybridized hundreds of botanicals that we depend on today.

Enterprising settlers developed early businesses based on native plant economies. Corn, beans, squash, tobacco, cotton, witch hazel, ginseng, sassafras, wintergreen, wild rice, cranberries, blueberries, strawberries, and so much more flourished in these rich new lands—which were actually quite old and sacred in the human register of native oral traditions and use. From maple syrup, lobster, and shellfish, to turkey, catfish, salmon, trout, and crayfish, American Indian foods fed this growing nation and led the field in dietary diversity.

Displaced native tribes were continually being pushed away beyond the spreading European settlements. For the hunting and horticultural tribes in the East, this period of change was earth-shaking. The language and legalities of these periods reflect it.

Native Vegetables ❧

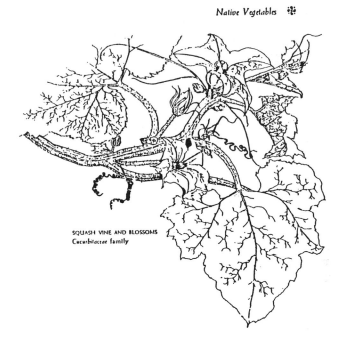

SQUASH VINE AND BLOSSOMS
Cucurbitaceae family

The increasing importance of and dependence on cultivated foods among Algonquian peoples in the Northeast affected their settlement patterns, political organizations, and trade relations long before the contact period. Colonization tipped this balance in every possible way, upsetting the sustenance patterns of foodways, hospitality, and reciprocity with nature. Most native systems could never recover balance. (Illustration by Barrie Kavasch. From *Native Harvests: Recipes and Botanicals of the American Indians.* New York: Random House, 1979.)

CONTACT PERIOD

The Eastern Algonquian Indians living in the Northeast at the time of early Puritan settlements in the 1630s had increased their populations and trade networks. Hunting, trapping, fishing, and wild foods provided rich, seasonally diverse diets augmented with significant horticulture, through direct trade and gardening. Tribal groups and bands in the Wabanaki Confederacy of Maine and the Canadian Maritimes included the Abenakis, Passamaquoddies, Penobscots, Maliseets, and Micmacs. Massachuset, Wampanoag, Natick, Nipmuc, and Pocumtuc tribal groups populated middle New England regions and what is now Massachusetts. The Pocumtuc Confederacy included the river tribes of the Tunxis, Podunks, Wangunks, and Sicaogs stretching down through the fertile Connecticut Valley, along with the Mattabesecs and Hammonassetts. The Wappinger Confederacy of western Connecticut regions included the Pootatucks, Paugussetts, Quinnipiacs, and Pomperaugs. The Pequots, Mohegans, and Niantics (Nehantics) populated the eastern Connecticut regions, along with the Narragansetts living in what would become the state of Rhode Island.

The turbulent centuries of contact brought cataclysmic changes to native settlements, economies, diets, and health—and, for many native Algonquians, annihilation. European diseases and killing epidemics combined with the recurring impact of warfare during early settlement periods caused catastrophic situations. The plague of 1616–1619 (the actual illness has never been sufficiently diagnosed), followed by outbreaks of smallpox by 1633 and continuing throughout the seventeenth into the eighteenth centuries, often reaching epidemic proportions, were crippling (Bendremer 1993:26). Yellow fever, scarlet fever, bubonic and pneumonic plague, and hepatitis, along with respiratory ailments of tuberculosis, whooping cough, pneumonia, and influenza, and recurring waves of nonrespiratory diseases of typhus, measles, and spotted fever decimated native Algonquian populations.

ETHNOBOTANY OF THE EASTERN WOODLAND INDIANS

American Indian sources of foods, beverages, healing, and technical needs have been largely developed through their diverse understandings of seasonal native plants. Indigenous plants provided foods, dentifrices, beverages, seasonings, preservatives, fumigants, dyes, poisons, medicines, insecticides, cordage, cosmetics, tools, and the substances for ceremonial, magicoreligious, symbolism, and technological needs. Ethnobotany,[3] the study of how a culture used or uses the floral environments, is scarcely 100 years old, yet herbalism, curing, and healing practices and foodways of the eastern woodland Indians span millennia. Plants of the regional Northeast have excited people's interests for almost five centuries of recorded history, and archaeological evidence shows a much more ancient record. The ancestors of today's Algonquian peoples managed rich wild resources. Early medicines, formulas, healing practices, and healing societies developed intertwined with native foods. It is important to look at the whole picture in order to understand key parts.

A considerable portion of American Indian botanical treatments evolved to treat the needs of women and children and to aid in childbirth. American Indians (principally women) devoted a great deal of attention to the necessities of what we now call gynecology, obstetrics, and pediatrics. Root, leaf, bark, and blossom extracts and decoctions and herbal infusions, with carefully worked-out formulas, enrich the herbal traditions of the eastern woodland Indians. Native medicines have demonstrated the treatments and virtues of countless botanicals, many of which have been included in various pharmacopoeias and formularies in the United States and abroad.

A pharmacopoeia is a list of drugs and their standard formulations. The first American pharmacopoeia was written in 1820, listing 217 drugs. The American Pharmaceutical Association began publication of the National Formulary in 1888, listing drugs that were considered effective but were not listed in, or had been dropped from, the United States Pharmacopeia. For countless centuries before formalized medicine, native American herbalism and holistic healing practices, like their native, natural counterparts around the world, treated various human diseases and disorders to the best of their indigenous understandings. Often this must have been accurate to possibly brilliant; their populations flourished and increased in many areas.

HEALING

Homeopathy, a school of medicine that has been practiced for nearly 200 years, seeks to cure by stimulating the body's own natural defenses against the illness or disorder. Homeopathic studies teach that the symptoms of a disease represent the body's efforts to cure itself. By administering very small doses of a select medicine (that if taken in large quantities by a healthy person can cause the same symptoms), the treatment reinforces the body's ability to overcome infections. It is similar to immunization, whereby a small dose of treated polio or measles virus given to a person produces immunity to the disease. Allopathic medicine seeks to treat disease by suppressing its symptoms or attempting to destroy the microbes associated in the condition.

One cannot fail to see interesting parallels between some current food and healing trends and those of recorded history in Eastern Algonquian Indian practices. Prior to formalized fields of research and study, native healers used similar pathways to healing—from most accounts. Herbalists, conjurers, curers, shamans, and powwows[4] (and rare individuals could fill all of these roles) sought tribal wisdom and training, often in healing societies. In many cases, native healers were considered so successful that colonial "doctors" during the late sixteenth to nineteenth centuries sometimes trained with native healers to learn the "secrets and simples"—uses of indigenous roots, barks, blossoms, berries, and herbs—to add to their own knowledge and esteem. They proudly called themselves "Indian Doctors" to reflect this noteworthy apprenticeship and enhance their range of practice. Generations of worthy doctors in the Northeast prospered in these early pursuits, both native and nonnative doctors on the threshold of modern medicine. Along with mainstream doctoring, there were colorful (and sometimes successful) snake oil medicine men, and every variation in between. Early nineteenth- and twentieth-century medications sometimes pictured an Indian on the label, to strengthen and authenticate the contents within. Other times, an illustration pictured an Indian woman indicating

THE

INDIAN DOCTOR'S
DISPENSATORY,

BEING

FATHER SMITH'S ADVICE

RESPECTING

DISEASES AND THEIR CURE;

CONSISTING OF PRESCRIPTIONS FOR

MANY COMPLAINTS:

AND A DESCRIPTION OF MEDICINES,

SIMPLE AND COMPOUND,

SHOWING THEIR VIRTUES AND HOW TO APPLY THEM.

DESIGNED FOR THE BENEFIT OF HIS CHILDREN, HIS FRIENDS AND THE
PUBLIC, BUT MORE ESPECIALLY THE CITIZENS OF THE WESTERN
PARTS OF THE UNITED STATES OF AMERICA.

BY PETER SMITH,
OF THE MIAMI COUNTRY.

Men seldom have wit enough to prize and take care of their
health until they lose it—And Doctors often know not how to get
their bread deservedly, until they have no teeth to chew it.

CINCINNATI:
PRINTED BY BROWNE AND LOOKER,
FOR THE AUTHOR.
1813.

The title page of Father Peter Smith's *Indian Doctor's Dispensatory of 1813,* although directed toward the "new" settlers of the West, was doubtlessly drawing heavily upon native healing plants of the Northeast. At this time, the greater portion of healing knowledge embraced botanicals native to regions in the East. This was one of the early self-treatment books founded, supposedly, upon American Indian medical secrets, which were popular in the nineteenth century, especially throughout New England.

the special healing plant(s) to her white companion, who looked on indulgently.

Native American Indian foods, especially certain cleansing, tonic, or restorative foods, were central to the healing pathway. This same wisdom is again being recognized, as today we realize the healing virtues of eating cranberries and drinking cranberry juice to treat liver and kidney complaints. To some extent, too, blueberries, especially the leaves as teas, and bearberry leaves and fruits are valued as foods, beverages, and medicines.

Ella Wilcox Sekatau, a Narragansett herbalist and medicine woman, remembers that during her youth, she and other Narragansett children would enjoy picking and chewing on or eating select needles of white pine, spruce, or fir trees on their walk to school in Rhode Island. Through the changing seasons, the tart-sour taste of the evergreen foliage (needles) was esteemed and recalled as being delicious (Sekatau, personal communication). Now we know that native coniferous foliage is mineral rich and very high in vitamin C content, especially when eaten raw, though the needles were also brewed as delicious, mineral-rich teas.

Penobscot winter foods are lovingly recalled by Stan and Sheri Neptune as they relate the virtues of cooked muskrat, especially choice after its late autumn feeding on sweet flag roots *(Acorus calamus)*, which made the meat taste so fragrant and sweet that muskrat stew was like a "delicious medicine" (Neptune and Neptune, personal communication).

Long before we labeled immune-deficiency disorders and looked at positive ways to strengthen the immune system, native northeastern Indians seemed to have grasped these principles and practiced them for longer than we could know.

Many wilderness beverages made from native plants, such as sumac *(Rhus glabra* and other species), spicebush *(Lindera benzoin),* joe-pye-weed *(Eupatorium purpureum),* goldenseal *(Hydrastis canadensis),* American ginger *(Asarum canadensis),* or Oswego tea (beebalm) *(Monarda didyma* and spp.) acted as preventative medicines and were enjoyed seasonally and specifically to help maintain good health. Algonquian Indian medicine people sought to understand and treat the broad range of native disorders, from headaches, toothaches, arthritis, and rheumatism, to wounds and diseases. Cadwallader Colden wrote to Peter Kalm in 1751 that the children of European immigrants commonly lost their teeth from scurvy, although the native Indians did not: "I have heard that the Indians use the roots of one kind of Nymphaea as a preventative." There are native species with several varieties that are widespread. The roots of the native fragrant water lily *(Nymphea odorata)* were a highly esteemed and abundant wild vegetable enjoyed year round by Algonquian peoples.

SACRED PLANTS

Native spiritual beliefs embraced the giving of special (often sacred) substances along with prayers in exchange for taking something of life-giving consequence, such as hunting game for food, harvesting food or medicine plants, or preparing planting fields to hold annual roots and seeds. When

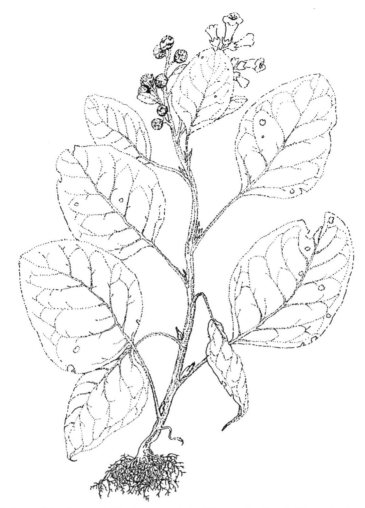

Native wild tobacco *(Nicotiana rustica)*. (Drawn by Barrie Kavasch from a 100-year-old specimen collected in the wild. In the collections of the Yale Peabody Herbarium, New Haven, CT.)

carried out in the proper manner, the results would give greater benefit. This was an essential aspect of native balance: the harmony among living things. The most sacred offering substances in tribal New England were tobacco *(Nicotiana rustica)*, sweet grass *(Hierochloe odorata)*, sweet vernal grass *(Anthoxanthum odoratum)*, bearberry "Kinnikinnik" *(Arctostaphylos uva ursi)*, and red cedar *(Juniperus communis)*, along with corn and cattail pollen and the ripe spores of various *Lycopodium* species. Sometimes a pinch of tobacco or kinnikinnik was offered to each of the cardinal directions, in prayer, or offered directly into the water or ground or wind, depending

Sweet Grass Braid
Northern Iroquois

(shiny green with
red stems)

Torresia odorate
now Hierochloe

Illustration by Barrie Kavasch, 1979.

upon intent and necessity, and occasionally burned, or smudged so that the rising smoke would carry the prayers up to the Creator. Honoring these ancient traditions adds energy and reverence to native foodways and healing practices. Certainly native foods continue to be enhanced by these enduring traditions.

MYCOLOGY

Fungi evolved during the Silurian period, more than 20 million years ago. They are one of the largest groups of organisms known to humanity and more widespread than green plants. As a group, fungi lack chlorophyll and therefore must obtain nourishment from other organisms—dead or alive. Once they were considered part of the plant kingdom; however, today they are recognized as the fungi kingdom.

The discipline dealing with the study of fungi is mycology, which developed as a science during the last half of the nineteenth century. Research has brought it into many areas of the food and pharmaceutical industries and phytopathology, the study of plant diseases. Ethnomycology is the study of a people's uses for their endemic fungi.

The part of the fungus we see, called a mushroom, is actually the fruiting part of a much larger, concealed body. This hidden mass is called the mycelium, with threadlike strands forming a network in the substrate. The mushroom is the reproductive organ of this system and contains the spores. Its growth is controlled by specific ecological requirements, such as temperature, moisture, and availability of plant material.

Mycologists generally include all fleshy fungi in the category mushroom—even such diverse fungi as puffballs, spongy boletes, brainlike morels, rubbery jellies, and the corals. Many mushrooms spring up overnight, especially after heavy dew or rainstorms; others take a season to grow. Theses evanescent organisms are strange, unearthly things to some people.

Mushrooms in Early History

Mushrooms are mentioned as food in the Talmud and in Chaldean writings that date from the dawn of civilization. The earliest literate concepts of plant diseases are recorded in ancient Vedas, 1200 B.C. More than twenty centuries ago, the eating of mushrooms "became a mania among the rich in Rome." It is recorded that the early Greeks delighted in eating wild mushrooms, although some poisonous ones were notoriously used, suspected in political assassinations. (Both an emperor and a pope supposedly succumbed to mushroom poisoning.) Throughout European history, the black arts of poisoning often involved the mushrooms (toadstools); they had heavy association with witchcraft during medieval times. The Dark Ages were noted for the use of numerous poisonous plants and mushrooms, and widespread mycophobia—a fear of eating mushrooms—developed in Europe. Anglo-Saxons had a fear of mushrooms, and from this background came the persecuted pilgrims to America.

The early British arrivals in the colonies feared nearly all mushrooms, derisively calling them toadstools, a term originating from the archaic belief that toads were poisonous and that mushroom caps were likely resting places for toads. Early settlers in the Virginia, Connecticut, and Massachusetts colonies came principally from Great Britain. The only mushroom they recorded using was the cultivated white agaric (since the sixteenth century), which was sometimes grown on spawn in colonial gardens.

Germanic peoples who settled regions of Pennsylvania, New York, and New Jersey had family traditions of eating and using wild mushrooms. Modern mycologists believe that these interests were perhaps shared and compatible with early American Indian mushroom uses, and some early ethnomycology was exchanged. Certainly during starving times and seasonal mushroom flushes, it is believed, abundances of wild mushrooms were important staple foods in colonial America.

The veritable year-round wealth of diverse wild mushrooms in what is now New England was not lost on the indigenous people, although sparse accounts show up in archaeological evidence. Wild mushrooms were not, however, ignored by native peoples in the Northeast.

John Josselyn, writing in "New England Rarities" in 1638, details cautery and moxa treatments among the Indians of the Southeast, using a dried, powdered *Polyporus* (possibly the birch polypore, *Piptoporus betulinus,* which has recorded historic use as an anaesthetic and as an igniting aid (to keep fires burning). It is edible when very young and is found growing on living or dead birch trees) species, which they referred to as "spunk" (the probable origin of our term *punk*): "an excrescence growing out of black birch," which was one of the "touchwoods" (a sacred wood) of the Indians. "They help the sciatica, or gout of the hip, or any great ache, burning the patient with it in two or three places upon the thigh and upon certain veins." A similar treatment was reported from regions of North Carolina.

Ethnomycology

F. W. Waugh, living with the Iroquois in 1916, noted that "a number of kinds of fungi are used by the Iroquois, and were probably employed even more extensively in former times." One of their most highly esteemed foods was the *Agaricus campestris,* which the Mohawk called *E'skan agohu da* ("ghost ears"). This common meadow mushroom was a favorite food in most of the environments where it was found growing. Arthur C. Parker, a noted Iroquois/Seneca anthropologist, remembered that his people ranked the pleasure of eating wild mushrooms almost equal to that of eating meat. Gladys Tantaquidgeon, a Connecticut Mohegan elder, records that Delaware and other eastern Algonquian peoples enjoyed this species, which they called "tripe form," and fried the mushrooms in hot fat or salted and boiled them in soups.

The little garlic mushroom *(Marasmius scorodonius),* which springs up quickly after summer rains, was collected and threaded on clean twigs to be dried as flavoring for foods.

Both the Iroquois and Algonquian Indians were known to enjoy eating morels *(Morchella esculenta)* and related species. Corn smut *(Ustilago maydis)* was a choice food of the eastern horticultural tribes. They called these corn "sores" or "blisters," and they were gathered as soon as they appeared, while firm and white, to eat, and when ripe and black to use in medicines.

A broad array of the polypores were perennially sought as foods by numerous tribes. The young, tender *Coriolus versicolor*—turkey tails or "tree ears"—were usually boiled. The natives never collected this species from ash trees because the fungi were considered too bitter to eat. The Algonquian and Iroquois people ate the hen of the woods *(Polyporous frondosus,* now *Grifola frondosa),* the umbrella polypore *(Polyporus umbellatas),* and chicken of the woods *(Laetiporus sulphureus),* which were choice and abundant and were most commonly boiled in soups. These edible fungi were said to taste different depending upon their tree hosts and were named according to the trees they were found growing upon. Indeed, the sulphur shelf (chicken of the woods) *(Laetiporus sulphureus)* was widely appreciated all across North America. It is still considered to be one of the tastiest of all woodland mush-

+=useful   *=Poisonous   o=edible

o 1. White Coral, *Ramariopsis Kunzei*

* 2. Ravenel's Stinkhorn, *Phallus ravenelii*

* 3. Stinky Squid, *Pseudocolus schellenbergiae*

4. Velvety Earth Tongues, *Trichoglossum hirsutum*

5. Moose Antlers, *Wynnea americana*

o 6. Zeller's Bolete, *Boletus zelleri*

o 7. Black Morel, *Morchella elata*

o 8. Black Trumpet, *Craterellus fallax*

* 9. Saddle-shaped False Morel, *Gyromitra influla*

10. Brown-Honey White Cup, *Humaria hemisphaerica*

o 11. Tree Ears, *Auricularia auricula*

12. Splash Cup, *Cyathus striatus*

13. Netted Rhodotus, *Rhodotus palmatus*

14. Coral Slime, *Ceratiomyxa fruticulosa*

o 15. Jelly Leaf, *Tremella foliacea*

o 16. Veiled Oyster, *Pleurotus dryinus*

o 17. Oyster Mushroom, *Pleurotus ostreatus*

o 18. Angel's Wings, *Pleurocybella porrigens*

o 19. Northern Tooth, *Climacodon septentrionale*

o 20. Bearded Tooth, *Hericium erinaceus*

o 21. Birch Polypore, *Piptoporus betulinus*

+ 22. Artist's Conk, *Ganoderma applanatum*

+ 23. Tinder Hoof Polypore, *Fomes fomentarius*

Not necessarily drawn to scale, but designed to illustrate diversity of woodland fungi usually found on or in association with hardwoods or mixed forest woods.

Illustration by Barrie Kavash, 1985.

rooms and usually is found growing in quantities on various different hardwoods, to be harvested from living trees or dead stumps in late summer and fall. This sometimes-vivid sulphur shelf was known to reappear in the same locations, always on wood, and up to fifty pounds could be collected in each location. The solid white to pale orange flesh of these brackets was likened to the tasty meat of choice fowl. The firm, white-meated young puffballs were collected and roasted, fried, smoked, boiled, or pickled— depending on native needs.

The *Lycoperdon* species and the common giant puffball *(Calvatia gigantea)* were sometimes regarded with apprehension as "ghost's make-up," "corpse," "ground ghosts," or "frog's navel." The Iroquois noted similar concerns yet collected and ate young puffballs, and their dusty puffball spores were saved to use as styptics, especially to treat nosebleeds, surface scratches, wounds, and abscesses. The Onondaga called them "smoking fungus," and the Mohawk referred to them as "devil's bread" and "devil's snuffbox." It is not surprising that these species of puffballs were so acclaimed. They do literally pop up overnight, and sometimes they can be enormous by midday. The word *Puhpohwee* is an old Algonquian (Ojibway) term meaning "to swell up in stature suddenly silently from an unseen source of power."

The honey mushrooms *(Armillariella mellea* and *A. ponderosa)* were eaten boiled or fried by the eastern woodland Indians. These gilled mushrooms, often growing densely, are fairly widespread throughout some hardwood forests and are associated with the shoestring rot disease, which afflicts oaks and maples. The mycelium of the honey mushroom is usually luminescent, causing a night-glowing phenomenon known as foxfire. This characteristic was both used to advantage and feared by various people, who believed it to be associated with witchcraft or visitors from the spirit world.

Many varieties of fungi are well camouflaged. Often the tastiest species are dark and unobtrusive and must be carefully searched out in their habitats, in just the right seasons, such as the morels, jelly mushrooms, and chanterelles. Many other fungi readily draw attention by their stunning colors, growth formations, sizes, and sudden appearance. Certain fungi have quite attractive odors and are mild tasting.

Remarkable varieties of tastes, textures, and fragrances in the fleshy fungi have long tantalized hungry people, and appreciation for these factors seems long-standing on the North American continent. The deep, rich, red beefsteak mushroom *(Fistulina hepatica)* is remarkable for its distinctive look of raw beefsteak, and the exact taste and flavor almost duplicates that of beef. The sulphur shelf mushroom *(Laetiporus sulphureus)* is remarkably close to the taste and texture of white breast meat of chicken. The oyster mushroom *(Pleurotus ostreatus)* is the woodland counterpart to fresh or smoked oysters. The dye polypore *(Polyporus schweinitzii)* is incredibly close to the taste of venison or beef liver when young. Highly perfumed fresh specimens of the bear mushroom *(Lentinellus ursinus)* exude the aroma of fresh fruit. Creamy white rippled layers of the northern tooth *(Climacodon septentrionale)* give off the odor of ham (when drying). Anise mushroom *(Clitocybe odora)* smells strongly of anise. Certain *Inocybe* and *Russula* species give off a fishy smell, while the lobster mushroom, *(Russula xerampelina)* possesses the aroma of lobster, and almond-scented russula *(R. laurocerasi)* usually smells very sweet. The bread dough entoloma *(Entoloma abortivum)* and sweet-bread mushroom *(Clitopilus prunulus)* come very close to the aroma of fresh yeast dough and cucumber, respectively. It would seem unlikely that early Algonquian people overlooked these freely available resources.

Fungi are unique and powerful in all their various forms: mushrooms, molds, blights, smuts, and rusts. They can feed and cure us, as well as in-duce visions and kill us. They contribute enormously to modern medicines. Those that are safe to eat make a fascinating, delectable group and have long been sought for their many flavors and textures. They dry easily, and many wild ones have more robust flavors after drying and aging. They are fine additions to year-round meals, and some species can provide a satisfying meal alone. Mushrooms are usually rich in folic acid and trace minerals and are particularly good sources of nitrogen and B vitamins.

The knowledge of mycophagy prior to written history is speculative. Contemporary estimates suggest there may be 200,000 species of fungi worldwide. There are a growing number of researchers who are giving spe-cial attention to the potential that fungi possess for making significant con-tributions to the world's food supply. Their findings, based upon the di-verse ethnomycology of the American Indians, might enable us to take the usage of our ambient fungi into the broadest realms of human ingenuity.

CONCLUSIONS

It is clear that Algonquian Indian foodways were (and continue to be) highly evolved and continually changing. The seasonal diversities of food resources in the Northeast, even in periods of drought, disease, and natural and humanmade disasters, supported growing populations, who learned in-tricate food concepts and have endowed American foods today with some of its richest culinary treasures. From scallops, oysters, and lobsters, wild duck, venison, and rabbit, to maple sugar, wild cherries, cranberries, blue-berries, strawberries, and mushrooms, native food economies birthed recur-ring waves of New England foods and successful businesses.

The impact of introduced plants and foods on native Algonquian Indian people and their ways of life continues to reverberate across the land. The fertile floodplains of the famous Tobacco Valley, stretching through central Connecticut and up through central Massachusetts, are growing more strawberries and pumpkins and native Christmas trees, as well as houses and communities, than its once-golden shade tobacco and prehistoric corn and cultigens, and wild foods. As we watch the changes, we need to hold on to our land-based foodways and examine wiser agricultural alternatives for the future. By examining the past, we may realize new implications and food possibilities for our contemporary society.

ACKNOWLEDGMENTS

It is THE PEOPLE who, through their many gifts, have made this work possible, and along with the folks noted within the text, I especially thank: Chink Sands, Helen A. Attaquin, Joan A. Tavares, Earl Mills, Sr., Slow Turtle, Nanepashamet, Gladys Widdiss, Eleanor and Paula Dove, Red Thunder Cloud, Barry Dana, Jane and Melissa Fawcett, Tsonakwa, Dale Carson, Ron and Cheryl Welburn, Mitzi and Jean Rawls, Marguerite Smith, Roddy and Josephine Smith, Jeff and Judy Kalin, Mikke Aganstata and Sherman Paul, and many others. . . . I honor the memory of Irene Richmond, Sara Ransom, Tom Ransom, Claude Medford, Barry Miles, Harold Tantaquidgeon, as well as Courtland Fowler, Clara Addison, and Richard Chrisjohn.

NOTES

1. Where necessary, I have used the taxonomy (binomials) within the text once, in order to note the exact animal, mushroom, or plant.

Binomial nomenclature is the system of classifying plants, animals, and mushrooms by a double name, usually of Latin or Greek origin, the first being the genus, the second that of the species within the genus.

In some cases, especially in the fields of botany and mushrooms, there have been (and continue to be) considerable changes in scholarly understandings of precise classifications of species. I have watched the binomials for some genus and species change three times since first recorded in ethnographic sources. Added to this, regional colloquial names of species, even within New England, are variable. For instance, the English, Dutch, French, and Portuguese settlers each had their own terms and concepts for a particular plant, like elderberry or mountain ash, based on native European species they knew and used. There were many parallels and similarities in use concepts, yet often native Algonquian Indians knew and used their own native species of these two examples in remarkably different ways. The ripe berries of American mountain ash *(Sorbus americana)* were generally eaten, especially to treat scurvy and worms, and the tender inner bark and buds were steamed and eaten as a cold remedy; the Maliseet boiled the inner bark for infusions to treat boils and other skin eruptions, among many other uses. The spring blossoms and late-summer ripe berries of one of our common elderberries *(Sambucus canadensis)* were esteemed by many Algonquian people for beverages and foods and to treat various disorders. The Micmac and Maliseet used the boiled bark (known to be toxic) to treat toothaches and as a purgative and emetic.

2. "Long before the introduction of maize, farming economies and an agrarian way of life had been established in eastern North America" (Selig 1993:1). American Indian women and men in the prehistoric northeast collected seeds from areas of "managed" wild resources, unique echoniches where certain cereal plants and wild vegetables were concentrated, and domesticated some of these plants between 3000 and 2000 B.C., according to various scholars working in this field. Although not all American Indian groups would become farmers, evidence shows that some of these

early horticulturists domesticated sunflowers, marshelders, chenopods, and wild gourds, *Cucurbita pepo*. The latter was developed into different varieties of edible squashes. In reality, we must see the northeast as one of the world's four major, independent centers of plant domestication, along with Meso America, China, and the Middle East.

3. The term *ethnobotany* was first used in 1891 by Professor John Harshburger to denote a special branch of anthropology.

4. Powwow (also Pawwoh, Pauwau, with numerous Algonquian variations), is one of the earliest documented and most enduring words, given to mean "conjurer," "medicine man," "sorcerer," "someone who devines the future" or "ceremonialist" by European interpretations. Powwow generally referred to a spiritual leader, healer, and counsellor who served to maintain balance and integrity in Algonquian societies. Years of training and special abilities enhanced the powers of select individuals, who often walked the medicine pathways of herbalism and healing. Powwow also designates special gathering places: rivers, ponds, hills, immense boulders, and clearings throughout New England where native people gathered since earliest times to celebrate important periods in their ceremonial year, establish strong alliances, palaver, and hold healing rituals.

REFERENCES

Bendremer, Jeffrey. 1993. "Late Woodland Settlement and Subsistence in Eastern Connecticut." Ph.D. dissertation, University of Connecticut.

Brothwell, Don, and Patricia Brothwell. 1969. *Food in Antiquity: A Survey of the Diets of the Early Peoples*. New York: Frederick A. Praeger Publisher.

Burk, William R. 1983. "Puffball Usages among North American Indians." *Journal of Ethnobiology* 3, no. 1:55–62.

Butler, Eva. 1948. "Algonquian Culture and the Use of Maize." *Bulletin of the Archaeological Society of Connecticut* 22:4–39.

Cassedy, Daniel, T. Webb, and H. Willis. 1993. "New Data on Maize Horticulture and Subsistence in Southwestern Connecticut." Paper presented at the Northeastern Anthropological Association, Western Connecticut State University, Danbury.

Cronon, William. 1983. *Changes in the Land: Indians, Colonists, and the Ecology of New England*. New York: Hill & Wang.

Deboer, Warren R. 1988. "Subterranean Storage and the Organization of Surplus: The View from Eastern North America." *Southwestern Archaeology* 7, no. 1:1–20.

DeForest, John III. 1851. *History of the Indians of Connecticut from the Earliest Known Times to the 1850's*. Hartford: W. J. Hammersley.

Gookin, Daniel. 1674, 1792, 1806. *Historical Collections of the Indians of New England*. Collections of the Massachusetts Historical Society, Boston.

Handsman, Russell G. "The Fort Hill Project—Native Americans in Western Connecticut and an Archaeology of Living Traditions." Research manuscript series of the American Indian Archaeological Institute.

———. 1990. "The Weantinock Indian Homeland Was Not a 'Desert.' " *Artifacts* 18, no. 2:3–7.

Handsman, Russell G., and Jeffrey H. Maymon. 1987. "The Weantinoge Site and an Archaeology of Ten Centuries of Native History." *Artifacts* 18, no. 2:3–7.

Huden, John C. 1962. *Indian Place Names of New England*. Vol. 18. New York: Museum of the American Indian–Heye Foundation.

Josselyn, John. 1988 [1674]. *John Josselyn, Colonial Traveler: A Critical Edition of an Account of Two Voyages to New England Made during the Years of 1638 and 1663,* edited by Paul J. Lindholdt. Hanover, N.H.: University Press of New England.

———. 1985. "Puphowee: The Mushrooms of the American Indians." New York Botanical Garden *Gardens* 9, no. 5:14–23.

Kavasch, E., and Barrie J. Kavasch. 1979. *Native Harvests: Recipes and Botanicals of the American Indians.* New York: Random House.

Keewaydinoquay. 1978. *Puhpohwee: For the People: A Narrative Account of Some Uses of Fungi among the Ahnishinaubeg.* Cambridge: Botanical Museum of Harvard.

Lincoff, Gary H. 1981. *The Audubon Society Field Guide to North American Mushrooms.* New York: Chanticleer Press.

McBride, Kevin A. 1990. "The Historical Archaeology of the Mashantucket Pequots, 1637–1900: A Preliminary Analysis." In *Pequots in Southern New England,* edited by Laurence M. Hauptman and James D. Werry. Norman: University of Oklahoma Press.

Maine Indian Program of N.E.R.O. of the American Friends Committee Service. 1989. *The Wabanakis of Maine and the Maritimes: A Resource Book about Penobscot, Passamaquoddy, Maliseet, Micmac, and Abenaki Indians.* Bath, Maine: Author.

Moeller, Roger W. 1980. *A Paleo-Indian Site in Western Connecticut.* The American Indian Archaeological Institute Occasional Papers 2. Washington, Conn.: American Indian Archaeological Institute.

Russell, Howard S. 1980. *Indian New England before the Mayflower.* Hanover, N.H. University Press of New England.

Salsbury, Neal. 1982. *Manitou and Providence: Indians, Europeans, and the Making of New England 1500–1643.* New York: Oxford University Press.

Selig, Ruth. 1993. "A Quiet Revolution: Origins of Agriculture in Eastern North America." *Anthro Notes—National Museum of Natural History Bulletin for Teachers* 14, no. 2:1–15.

Smith, Bruce. 1992. "Prehistoric Plant Husbandry in Eastern North America." In *The Origins of Agriculture: An International Perspective,* edited by C. Wesley Cowan and Patty Jo Watson. Washington, D.C.: Smithsonian Institution Press.

———. 1993. *Rivers of Change: Essays on Early Agriculture in Eastern North America.* Washington, D.C.: Smithsonian Institution Press.

Tantaquidgeon, Gladys. 1977. *Folk Medicine of the Delaware and Related Algonquian Indians.* Historical and Museum Commission, Anthropology Series No. 3. Harrisburg, Pa.

Trumbull, James Hammond. 1881, 1974. *Indian Names in Connecticut.* Facsimile ed. Hartford: Archon Books.

Vogel, Virgil J. 1970. *American Indian Medicine.* Norman: University of Oklahoma Press.

Warner, Frederic W. 1972. "The Foods of the Connecticut Indians." *Bulletin of Archaeological Society of Connecticut,* no. 37:27–47.

Waugh, F. W. 1916. *Iroquois Foods and Food Preparations*. Ottawa: Government Printing Bureau, National Museum of Canada.

Willoughby, Charles C. 1935. *Antiquities of the New England Indians—with Notes on the Ancient Cultures of the Adjacent Territory*. Cambridge: Peabody Museum of American Archaeology and Ethnology.

2

The Source and Mother of the Fur Trade: Native-Dutch Relations in Eastern New Netherland

Kevin A. McBride

This chapter examines the nature of Dutch exploration and trade in eastern New Netherland and its effects upon native cultures in the region during the first half of the seventeenth century. Eastern New Netherland is defined as coastal and near interior areas of southern New England from the Connecticut River to Narragansett Bay, as well as eastern Long Island and Block Island (Map 2.1). This region was part of a larger area referred to by the Dutch as New Netherland, which stretched from Cape Cod to the Delaware River. Although the Dutch were active in eastern New Netherland for only thirty-five years, they had a tremendous impact on native cultures. The processes that initially altered native political, social, and economic patterns in the region are best understood in the context of Dutch participation in the fur and wampum trade in the early decades of seventeenth century. These changes in native society were not solely a response to new economic opportunities afforded by trade with the Dutch; native social and political agendas among both coastal and interior groups strongly influenced the nature of Dutch trade throughout New Netherland.

The acquisition of furs in New Netherland was the primary activity throughout the period of Dutch trade (ca. 1610–1664), but furs were largely depleted in coastal regions of New Netherland within a decade of the establishment of the Dutch West India Company in 1621. By the mid-1620s, the nature of Dutch trading activities in eastern New Netherland changed dramatically, shifting in focus from furs to the acquisition of wam-

Map 2.1
Eastern New Netherland: Fortified Places, Trading Posts, and Areas of Wampum Production

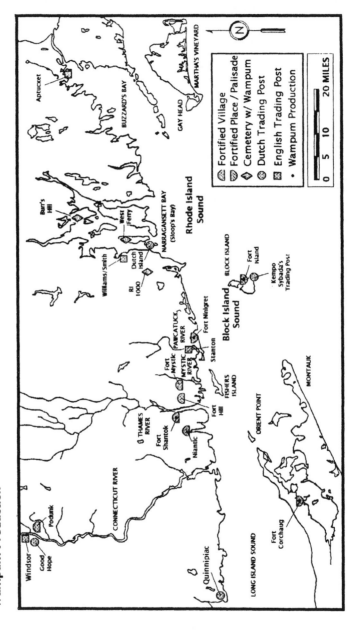

pum for use in interior areas of New Netherland. Subsequently, a special-
ized wampum trade developed in eastern New Netherland as the Dutch
sought to maintain a competitive edge in the fur trade and to support the
economy of New Netherland. Between approximately 1620 and 1650,
wampum from coastal regions of eastern New Netherland became one of
the most important elements in the Dutch fur trade. In the process, the
wampum trade, more so than the fur trade, transformed native social, political, and economic patterns in the region.

Although the Dutch were not the first Europeans in the region, they were
the first to develop and sustain long-term trade with native populations and
the first to have a detectable impact on native cultures. The first documented
European presence in the region was Giovanni de Verrazanno in 1524,
whose two-week stay in Narragansett Bay resulted in the earliest description
of native cultures in southern New England (Wroth 1970). Although gifts
were exchanged between Verrazano and the Narragansetts, no real trade
was conducted, and it appears that this was the initial encounter between
natives and Europeans in southern New England. There are few recorded
contacts between Europeans and native Americans for the remainder of the
sixteenth century, although cartographic details added to the coastline during this period are indicative of a continued European presence in the region. The recent identification of a possible sixteenth-century Iberian ceramic pot from Block Island is also suggestive of a continuous, though
perhaps limited, European presence in the region through the sixteenth century (Ivor Noel Hume, personal communication 1987).

The French appear to have been active in southern New England during
the late sixteenth and early seventeenth centuries. A number of documents
specifically reference French traders on the Hudson River, Narragansett
Bay, Massachusetts Bay, and Cape Cod (Morison 1987; Hart 1959; Jameson 1909). A limited English presence is also suggested by a description
and map of New England by John Smith. Smith's knowledge of the region
was likely passed on to Henry Hudson prior to Hudson's voyage to New
England in 1609–1610 (Rink 1976).

The Dutch appear to have been the first Europeans to explore the region
systematically and to initiate regular trade with natives. The four voyages of
Adrian Block between 1611 and 1614 provided a great deal of information
on the geography and native inhabitants of southern New England (Jameson 1909; Hart 1959). Block's description of native groups and the figurative map produced from these voyages (see Map 2.2) could have been obtained only through extensive exploration and contacts with natives
(Jameson 1909). A comparison of the 1610 Velasco map of southern New
England and coastal New York, presumably based on Hudson's 1609–1610
voyage, and Block's 1614 figurative map indicates that an enormous
amount of cultural and geographic information was added in a five-year
period (Ceci 1990; Stokes 1915–1928).

Map 2.2
Nova Belgica et Anglia Nova

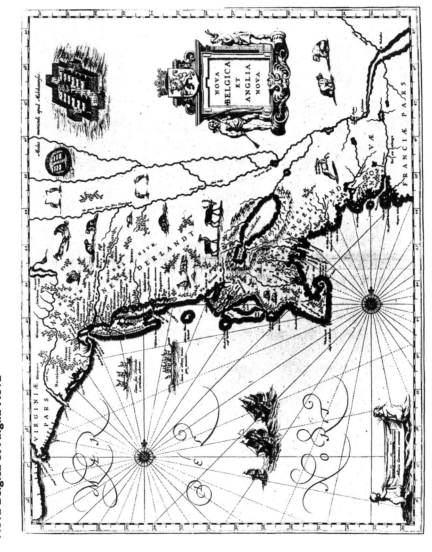

Source: From J. Blaeu's *Grooten Atlas*, vol. 8, 1648–1664, Africa and America. Courtesy of Map Division, The New York Public Library, Astor, Lenox and Tilden Foundations.

By 1614 the Dutch had already established trading relationships with several native groups in southern New England, including the Wampanoags of Cape Cod, the Mohegans of the Thames River, and the Quinnipiacs of New Haven harbor. By 1620 the Dutch had explored and charted the entire coastline from Cape Cod to the Delaware River (Jameson 1909; Hart 1959).

With the establishment of the New Netherland Company in 1614 and the West India Company in 1621, the Dutch began to construct an extensive trade network throughout the region. The easternmost area involved in the Dutch trade was Cape Cod, although Massachusetts Bay was likely visited periodically before 1620. Sloops Bay (the west channel of Narragansett Bay) is the most frequently mentioned location on the eastern frontier of New Netherland, usually in the context of the wampum trade. Although most of the Dutch effort focused on the Hudson and Delaware drainages, available documentation indicates that coastal areas of eastern New Netherland were intensively exploited for furs when private companies such as the New Netherland Company were active (1611–1621) and for furs and wampum during the early years of the Dutch West India Company (1621–1664). By 1625 and possibly earlier, the focus of the trade in eastern New Netherland was no longer furs but wampum. Although the fur trade had moved into northern interior areas of the Northeast by the third decade of the seventeenth century, wampum from eastern New Netherland became one of the most important commodities in this trade.

In 1633 John Winthrop of Massachusetts Bay stated that out of the northern Connecticut Valley and Lake Champlain "come most of the beaver which is traded between Virginia and Canada. . . . There comes yearly to the Dutch about ten thousand skins, which might easily be diverted if a course of trade were settled above in that river" (Hosmer 1908:1:110). Winthrop also reported in 1634 that twenty hogsheads of beaver were sent to England, "the greatest part whereof was traded for Wampampeage" (Morison 1987:190). While the figure of 10,000 furs per year may be somewhat of an exaggeration, it does suggest the extent of the fur trade in New Netherland. Most sources indicate that no more than 10,000 furs per year were being shipped from New Netherland, and usually between 7,500 to 8,000 furs per year (Fernow 1883; O'Callaghan 1848; van Laer 1924; Hosmer 1908). The statements by Winthrop indicate not only the northward movement of the fur trade and the importance of the Connecticut River as a conduit for the trade but an English strategy for acquiring a greater share of the trade. It is no coincidence that the Dutch, English, and Pequots all converged on the middle Connecticut River Valley in the early 1630s. The Dutch and English were pursuing the northern fur trade by establishing permanent trading posts at or near the confluence of the Farmington and Connecticut rivers, major routes into northern interior areas. At the same time the Pequots were attempting to maintain their control of the

European trade. Just prior to the establishment of trading posts by the Dutch and Plymouth Colony in 1633, the Pequots brought the local native groups into a tributary relationship following the defeat of a local sachem in battles (de Heeren 1725).

There are numerous references to individual Dutch traders operating in the eastern sections of New Netherland, with the Pequots, Narragansetts, Mohegans, Quinnipiacs, and Wampanoags mentioned as trading partners (Jameson 1909). Jaques Elckins, a supercargo (trader) for the New Netherland Company and commander of Fort Nassau for a short period of time, carried on trade along the Connecticut River and Long Island Sound with the Pequots and other native groups. In 1622 he extorted 140 fathoms of wampum from the Pequots by kidnapping the Pequot sachem Tattobam and holding him for ransom (Jameson 1909). Pieter Barentsz, commander of Fort Orange for a brief period, was active in the fur and wampum trade in the region and understood many of the local native languages (Jameson 1909). Barentsz is usually mentioned as being sent "upwards and along the coast with the sloops" (Jameson 1909:85).

Kempo Sybada, originally a pilot on a Dutch ship for the West India Company, became an independent trader in Long Island Sound during the mid-seventeenth century (Burgess 1926). During the Dutch-English war of 1653, an English privateer by the name of Edward Hull captured a ship belonging to Kempo Sybada on the Connecticut River. Sybada, described as a "Dutchman" but actually an Italian from Liverno, also had a trading post on Block Island where his agent, William Baker, and his wife, Mary, kept the post (Chapin 1926). Hull seized Sybada's goods and ship, and then went to Block Island and seized the goods at Sybada's trading post and transported Baker and his wife off the Island.

Kempo Sybada first appears in 1649, mentioned in the notarial records for New Amsterdam as a pilot of the Dutch ship *La Garce* involved in the capture of a Spanish bark, the *Tabasko* (Chapin 1926). Sybada's share of the prize, the *Tabasko,* provided him the means to pursue the trade in Long Island Sound, and it is this ship that Hull seized on the Connecticut River in 1653. Sybada probably established his trading post on Block Island shortly after he received the Spanish ship in the summer of 1649. His selection of Block Island as the location for a post is curious; it was relatively isolated and certainly would not have had easy access to furs. Undoubtedly, the most important factor in Sybada's selection of Block Island as a location for the post was access to wampum. The only commodity the Manisses Indians of Block Island had to offer during the seventeenth century was wampum, and wampum was likely the reason for the presence of Sybada's post and a native palisade (Fort Island) on the island. The Fort Island site was used and occupied at the same time Sybada's post was in operation. These two sites are located approximately one mile apart, and their geographic and temporal congruence was likely not a coincidence (Map 2.3).

Map 2.3
Site RI-118: Fort Island, Block Island, Rhode Island

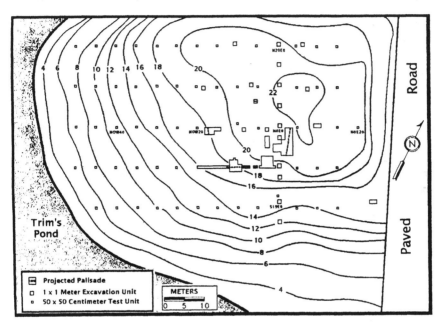

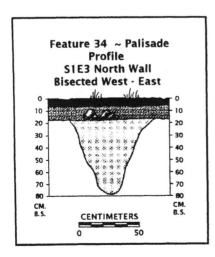

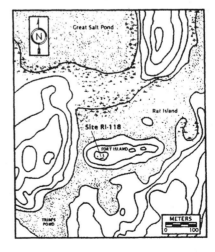

The ability of these traders to carry on the trade depended on good relationships with the natives. Presumably this is why the Dutch West India Company declined to hire Jaques Elckins, who kidnapped the Pequot sachem Tattobam in 1622 (Jameson 1909). Pieter Barentsz developed such a good relationship with the Pequots in 1626 that "the chief of this nation has lately made an agreement with Pieter Barentsz not to trade with any other than him" and has "no confidence in any one but this one now" (Jameson 1909:86).

As early as 1623, the Dutch and English began to engage in direct competition for furs in Narragansett Bay and Cape Cod (Morison 1987). In 1627, the English at Plymouth requested that the Dutch "forbear to trade with the natives of this Bay (Buzzards) and River of Narragansett" (Nassau or east passage of Narragansett Bay) (Fernow 1883:1:174). During the first quarter of the seventeenth century, the Dutch were able to gain an advantage in the fur trade against the English because of the better-quality trade goods they could offer. In 1623, Plymouth Colony outfitted the *Little James* for "trade and discovery to the southward of Cape Cod" (Morison 1987:324). Sailing to the east passage of Narragansett Bay, the English found that the Dutch had already been there. The English reported that "the Dutch used to furnish them [Narragansetts/Wampanoags] with cloath and better commodities, they [English] having only a few beads and knives which were not there much esteemed" (Morison 1987:343–344). Just a few years earlier, these same items were traded to natives on Cape Cod by the English and "were then good trade" (Morison 1987:277). Even the Dutch in the earliest years of trade along the Hudson River were very successful with beads, knives, and a few hatchets (Jameson 1909; Morison 1987). Items that were commonly traded to natives for furs and wampum included glass beads, knives, adzes, axes, hoes, copper and iron kettles, and duffel cloth (Jameson 1909). In coastal areas, duffel cloth was the most important trade item. Without it, the Dutch were apparently unable to acquire as much wampum as they needed for the interior fur trade. Isaack de Rasiere, general secretary of the West India Company in New Netherland, reported to the directors of the company in 1626 that if they were "to supply me continually with duffels I shall know how to get wampum to stock Fort Orange in such a way that the French Indians will never again come here in vain" (van Laer 1924:227). The English, squeezed between the French to the north and the Dutch to the south, were losing out in the fur trade "for want of means to gather them [furs] . . . , seeing the Dutch on one side and the French on the other side . . . and doe furnish the savages, not with toys and trifles, but with good and substantial commodities, as kettles, hatchets, and clothes of all sorts" (Morison 1987:345). Eventually, by investing some of their profits from the fur trade to purchase better-quality trade goods rather than to pay off their debts to the backers of the colony or to purchase corn, the English became more competitive in the region.

The primary advantage the Dutch had against the French was their ability to acquire large amounts of wampum, without which they could not attract "French Indians" southward (van Laer 1924:227). Isaack de Rasiere stated in 1626 that the French Indians "come to us for no other reason than to get wampum, which the French cannot procure unless they come to barter for it with our nations in the north, just as the Brownists (English) of Plymouth Colony [come] near our places to get wampum" (van Laer 1926:223–224).

De Rasiere outlined the Dutch strategy to the directors of the West India Company for maintaining an advantage in the fur trade with respect to both the English and French:

I beg to submit to your honors whether, if we could overtake French or English sloops here, it would not be well by some means or other to take the trade away from them, either by force or by spoiling their trade by outbidding them with duffels or hatchets, in order that they themselves would have to come to us to get wampum, or that we in going to them could exchange the wampum for skins in their possession. And instead of giving the Indians 2 1/2 hand-lengths, we could give them three or four hands. (Isaack de Rasiere to the Directors of the West India Company, 1626, van Laer 1926:227)

Dutch strategy in eastern New Netherland was also designed to prevent the English from trading south and west of Cape Cod, thereby discovering the wampum trade. Of critical importance was control and access to the west side of Narragansett (Sloop's) Bay, the eastern boundary of the wampum-producing region. This may explain why the Dutch purchased Quetenis (Dutch) Island on the west side of Narragansett Bay from the Narragansetts and established a short-lived trading post in 1637 (Chapin 1926; Fernow 1883:1:544). In 1627 Plymouth Colony built a small pinnace at their trading post at Buzzards Bay (Aptuxet) to pursue the fur trade to the west of Cape Cod in Narragansett Bay. Prior to this, the English had confined their trading activities to Massachusetts Bay, Cape Cod, and northern New England. When this information was received by officials in New Amsterdam, it precipitated a letter and visit by Isaack de Rasiere, the first official contact between the Dutch and Plymouth Colony since Plymouth was settled seven years earlier. In an attempt to prevent the English from pursuing the fur trade and discovering the growing wampum trade, the Dutch offered to sell the English any goods they required and purchase their furs at a good price (Morison 1987). More important, de Rasiere sold the English fifty fathoms of wampum and encouraged them to use it in northern New England to obtain furs. As de Rasiere explained to officials of the West India Company, the Dutch did not want the English trading in Narragansett Bay "because the seeking after wampum by them is prejudicial, inasmuch as they would, by doing so, discover the trade in furs; which if they were to find out, it would be a great trouble for us to maintain" (Jameson 1909:110). Providing the English with wampum was a calculated risk by the Dutch; they hoped that the English would employ the wampum elsewhere (presumably in northern New England) and not pursue either the wampum or fur trade in eastern New Netherland. This strategy worked for a time; "it was two years before they [English] could put of this small quantity, till the inland people knew of it; and afterwards they cold scarce ever gett enough for them, for many years together" (Morison 1987:43). By the early 1630s the English were very active in Long Island Sound and the Connecticut River Valley and had begun to trade for both furs and wampum (Hosmer 1908).

With the English trading more frequently in Long Island Sound and the Connecticut River by the early 1630s, Dutch access to wampum became increasingly problematic. This difficulty was further increased after the Pequot War, when much of the wampum-producing areas came under direct or indirect English control, and large amounts of wampum in the form of tribute were being acquired by the English colonies. The incursion of English traders and settlers into eastern New Netherland precipitated the establishment of the only major permanent Dutch trading post in the region.

The House of Hope was constructed in 1633 along the Connecticut River at Hartford to intercept furs coming downriver from the north and to establish a Dutch presence in an area in which the English were becoming increasingly interested. Plymouth Colony constructed a permanent post a few miles upriver from the Dutch trading post two months later, effectively circumventing any Dutch trading advantage. With the establishment of the Plymouth post in 1633 and English settlements at Hartford, Wethersfield, and Windsor in 1635, the fortunes of the Dutch at the House of Hope declined further. In a 1639 visit to the fort, De Vries noted that the English at Hartford were encroaching on Dutch lands and abusing the West India Company farmers and soldiers at the fort (Jameson 1909:208). In 1640 it was reported that the English had seized Dutch lands at the fort, beat the inhabitants with sticks and clubs, and threw farm implements into the river (Jameson 1909:308). By 1647 the commissary of the fort reported that it "is in great need of repair and requires more attention than it has hitherto received" (van Laer 1924:365). The situation at the House of Hope continued to decline, probably indicating that the post was no longer economically viable. The arguments for repairing the fort were political, not economic; the Dutch wished to maintain the post as a tenuous claim on the Connecticut River against the English. In 1648 it was estimated that 6,000 guilders would be necessary to repair the Fort of Good Hope, in its old form "with four points" (O'Callaghan 1848:65). This money was never authorized, and shortly after 1650 the post was abandoned (O'Callaghan 1848:234).

Permanent posts such as the House of Hope were rare in coastal areas of eastern New Netherland because they were not an effective strategy for pursuing the wampum trade. Such posts were established as much for pursuing the fur trade as to establish a Dutch presence on the eastern frontier of New Netherland. A small trading house and perhaps a settlement may have been constructed at the mouth of the Connecticut River as early as 1623 (Rink 1976), and the House of Hope was built along the Connecticut River at the present site of Hartford in 1633 (Morison 1987). The Dutch purchased Connittekock (Connecticut) from the Pequots (who claimed it by right of conquest) and Kievets-Hoeck (Saybrook Point) "from the Indians" in 1632, presumably in response to English activity along the Connecticut River (Jameson 1909; de Heeren 1725:607). Quetenis or Dutch Island was purchased by the Dutch from the Narragansetts in 1637, and a trading post was established (Fernow 1883:1,544; Chapin 1926). A trading post was also located on Block Island in 1649, but this was likely a private enterprise and not directly associated with the West India Company (Burgess 1926).

The Dutch monopoly in the wampum trade was effectively broken when the English defeated the Pequots in 1637, thereby gaining direct or indirect control of most of the wampum-producing regions in eastern Long Island Sound (Ceci 1990). An additional advantage the English had after the Pequot War was their acquisition of large amounts of wampum through tribute payments. Not only were the surviving Pequots paying yearly tribute in wampum to the English, but many of the other native groups were doing so as well, including the Mohegans, Narragansetts, Manisses (Block Island), Eastern Niantics, Montauk, and Connecticut River Indians (Morison 1987; Hosmer 1908). Although it is not entirely clear where all of this wampum was ending up, presumably the English used it in the northern fur trade.

The importance of shell to native groups has been well documented, and exchange of marine shell to interior areas extends well back into prehistory (Ceci 1990). Marine shell and particularly wampum served a number of social, political, and ritual functions in native society (Ceci 1977, 1983, 1990). Wampum is manufactured from two types of shells. The small northern whelk (*Busycon canaliculatum* and *B. carica*) produces a white bead manufactured from the inner columella of this shell. Quahog (*Mercenaria mercenaria*) produces a purple bead from the purple segments of the shell (Ceci 1990). Wampum is tubular in shape, well finished and smooth from grinding. The beads average 5.5 mm in length and 4 mm in width. The bore diameters, drilled with European iron drills, average 1 mm in diameter (Ceci 1990).

The amount of wampum available to native groups in the interior increased dramatically after the second quarter of the seventeenth century. Late sixteenth- and early seventeenth-century archaeological sites in central

New York yielded only a few hundred wampum beads at most. Some archaeological sites in this region dating from the mid-seventeenth century yielded between 100,000 to 250,000 beads (Ceci 1977, 1983). Production increased as much from the introduction of certain European technologies such as iron drills as from increased demand by interior native groups. Transport and dispersal of wampum were facilitated by Dutch traders operating out of small coastal sloops, acquiring wampum along coastal areas of eastern New Netherland, and transporting it up to Albany, where it was traded to interior tribes such as the Mohawk and Northern Algonquians.

There has been a great deal of debate concerning the role of the Dutch in the introduction of wampum and its use as currency in New Netherland (Ceci 1977, 1990). It has been suggested that Dutch involvement in the West African slave trade and their experience there with trading coastal shell to inland groups for slaves was the impetus for its use as a trade item and currency in New Netherland (Ceci 1977, 1990). A review of documents associated with Hudson's initial encounter with natives in the Hudson River indicates that natives initiated wampum and shell exchange several times during Hudson's stay (Jameson 1909). The context in which this exchange took place was social in nature and clearly indicates the importance of shell to natives, particularly interior groups. One example was an attempt by natives to ransom a sachem who got drunk and was inadvertently left behind on Hudson's ship. Apparently thinking that Hudson meant to kidnap the sachem, "some of them came again, and brought stropes of beads" (Jameson 1909:22). On two other occasions, Hudson was presented with "stropes of beads" by a sachem. In one instance, this exchange was followed by an oratory by the sachem, who then "shewed him [Hudson] all the country there about, as though it were at his command" (Jameson 1909:24). Both tobacco and shell beads are mentioned by Hudson in a context of gift giving, reciprocal exchange, and ransom. The Dutch likely noted the importance of shell beads to interior groups and later used their experience in Africa to initiate the wampum trade (Ceci 1977, 1990).

The Dutch referred to wampum as the "source and mother of the fur trade" (O'Callaghan 1848, 2:543). Within a decade of initiating trade with natives in New Netherland, wampum became the most important item in the fur trade. Jaques Elckins, who kidnapped the Pequot sachem Tattobam in 1622, demanded 140 fathoms of wampum, not furs, as ransom (Jameson 1909). The need for wampum became so great by 1626 that Isaack de Rasiere requested funding from the Netherlands to construct two or three sloops to pursue the wampum trade. He estimated that a thousand yards of wampum (approximately 150,000 beads) would be necessary during the winter of 1626 to pursue the trade (van Laer 1924). The Dutch in New Netherland, not able to acquire as much of this material as they needed, also sought to produce wampum in the Netherlands. De Rasiere sent two strings of wampum (one white and the other black or purple) to the Netherlands as a sample and requested that the company "kindly send me of each sort 200 or 300 pounds, strung to the same length and of the same size, as these are much sought after and there are no more here" (van Laer 1924:232). There is no evidence that beads were ever produced in the Netherlands, although they were produced in Albany in the seventeenth and eighteenth centuries (Pena 1990).

The 1650 Treaty of Hartford between the Dutch and the English denied Dutch rights to any lands east of the Connecticut River, effectively eliminating the Dutch supply of wampum from this region and threatening to ruin the fur trade. By the late 1650s, and possibly earlier, the Dutch were importing large amounts of conch from the Caribbean to New Netherland, presumably to manufacture wampum. Between 1659 and 1664 over ten barrels of conch are listed in various ships' manifests going from Curaçao to merchants in New Amsterdam (Gehring and Schilikamp 1987). Charles Gehring has suggested that these are shells, not food, likely meant for wampum production in New Netherland (Charles Gehring personal communication, 1990). Elizabeth Pena (1990) has documented several instances of Dutch wampum production in Albany during the seventeenth and eighteenth centuries, further supporting the contention that the demand for wampum was exceeding the supply.

The establishment of permanent trading posts such as the House of Hope was the most effective means to facilitate the collection of furs, which were distributed and obtained over a wide geographic area. However, the wampum trade required a different strategy. Rather than fixed or permanent European trading posts and mobile native hunters as in the fur trade, the wampum trade required the reverse: a mobile European collection strategy and fixed native places of production. This strategy is illustrated by the number of small coastal sloops and yachts that visited fixed native fortified places and villages along the coast to trade for wampum. The nature and distribution of shellfish beds that produced wampum and the need to protect these resources resulted in the establishment of a number of native fortified places along the coast. In such places, wampum was produced and protected in the relative safety of a stockade (Map 2.1).

Native fortifications have not been identified archaeologically in coastal areas of Long Island Sound or Narragansett Bay prior to European contact, and it has been argued that these kinds of sites did not exist prior to the early seventeenth century in this region (McBride 1990). Adrian Block described a fortified native village in the middle Connecticut River Valley in 1614 but not in coastal regions of southern New England. The presence of a fortified village in the middle Connecticut Valley at this time may be the result of Iroquoian (Mohawk) raids into the Connecticut Valley, a frequent occurrence in the seventeenth century following contact with Europeans and the development of the fur trade. The presence of such sites in southern

New England indicates increased conflicts among native groups in the early seventeenth century. Support for this hypothesis is based in part on evidence from burials, which indicate an increase in death by trauma in the first half of the seventeenth century, as well as changes in native settlement patterns during this same period.

No cases of death by trauma are reported from precontact burials from the area (southeastern Connecticut). Several contact period burials from Pequot territory have been reported that indicate the individuals died as a result of warfare. One instance was a double burial of two adult males from Niantic, with "both skeletons riddled with arrowheads" (Rogers 1935:1). One skeleton had fifteen arrowheads embedded in the skull, vertebrae, pelvis, and ribs. The second skeleton had six arrowheads associated with the ribs, groin, and pelvis. Although the projectile points were not made of metal, the site where these individuals were interred dates to the early Historic period.

The files of the Department of Anthropology, National Museum of Natural History, Smithsonian Institution, list the skeleton of an adult male recovered in 1916 from the east bank of Connecticut's Thames River (Accession Number 00062729). Embedded in the pelvis and vertebrae of the individual were two "bronze" projectile points. Because no Pequots were allowed on the east side of the river following the Pequot War, the burials likely date after contact with Europeans but no later than the war (ca. 1600–1637). The temporal, geographic, and archaeological context of the Niantic and Thames river burials indicates that the individuals were the victims of conflict with other natives during the first half of the seventeenth century as they began to compete for control of the European trade.

Reconstructions of pre- and postcontact Pequot settlement patterns also indicate increased conflicts among native groups in the region following the initiation of sustained trade with Europeans. The nature and distribution of postcontact Pequot settlements are very similar to precontact settlement patterns from the region (McBride 1984, 1990). Late Prehistoric and Early Historic period Pequot coastal villages (ca. A.D. 1400–1637) were located immediately adjacent to saltwater marshes along Long Island Sound or on tidal estuaries such as the Mystic, Thames, and Pawcatuck rivers. The only sites that do not fit this pattern are the two Pequot fortified villages (Mystic and Weinshauks; Map 2.4) (McBride 1990), located on high hills with steeply sloping sides, some distance from a saltwater marsh or estuary. No precontact period Pequot villages have been identified in such locations. The locational criterion for Pequot fortified villages was clearly defensive and not based on accessibility to saltwater marshes or estuaries. This evidence strongly suggests that fortified villages are a postcontact phenomenon in coastal regions of southeastern Connecticut.

Seventeenth-century native fortifications consisted of both fortified villages, such as Fort Shantok (Salwen 1966; Williams 1972), Weinshauks,

Map 2.4
Prewar Pequot Settlement Pattern in Southern Connecticut

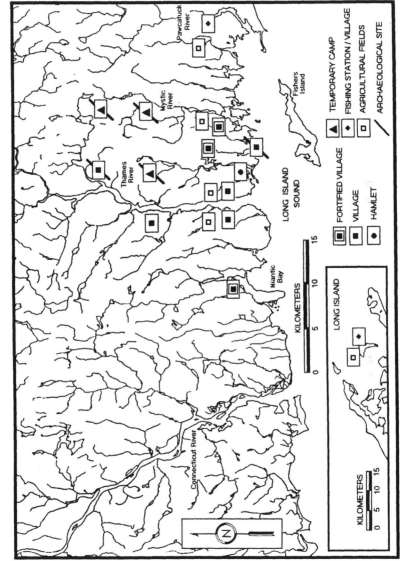

and the Mystic Fort (McBride 1990), and fortified places or palisades such as Forts Corchaug and Ninigret (Solecki 1950; Goodwin 1932; Map 2.1). The recent discovery and partial excavation of a native (Manisses) fortified place or palisade on Block Island is a good example of this type of site. The Fort Island site is located on a small island in the Great Salt Pond on Block Island (Map 2.3). The palisade is approximately 25 meters by 30 meters square and is situated on the highest, most defensible portion of Fort Island. The palisade construction is typical of native fortifications in the region. A small ditch was excavated measuring approximately 80 cm deep by 40 to 50 cm wide (Map 2.2). A series of large and small posts were then placed in the ditch to form a stockade. The activities that took place within the palisade were somewhat limited. Some domestic activities such as food processing and consumption are evident, but the domestic features and activities usually associated with villages were not identified. Evidence of wampum production is indicated by the occurrence of square fragments (blanks) of hardshell clam (quahog) and the presence of wampum beads. A number of European trade goods were also recovered, including glass beads, kaolin pipes, a mouth harp, ceramics (redwares), and unidentified brass and iron objects. Documentary evidence and the material culture recovered from the Fort Island site suggest a mid-seventeenth-century occupation (ca. 1640–1670). Block Island is frequently mentioned as an important source of wampum, and the palisade at Fort Island represented a phenomenon occurring throughout the region as conflicts between native groups increased with the competition for control of the wampum trade.

This process is illustrated by the expansion of Pequot social, economic, and political influence and the acquisition of tributary territory in southern New England during the second quarter of the seventeenth century (Map 2.5). Part of this process involved the subjugation of neighboring tribes by the Pequots. Within a ten-year period, between 1625 and 1635, a number of native groups were brought into a tributary relationship with the Pequots:

> Their chief sachem held dominion over divers petty sagamores; as over part of Long Island, over the Mohegans, and over the sagamores of Quinapeake (Quinnipiac-New haven), yea over all the people that dwelt upon Connecticut River, and over some of the southerly inhabitants of the Nipmuck country, about Quinabaag. (Gookin 1970:147)

The timing, nature, and geographic extent of the acquisition of tributary territory by the Pequots appear to correlate with the increased demand for wampum by the Dutch in the early 1620s, and Pequot attempts to control the wampum-producing areas of Long Island Sound. By the early 1630s, with the attention of the Dutch and English focused on the middle Connecticut River Valley, the Pequots also moved to control this area, which

Map 2.5
Pequot Settlements and Tributary Territory

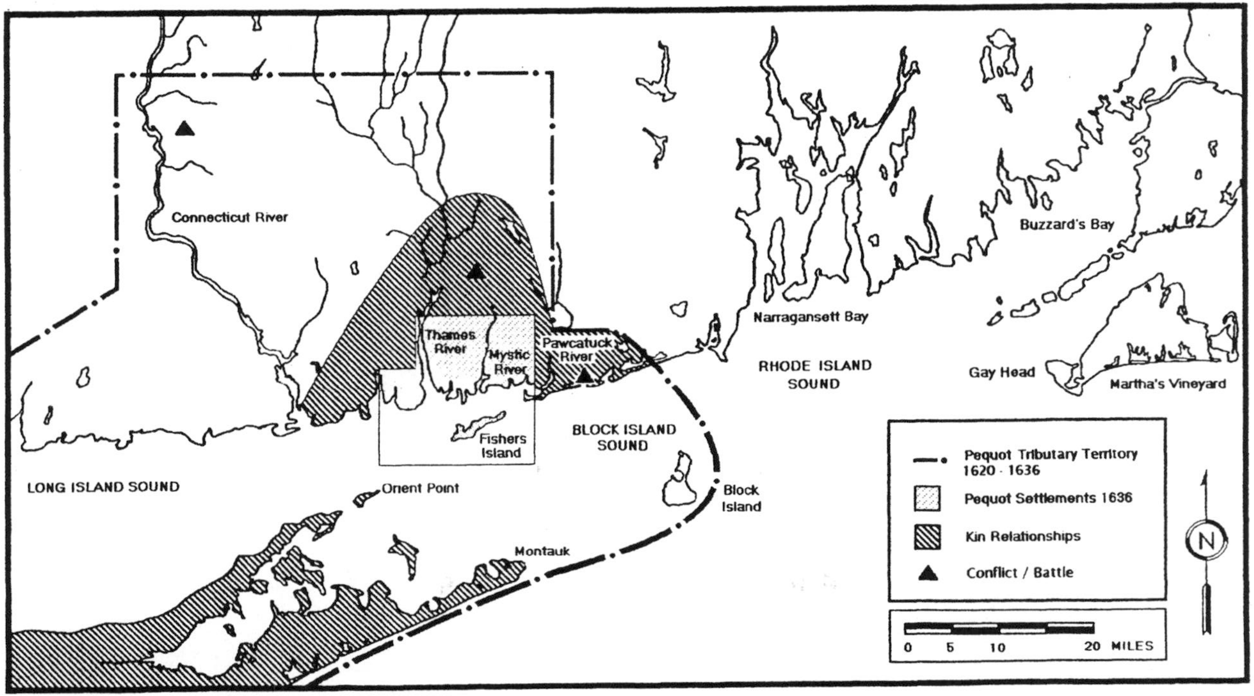

Legend:
- Pequot Tributary Territory 1620 - 1636
- Pequot Settlements 1636
- Kin Relationships
- ▲ Conflict / Battle

Scale: 0   5   10   20 MILES

N

Labels: Buzzard's Bay, Martha's Vineyard, Gay Head, Narragansett Bay, RHODE ISLAND SOUND, Block Island, BLOCK ISLAND SOUND, Pawcatuck River, Mystic River, Thames River, Fishers Island, Montauk, Orient Point, Connecticut River, LONG ISLAND SOUND served as the primary collection point for furs moving down the Connecticut River from the interior. In 1630, the English stated that the Pequots and Narragansetts "grew rich and potent" through the manufacture of wampum (Morison 1987:43). Unlike the Narragansetts, who were referred to by the Pequots as "Women-like men" and "not desirous to take in hand any martiall enterprize, or expose themselves to the uncertaine events of warre . . . and seeke rather to grow rich by industrie, than famous by deeds of chevalry," the Pequots chose a more aggressive means to extend their political, social, and economic influence (Wood 1865:70). Even the Narragansetts, the largest native group in the region, "whom until this year [1634] they [the Pequots] had kept under," were affected by Pequot expansion (Hosmer 1908:139).

This process appears to have begun shortly after the initiation of trade with the Dutch. By the early 1620s, the Pequots are mentioned frequently in Dutch records as trading partners (Jameson 1909). Presumably through their control of the wampum trade, the Pequots were able to control the trade with the Dutch and influence the distribution of European trade goods to native groups in the region. It may be that the West India Company, through Pieter Barentsz, entered into an exclusive trading agreement with the Pequots because they controlled the territory that produced most of the wampum in the region. By 1626, Dutch records indicate that eastern Long Island was tributary to the Pequots, and by 1628 "the whole north coast" was tributary (Jameson 1909:87). By the early 1630s Pequot control extended up the Connecticut River to Hartford and eastward along the coast to Weekapaug (Charlestown, Rhode Island; McBride 1990).

Documentary sources indicate that Pequot success was achieved largely through warfare. Although it is not clear precisely when this process began, Adrian Block mentioned as early as 1614 that the Pequots "are enemies of the Wampanoos," suggesting that to some extent, these conflicts began shortly after contact with Europeans, or perhaps even before (Jameson 1909:43). Although the "Wampanoos" appears to indicate the Wampanoag of Massachusetts, the Narragansetts are also a likely possibility in this context. De Rasiere reported in 1628 that the Siwanoys and Shinnecocks of eastern Long Island Sound "support themselves by planting maize and making sewan [wampum]. . . . The tribes are held in subjection by, and are tributary to the Pequots (Jameson 1909:103). In 1631 John Winthrop reported that the "Wahginnacut, a sagamore upon Quonehtacut [Connecticut] . . . was at war with the Pekoath [Pequot]" (Schlesinger 1929–47: vol. 3, 52). This event is also reported in a letter from the States General of the United Netherland to the Republic of England (de Heeren 1725). In it, Wouter van Twiller, director of New Netherland, related that the Dutch purchased Connecticut from the "victorious Pequots" who defeated the Sequeens of Connecticut "after three different battles, in open field." The Pequots were victorious and "kept the land" (de Heeren 1725:607). Even the Mohegans, who were closely related to and allies of the Pequots, were also subjugated by the Pequots. The Mohegan sachems "grew so great and so proud . . . at which the great Pequot sachem being angry with them made warr upon them and conquered them and their country" (Means 1947:26). The Pequots were also in conflict with the Narragansetts for a number of years. As early as 1632, the Dutch informed John Winthrop through Miles Standish that "many Pequins [Pequots who were professed enemies to the Anagansetts Narragansetts] had been there [Narragansett Bay] many days, and advised us to be watchful" (Hosmer 1908:79). In 1634, John Winthrop reported that the Pequots "were now in a war with the Narragansetts, whom until this year, they had kept under, and likewise with the Dutch" (Hosmer 1908:139). The "war" with the Dutch was precipitated by the Pequots, who "killed some Indians, who came to trade with the Dutch," probably in an attempt to retain their control of the Dutch trade (Hosmer 1908:139). In retaliation, the Dutch killed the Pequot sachem Tattobam, severing Dutch-Pequot trade relations. The Pequots then turned to the English, requesting that they "send a pinnace with cloth, and we should have all their trade" (Hosmer 1908:139). In return, the Pequots offered "all their right at Connecticut" (Hosmer 1908:139).

With the English heavily involved in the trade in the Connecticut Valley, Dutch control of the European trade and Pequot influence over other native groups began to wane. The conflict with the Dutch initiated a steady erosion of Pequot power and influence, culminating with the Pequot War in 1636. In addition to losing the middle Connecticut Valley to the English, the Pequots lost the Misquamicut area of southwestern Rhode Island following a battle and a Narragansett victory over the Pequots. Both the Dutch and the Pequots prospered when each was in a position to control their respective elements of the trade.

With the English entry into the trade in the early 1630s, the Dutch and the Pequot monopolies over the trade were effectively broken. To some extent, the causes of the Pequot War can be viewed in the context of Pequot attempts to maintain their monopoly of the European trade. Although the Dutch were active in eastern New Netherland for only thirty-five years, they had a tremendous impact on native cultures throughout southern New England. These changes in native social, political, and economic patterns are best understood in the context of native political and social agendas. During the early decades of the seventeenth century, native tribes in the region pursued their own agendas. Dutch activity in eastern New Netherland must be viewed, in part, as responses to these native goals and agendas.

REFERENCES

Burgess, George. 1926. *The Earliest Known White Settlement on Block Island*. Rhode Island Historical Society Collections, Vol. 19, no. 3, 81–91.

Bushnell, David, Jr. 1906. "The Origin Of Wampum." *Journal of the Royal Anthropological Institute of Great Britain and Ireland* 36:172–177.

Ceci, Lynn. 1977. "The Effect of European Contact and Trade on the Settlement Pattern of Indians in Coastal New York, 1524–1665: The Archaeological and Documentary Evidence." Ph.D. dissertation, City University of New York.

———. 1983. "Tracing Wampum's Origins: The Shell Bead Evidence from Archaeological Sites in Western and Coastal New York." In *Proceedings of the 1986 Shell Bead Conference,* edited by Charles Hayes III, 63–80. Rochester Museum and Science Center Research Records No. 20. Rochester, N.Y.

———. 1990. "Native Wampum as a Peripheral Resource in the 17th-Century World System." In *The Pequots in Southern New England: The Fall and Rise of an American Indian Nation,* edited by Laurence Hauptman and James Wherry. Norman: University of Oklahoma Press.

Chapin, Howard, M. 1926. *Quetenis Island or Dutch Island.* Rhode Island Historical Society Collections, Vol. 19, No. 3, 88–91.

de Heeren, V. 1725. Verbael Gehouden door de Heeren H. van Bevernigk, W. Nieupoort, J. van de Perre, en A. P. Jongestal, als Gedeputeerden en Extraordinaris Ambassadeurs van de Heeren Staeten Generael der Vereenigde Nederlanden aen de Rebublyck van Engelandt. Gravenhage.

Fernow, Berthold, ed. 1883. *Documents Relating to the Colonial History of the State of New York,* 15 vols. Albany, N.Y.: Weed, Parsons and Company.

Gehring, Charles, and J. Schiltkamp. 1987. *New Netherland Documents.* Vol. 17: *Curaçao Papers 1640–1665.* Interlaken, N.Y.: Heart of the Lakes of Publishing.

Goodwin, William. 1932. *Notes Regarding the Origin of Fort Ninigret in the Narragansett Country at Charlestown.* Rhode Island Historical Society Collections Vol. 25, no. 1, 1–16.

Hart, Simon. 1959. *The Prehistory of the New Netherland Company: Amsterdam. Notarial Records of the First Dutch Voyages to the Hudson.* Amsterdam: City of Amsterdam Press.

Hosmer, James K., ed. 1908. *Winthrop's Journal: History of New England,* Vols. 1–2. New York: Charles Scribner's Sons.

Jameson, J. Franklin, ed. 1909. *Narratives of New Netherland, 1609–1614.* New York: Barnes and Noble. Reprinted 1967.

McBride, Kevin A. 1984. "Prehistory of the Lower Connecticut River Valley." Ph.D. dissertation, University of Connecticut.

———. 1990. "Historical Archaeology of the Mashantucket Pequot, 1637–1900." In *The Pequots of Southern New England,* edited by Lawrence Hauptman and James Wherry. Norman: University of Oklahoma Press.

Means, Carroll A. 1947. "Mohegan-Pequot Relationships." *Bulletin of the Archaeological Society of Connecticut* 21:26–34.

Morison, Samuel, ed. 1987. *William Bradford's History of Plymouth Plantation, 1620–1647.* New York: Alfred A. Knopf.

New York State Archives. 1650. Notorized Copy of the Bill of Lading of De Nieu Nederlantse Fortuyn. Vol. 11: Document 51, Dutch Colonial Manuscripts, New York State Archives. Translated by Charles Gehring, Director, New Netherlands Project.

O'Callaghan, Edmund. 1848. *History of New Netherland, New York under the Dutch.* Vols. 1–3. New York: Bartlett and Welford, D. Appleton and Company.

Pena, Elizabeth. 1990. "Wampum Production in New Netherland and Colonial New York: The Historical and Archaeological Context." Ph.D. dissertation, Boston University.

Rink, Oliver. 1976. "Merchants and Magnates: Dutch New York, 1609–1664." Ph.D. dissertation, University of Southern California.

Rogers, E. H. 1935. "A Double Burial near Niantic." *Bulletin of the Archaeological Society of Connecticut* 1:2–3.

Salwen, Bert. 1966. "European Trade Goods and the Chronology of the Fort Shantok Site." *Bulletin of the Archaeological Society of Connecticut* 34:5–39.

Schlesinger, Arthur M., ed. 1929–47. *Winthrop Papers.* 5 volumes. Boston: Massachusetts Historical Society.

Slotkin, James, and K. Schmidt. 1949. "Studies in Wampum." *American Anthropologist* 51 (April):223–236.

Solecki, Ralph. 1950. "The Archaeological Position of Historic Fort Corchaug, LI, and Its Relation to Contemporary Forts." *Bulletin of the Archaeological Society of Connecticut* 24:3–40.

Stokes, I. N. Phelps. 1915–1928. *The Iconography of Manhattan Island, 1498–1909.* Vol. 2. New York: R. H. Dodd.

Van Laer, A. J. F., ed. 1924. Documents Relating to New Netherland, 1624–1626. San Marino: Henry E. Huntington Library and Art Gallery.

Williams, Lorraine. 1972. "A Study of 17th-Century Culture Contact in the Long Island Sound Area." Ph.D. dissertation, New York University.

Wood, William. 1977 [1634]. *New England's Prospect,* edited by Alden T. Vaughan. Amherst: University of Massachusetts Press.

Wroth, Lawrence. 1970. *The Voyages of Giovanni de Verrazano, 1542–1528.* New Haven: Yale University Press.

Part II

Survival through the Ages

With increased European settlement of the Northeast came increased conflicts with the native peoples. The Pequot War in 1637 and King Philip's War in 1675 were two of the bloodiest battles between Indians and colonists. As Chapter 2 indicated, the Dutch and English became heavily invested in coastal New England during the first quarter of the seventeenth century. More and more trading posts were established throughout New England along major river thoroughfares, like the Connecticut River, and along the coastline. European immigrants continued to stream into New England. As colonial settlements grew and pushed beyond their bounds, colonists began to leave their initial homes and move westward to settle new lands and establish new colonies.

The Pequot War was a conflict that posed a number of complex issues: the competition between Indians and Europeans for access to the wampum and fur trades and the wider competition among all parties to establish hegemony in coastal New England. The war demonstrated the ferocity of English claims to the region: 300 to 700 Pequots were massacred, most of them women, children and the elderly (see Hauptman 1990 for a discussion of this war and the brutality of the English).

By the time of King Philip's War, the Dutch had forfeited their claims to the English colonists, and the English had quickly established hegemony throughout much of the Northeast by acquiring ever more Indian lands. The English colonies of New York, Plymouth, Connecticut, and Massachusetts Bay were all competing against each other for these lands. The Wampanoags' supreme sachem, King Philip, however, wanted to put an end to the tide of English land greed. His people were starving, for they did not have enough planting and hunting lands to sustain themselves.

The war began when Philip's forces destroyed a newly settled village on the edge of Plymouth Colony. The war quickly spread northward and westward, with English and Indian communities throughout New England becoming engulfed in the conflict. In the end, many English settlements were destroyed by Philip's confederated forces of Wampanoags, Nipmucks, Abenakis, and others. Despite his early successes, King Philip lost. The Narragansetts, who were pushed into the war by the English, suffered a huge massacre, not unlike the one suffered by their Pequot brethren decades before. Many native peoples who sided with Philip were punished by being sold into slavery or indentured, or confined to reservations within the ever-growing colonies (see Chapter 4 for a discussion of the Narragansetts during and after the war; see Leach 1958 and Jennings 1975 for a full account of King Philip's War; see Weinstein 1983 for a discussion of how the alienation of Wampanoag land led up to the war).

One can only imagine the incredible sense of despair and hopelessness that native peoples felt after King Philip's War. Despite near extermination, native communities survived the seventeenth century. During the next two centuries, the Wampanoags, Mohegans, Pequots, Narragansetts, Schaghticokes, Passamaquoddies, and other nations combined old and new strategies to promote their cultural survival. Coastal groups, like the Wampanoags, became involved in the whaling industry. Native men were hired to join the crews of large sea vessels and consequently were gone for months at a time. Herman Melville's *Moby Dick* glorifies the Indian presence in this industry.

Many natives throughout New England found another source of income: they sold their arts for profit. Basket weaving was an especially important industry. Weavers would go to white communities to peddle their wares house to house. When tourist resorts in the White Mountains and coastal Maine were opened in the nineteenth century, native weavers found a new market for their decorative and utilitarian baskets (see Lester 1987). Some individuals, like the Schaghticoke Henry Harris, combined itinerant farm labor with peddling his baskets (Handsman and McMullen 1987:33).

Native dress in the eighteenth century gradually gave way to European-style clothing. The native house—the wigwam—also gave way to the European frame house on many reservations during that century. Indians attempted to practice subsistence farming, adding European crops and cattle to their native repertoires. Life was tough, however, as all groups attempted to eke out a living on dwindling amounts of land. Indians suffered discrimination, poverty, and starvation. Indian communities were never economically or politically integrated into the mainstream white societies. These small communities fought back as best they could against all of these problems; they continually sent petitions to the general courts of the towns protesting the alienation of their lands and other injustices. Alienation of lands was often expedited by the white-appointed overseers and guardians (to the Indian reservations), the very officials who were supposed to be protecting the integrity of the reservations. Put quite plainly, Indian communities were "expected to become extinct" (Brodeur 1985:131 writing about the Passamaquoddy settlements).

The Great Awakening of the eighteenth century inspired many southern New England native groups to join in a religious revival that promised to turn despair into hope. Although the movement was initiated by white ministers who thought that colonists had strayed from the Christian gospel, it quickly spread to native communities as well, in large part because of the work of Samson Occom (see Chapter 5). Individuals from many southern New England Indian groups began to leave their homelands to join a growing trek westward to New York to establish the Christian Indian communities of New Stockbridge and Brothertown.

During the eighteenth and nineteenth centuries, native groups were in a state of flux as a result of both migration and intermarriage. The Great Awakening became a catalyst for migration, as did white land encroachment. Potatucks and Paugussets, for example, left their homelands in west-central Connecticut and moved farther west to found Schaghticoke (see Chapter 6). Many natives throughout New England intermarried with blacks, Portuguese, and whites and either moved out of the Indian communities or brought their spouses back home with them. Intermarriage, even with whites, did not dispel prejudice, however, and it did not make the natives more visible. Children of all such unions were listed as either "coloreds" or "mulattoes" in the census materials.

The chapters in Part II document aspects of native survival after European contact. Paul Robinson (Chapter 4) and Ken Feder (Chapter 3) combine archaeology and history to demonstrate the continuities and changes in native life. Whereas Robinson looks at the wide expanse of Narragansett history in Rhode Island, Feder examines a specific community founded in Connecticut. In Chapter 5, I examine how the Christian revivalism of the eighteenth century affected native groups throughout New England, especially the Mohegan. Finally, Trudie Lamb Richmond (Chapter 6) examines the unique history of the Schaghticokes.

REFERENCES

Brodeur, Paul. 1985. *Restitution: The Land Claims of the Mashpee Passamaquoddy and Penobscot Indians of New England.* Boston: Northeastern University Press.

Jennings, Francis. 1975. *The Invasion of America: Indians, Colonialism, and the Cant of Conquest.* Chapel Hill: University of North Carolina Press.

Handsman, R., and A. McMullen. 1987. "An Introduction to Woodsplint Basketry and Its Interpretation." In *A Key into the Language of Woodsplint Baskets,* edited by R. Handsman and A. McMullen, 16–35. Washington, Conn.: American Indian Archaeological Institute.

Hauptman, Laurence. 1990. "The Pequot War and Its Legacies." In *The Pequots in Southern New England,* edited by L. Hauptman and J. Wherry, 69–80. Norman: University of Oklahoma Press.

Leach, D. E. 1958. *Flinthook and Tomahawk: New England in King Philip's War.* New York: W. W. Norton & Company.

Lester, Joan. 1987. " 'We Didn't Make Fancy Baskets until We Were Discovered': Fancy Basket Making in Maine." In *A Key into the Language of Woodsplint Baskets,* edited by R. Handsman and A. McMullen, 38–59. Washington, Conn.: American Indian Archaeological Institute.

Weinstein, Laurie. 1983. "Indian vs. Colonist: Competition for Land in 17th-Century Plymouth Colony." Ph.D. dissertation, Southern Methodist University, Dallas, Texas.

3

Material Culture at the Lighthouse Village: The Legend and the Evidence

Kenneth L. Feder

It was the desire to determine the truth behind the "Legend of the Bark-hamsted Lighthouse" that inspired reporter J. E. Mason (1855a, 1855b) to investigate the story in 1855. Concerning that legend of a village established by James Chaugham, a Narragansett Indian, and his white wife, Molly Barber, Mason was to write: "The millionaire in his mansion, with more money than brains, and the laborer in his cottage, with more children than dollars, have all heard of Barkhamsted Light-House and wondered whether it was a real or an ideal structure" (1855a). And indeed, the story of the romance between an Indian and a wealthy young white woman, their secret marriage, their flight into the sparsely inhabited hills of western Connecticut, their settling on the slopes of a rugged mountain adjacent to the Farmington River, and their establishment of an outcast community that attracted Indians, freed slaves, and disenfranchised whites has long captured imaginations (Feder 1993).

Mason was to find out firsthand that the legend of the Lighthouse was largely a veritable history when he explored the slope of Ragged Mountain in the town of Barkhamsted in northwestern Connecticut. Probing a wooded terrace just above the Farmington River, he happened upon a cluster of inhabited wigwams and cabins. This was, in fact, the Lighthouse village itself, the source of the well-known legend, and still occupied in the mid-nineteenth century by descendants of the original settlers.

While Mason may have been correct in the nineteenth century that brainless millionaires and poor laborers had all heard of the Lighthouse, the same cannot be said for at least one archaeologist, until the middle of the summer of 1986 anyway. During that summer, the eighth field season of the Farmington River Archaeological Project (FRAP), I first confronted the legend in an encounter that set in motion my own quest, through documentary analysis and archaeological excavation, to illuminate the engaging tale of the Lighthouse.

While surveying the western part of People's State Forest in 1986, we came across a site that both excited and perplexed us. On a flat, wooded terrace overlooking the floodplain of the Farmington River, we found some rather peculiar-looking stone foundations. They clearly were not aboriginal, but they equally clearly were not the remains of standard colonial structures; the foundations were quite small and irregular, and the stonework was extremely crude.

We were fascinated by this discovery, and our imaginations ran wild. Had we located a nineteenth-century camp of freed slaves? Had we stumbled upon the village site of an ancient band of turnpike robbers? After all, the site was adjacent to East River Road, which had been part of the Farmington River Turnpike, a tributary to the old Albany Turnpike that connected Albany, New York, to Hartford, Connecticut. We were quite excited about our obviously significant discovery until one of the crew crossed back over the road, walked over to a boulder by the roadside, and called out to me, "Hey, Kenny, is this important?" I ambled over to see what was so interesting about the rock and then saw the plaque set into it. It bore the following inscription:

THIS PORTION OF THE PEOPLE'S FOREST
WAS GIVEN BY THE CONNECTICUT
DAUGHTERS OF THE AMERICAN REVOLUTION
1929
NEAR THIS SPOT WAS THE
SITE OF AN INDIAN VILLAGE.

Apparently we had made a remarkable archaeological discovery—one that the DAR, J. E. Mason, and, as it turned out, most other people in northwestern Connecticut were already aware of! We soon found out that though it is some sixty miles from the coast, the location of the crude foundations was locally known as the Lighthouse. Moreover, the site is at the core of a legend repeated for more than one hundred years in the northwestern corner of Connecticut. Perhaps most remarkable, through our investigation of primary historical documents as well as the archaeological record, we have been able to show that the legend of the Lighthouse is essentially true.

THE LIGHTHOUSE LEGEND

The most complete rendering of the legend is found in a poem first published in 1952 by Lewis Sprague Mills (Mills 1952), a well-known Connecticut educator. According to the legend as presented in the poem, in 1740 Molly Barber, a strong-willed young woman living in Wethersfield, Connecticut, rebelled against her wealthy father's command forbidding her marriage to a young suitor. To punish and embarrass her father, Molly eloped with another man, James Chaugham. If the scandal of elopement were not enough, Chaugham was a Narragansett Indian, born on Block Island.

Mills describes Chaugham as an accomplished hunter with a bow and arrow and a fine fisherman who was raised as an Indian but who lived, for a time, along the Connecticut River, where he became educated in the ways of the white settlers. As the Mills rendering goes, after her father forbade her marriage, Molly promised to marry the next man who asked her: "Cross me now and I will marry," Mills has her threaten her father, "The man who first may seek my hand, whether white or any color" (p. 16). Chaugham heard of Molly, asked for her hand in marriage, and she assented. After secretly being married by a justice of the peace, the two ran off to the densely forested northwestern hills of Connecticut.

According to the poetic account, they stayed for a time in an Indian village in what is now the town of Canton, Connecticut, living among the ninety or so inhabitants of this village of twenty wigwams. Writing in 1952, Mills claimed that evidence of their fireplaces (p. 27) could still be seen on the hillside. According to Mills, they stayed there for about a month until word reached them that the sheriff and constable were on their trail. They left the village, going deeper into the forested hills until they reached a secluded spot in what is now the town of Barkhamsted, Connecticut. There they settled on a terrace above the Farmington River (Map 3.1).

According to the legend, Molly and James raised a large family of eight children in their wooded hideaway. Supposedly, other displaced people, white, Indian, and black, settled in their village. According to the legend, the settlement thrived for awhile, with several of Molly's and James's children remaining in the Lighthouse village, building additional houses, marrying, and having children of their own. The inhabitants, as the story goes, hunted in the forest and fished in the river following the old Indian ways.

The story indicates that the inhabitants also raised crops and made baskets to sell to the ever-increasing number of white settlers moving into northwestern Connecticut in the nineteenth century. As many as forty cabins or wigwams are supposed to have dotted the hillside, and the village flourished.

The Lighthouse people buried their dead on a small knoll just south of the village; about fifty are supposed to be interred in the Lighthouse ceme-

Map 3.1
Connecticut

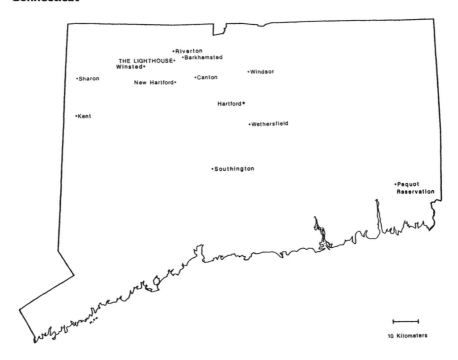

tery. The Mills poem states that James Chaugham died in about 1800 and Molly lived to be 105 years old, dying in 1820. Both, says the legend, are buried on that knoll.

In the Mills version of the legend, the strong personality of Molly was the glue that kept the settlement together. After her death, the village began to fall into decline, though it was inhabited for some time thereafter. Mills ends the poem with a rather touching tribute to the lives of James and Molly, maintaining that their struggle left a lasting impression on all those who heard the tale.

Although myriad versions of this legend have long been told, including a dramatic rendering by an aspiring nineteenth-century Connecticut playwright, as well as the rather lengthy poem by Mills, the possibility of the legend's ever being clarified has been questioned for just as long. On January 29, 1900, the *Connecticut Courant* published a feature article on the Lighthouse legend containing an interview with a Sol Webster and his wife, Mary, a couple who asserted they were the only survivors of the "Lighthouse tribe." The Websters could shed only a dim light on the story, and the reporter questioned whether the Lighthouse legend would ever be illuminated: "Inquiries into its history, when they were made by curious eyes, came too late; the true story of one of the last Indian resorts in the State will, perhaps, never be unearthed."

Unearthing the story of the Lighthouse—both literally and figuratively—however, is precisely what we have been doing since that day in 1986 when we fell upon it. The primary documentary record along with the material record at the archaeological site produced by the village inhabitants are allowing us to assess the legend itself and to describe the lives of the residents of this fascinating community.

CULTURE CHANGE AT THE LIGHTHOUSE

Occupation of the Lighthouse can be divided into three chronological phases regarding contact with the outside world. The first period begins with the inception of the village circa 1740, the date mentioned in legendary accounts, though, admittedly, there is no hard evidence for this date. The first period lasts until 1789 when the Farmington River Turnpike adjacent to the village was improved for stage travel (Wood 1919).

From 1740 to 1789, the village largely was isolated from the outside world. The relatively small number of village inhabitants would, of necessity, have been essentially self-sufficient. Contact would have been restricted to Indians living in scattered settlements in the northwestern hills of Connecticut and the small number of white settlers in the area. Artifacts of Euro-American origin should be limited to those items James and Molly brought with them and whatever they could obtain through trade with intermediary Indians or from the few white settlers.

The second phase of occupation begins with the opening of the Farmington River Turnpike for regular stage travel in 1789 and lasts until about 1815. This period almost certainly was marked by accelerating and intensifying contact with the outside world as stagecoaches regularly drove by the village. In fact, it was the stage drivers who began calling the village "the Lighthouse," because the light from the hearth fires of village residents served as a landmark for them. The artifact assemblage should reflect this as Euro-American artifacts increasingly became available to the Lighthouse inhabitants as a result of this stage travel.

The third phase of occupation begins roughly in 1815 and lasts until the village was abandoned sometime in the early 1860s. The 1815 date is an approximation; it represents the inception of rather rapid expansion in population and industry in the village of Riverton (first called Barkhamsted Forks, then Hitchcock's Mill, next Hitchcocksville, and finally Riverton, a village within the incorporated town of Barkhamsted). The first white settlement of Riverton occurred in 1782, but it remained sparsely inhabited until the second decade of the nineteenth century. Then began a period of the growth of Riverton as an industrial base in northwestern Connecticut with the opening of the Hitchcock Chair factory, the Stephens Ruler factory, and the Eagle Scythe Company. The population of Riverton grew from a few families in the early nineteenth century to 700 individuals by 1846 (Smiley 1934). The center of Riverton is fewer than two miles north of the Lighthouse, along the Farmington River Turnpike. Almost certainly, contact between inhabitants of the Lighthouse and Euro-American society after 1815 became no longer an occasional or even a fairly regular event but an everyday occurrence. Inhabitants of the Lighthouse were no longer physically at the margins, and within a short period they were to become incorporated into the dominant culture.

An examination of the material record at the site itself will show how well it conforms to our expectations based on the legend.

STRUCTURAL REMAINS

Structural remains were the first features we encountered at the Lighthouse. These stone or earth foundations, as well as their cellar holes, do not conform to the English 16-foot standard. Like the African-American communities at Parting Ways and Black Lucy's Garden, the home site of freed slave Lucy Foster, both in Massachusetts, the Lighthouse structures are uniformly smaller than 16-foot squares.

Although precise measurement is impossible, particularly for the six foundations at the site that are demarcated by little more than eroded depressions, it can readily be seen that the houses are a hodgepodge of sizes and shapes. The stone-lined foundation walls of Structures 1, 5, 6, and 7 range in length from 6 feet to more than 15 feet (Figure 3.1). The walls of the cellar holes of Structures 2, 3, 8, 9, and 10 range from less than 5 feet to nearly 10 feet in length. The cellar hole marking Structure 4 was too vague to obtain even an approximate measurement for size.

Certainly foundations or cellar holes need not be perfectly rectangular, but even in crude colonial architecture, opposite walls ordinarily are of nearly equal length, and adjacent walls meet at nearly right angles. This was not the case at the Lighthouse. Not only was there no standard size to the Lighthouse structures, there were few right angles, and rules of symmetry were not adhered to. Only Structure 5 has a rectangular foundation. The rest are only vaguely rectangular.

The findings should not be surprising. After all, the inhabitants of the Lighthouse were certainly not eighteenth- and nineteenth-century middle-class Euro-Americans. Although English individuals married into the family, the ethnic blend of native American and African-American contributed to a mixture of material cultures and building practices. Add this to the fact that the settlers were poor and, at least initially, had little access to outside technology, and it is to be expected that their house remains would be unlike those of contemporary, mainline English settlers.

Figure 3.1
Structure 7 at the Lighthouse

In many ways the foundations at the Lighthouse are reminiscent of seven-teenth-, eighteenth-, and nineteenth-century examples found in the south-eastern part of Connecticut on the Pequot Indian reservation. In both cases, foundations are smaller than the European 16-foot standard, are crudely constructed, and are often excavated into the sides of hills. In fact, when archaeologist Kevin McBride (1990a,1990b), who has focused much of his research energies on Pequot culture history, visited the Lighthouse site in 1990, he was immediately struck by the similarities between the architec-tural styles of reservation structures and at least some of those at the Light-house.

As McBride describes them, Pequot houses in the mid-eighteenth century

were built into south-facing hillsides with a fieldstone retaining wall constructed against the hillside. A low stone wall two to three feet wide was then built in a U or D shape from the back of the retaining wall. It is not known whether a sapling frame and mats were used in these structures, or if they supported some kind of more formal frame structure with shingles. (McBride 1990a:113)

His description of mid-eighteenth-century Pequot dwelling foundations matches quite closely the appearance of Lighthouse Structures 5 and 6.

Houses on the reservation and at the Lighthouse thus appear to have been an amalgam of English and native architectural forms. J. E. Mason calls the Lighthouse structures that he saw "wigwams," and a later reporter for a local newspaper, *Mountain County Herald* (1854), described the dwellings at the Lighthouse as being "built after a style of architecture about half-way between a wood-pile and a log fence." McBride is far more charitable—and likely more accurate—when he describes the eighteenth-century houses on the Pequot reservation as being "intermediate between wigwams and Euro-American frame houses" (1990a:113). This description is probably quite apt for Lighthouse village houses as well. A similar process of "creolization" of house construction is noted by historical archaeologist Leland Ferguson (1992) on plantations in South Carolina, where the cultures of Africans, native Americans, and Europeans intersected.

CEMETERY

The Lighthouse cemetery is another aspect of culture that reflects the multicultural or creole nature of the Lighthouse village. Individuals were interred in typical European fashion with bodies extended and marked with stone memorials. The markers, however, are crudely hewn, flat, rectangular stones, only roughly following a European pattern. Most of the stones are made of the same granite-schist used in foundation construction at the site. A few of the markers are made of red sandstone, another rock type abundant in the Farmington Valley.

There is no writing on the gravestones. We know from the land records that every time a Lighthouse inhabitant was required to sign a deed, he or she did so with an "X," a good indication of the lack of even signature literacy among Lighthouse inhabitants. The people of the Lighthouse did not exhibit even this ability, and this explains, along with their apparent poverty, why their gravestones bear no written inscriptions.

We identified close to one hundred stones in our cemetery survey that are potential grave markers. Almost certainly not all of these mark individual graves; some may simply be fortuitously shaped stones, and others may be footstones. Fifty graves is likely an accurate, conservative estimate for the number of graves in the Lighthouse cemetery; there may be as many as seventy-five.

MATERIAL CULTURE

When archaeologist Vern Baker (1978) analyzed the ceramic assemblage from the Black Lucy's Garden site (Bullen and Bullen 1945), he was struck by how similar that element of the material culture of freed slave Lucy Foster seemed to the ceramics of local white inhabitants: "Upon initial examination, the ceramics as well as other cultural materials retrieved from

Table 3.1
Lighthouse Artifact Assemblage

Artifact	Count	Percent of Total
Ceramics	4733	38.47
Pipes	398	3.23
Coins	5	0.04
Bricks	191	1.55
Glass:		
Window glass	737	5.99
Bottle glass	876	7.12
Lamp glass	745	6.05
Glass beads	4	0.03
Unidentifiable/Burned	461	3.75
Gun related	45	0.37
Stone tools	71	0.58
Buttons	178	1.45
Metal fragments	1396	11.35
Nails	2439	19.82
Cutlery	22	0.18
Slate pencils	3	0.02
Total	12304	

Black Lucy's Garden appear identical to those from Anglo-American sites" (p. 110). After more detailed scrutiny of the patterns reflected in the ceramic assemblage, however, Baker concludes, "Compared to recent findings from other Afro-American sites, these materials are seen to fit patterns not previously observed on sites of Anglo-Americans" (p. 110).

At first glance too, the material culture of the Lighthouse seems nearly indistinguishable from that of poor people of European ancestry in eighteenth- and nineteenth-century southern New England. However, just as was the case for poor, nineteenth-century African-Americans, the material culture of the Lighthouse, like the foundations of their houses and the stones they used to mark their graves, reflects their different cultural character.

There are more than 12,000 artifacts in the Lighthouse assemblage (Table 3.1). The most abundant artifacts (4,733 individual fragments) are ceramic sherds, which make up more than 38 percent of the assemblage. The next most abundant artifact are nails, with almost 20 percent of the total, followed by other metal fragments with a little more than 11 percent. Also found was bottle glass (about 7 percent) and window and lamp glass fragments (about 6 percent for each). Together, all of the rest of the labeled artifact categories make up the remaining 11 percent of the total.

The assemblage is overwhelmingly European in its content. Only a little less than 0.6 percent of the total assemblage (71 items) consists of stone tools, almost certainly made by Lighthouse inhabitants. The other 99.4 percent of the assemblage is made up of items obtained from the outside. In other words, virtually everything we found at the Lighthouse were Euro-American manufactured goods, purchased or traded for by Lighthouse residents. This finding provides an interesting insight about life in the village. Although they were a marginal group in both the literal and figurative sense—that is, the inhabitants of the Lighthouse were at the geographic and social margins of eighteenth- and nineteenth-century Connecticut—the vast majority of their material culture was obtained from the larger society. In other words, at least in terms of categories of items and their percentages, material culture at the Lighthouse was not unlike that in Euro-American society.

Ceramics

The ceramics at the Lighthouse are a varied lot (Figure 3.2). The types represented include redware, stoneware, creamware, pearlware, whiteware (including graniteware), yellowware, and ironstone. Included in the ceramic assemblage of the Lighthouse are the fragmentary remains of plates, saucers, cups, bowls, pans, jars, jugs, bottles, pitchers, teapots, and mugs (Table 3.2).

There were only seven identifiable maker's marks in our assemblage of more than 4,700 ceramic fragments. We identified four Canova ware marks; the term *Canova* was used by several different potteries as a designation for a style of transfer-print whiteware with a classical motif. Two of the Canova marks were from the pottery of T. Mayer in Staffordshire, England. One of the Canova marks, "Canova Stoneware" was a trademark name for a variety of pottery made by the American Pottery Company of Jersey City, New Jersey (Ripley 1942; Lehner 1988:228).

We also recovered a partial Canova mark (specifically, "anovan") of a potter named Clews. There were several potters in the Clews family, so we cannot tell definitively whose mark it was. However, based on the style of the ceramic, it almost certainly was manufactured by the English potters James and Ralph Clews, who were in business between 1818 and 1834.

Another mark seen was that of John Ridgway, a British potter; the particular mark seen here dates to after 1841. Finally, we recovered two partial marks that we have not yet been able to identify. On one we could make out only the name of the ceramic style: "Venture." On the other were the blue letters "CA." Because the sherd broke at that point, the letters may be part of a word, again indicating a Canova pattern. We cannot ascribe these marks to a particular potter or specific year or range of years.

Thus, all of the marks date to the nineteenth century, covering the years from about 1818 to 1855. Certainly, some of the ceramics found at the site predate this—according to the legend, the village was first occupied in the

Figure 3.2
Ceramics at the Lighthouse

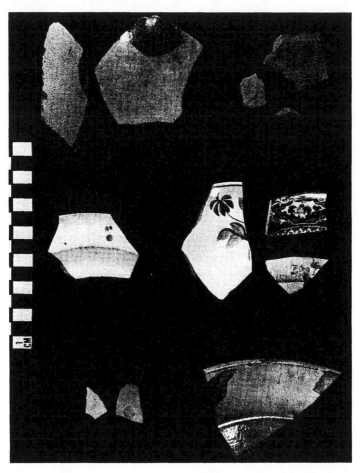

middle of the eighteenth century—but the evidence of the maker's marks is likely an indication that the inhabitants of the site became fully incorporated into a Euro-American economic sphere beginning only in the early years of the nineteenth century.

A mean ceramic date can also help date the appearance of Euro-American ceramics at the village (Table 3.3). The mean is a statistical procedure, developed by Stanley South (1977), which is based on the mean date and frequency for vessel types found at a site. The ceramic assemblages from individual structures produced dates ranging from 1814 to 1841. This conforms well with the maker's marks and supplies further evidence of the incorporation of the Lighthouse people into a broader economy only during the second half of occupation of the village.

Table 3.2
Ceramic Functional Types at the Lighthouse

Structures	1		2		3		4		5		6		7		8		Whole Site	
Functional Types	Vessel Count	%	Vessel Count	%	Vessel Count	%	Vessel Count	%	Vessel Count	%	Vessel Count	%	Vessel Count	%	Vessel Count	%	Vessel Count	%
plate	11	19.3	5	62.5	25	31.6	12	32.4	8	30.8	29	34.9	21	26.3	9	15	120	27.9
saucer	6	10.5	0	0	14	7.7	3	8.1	4	15.4	18	21.7	18	22.5	11	18.3	74	17.2
cup	2	3.5	2	25	10	12.7	5	13.5	2	7.7	9	10.8	10	12.5	11	18.3	51	11.9
bowl	15	26.3	1	12.5	12	15.2	7	18.9	1	3.8	10	12	12	15	15	25	73	17.0
pan	2	3.5	0	0	2	2.5	3	8.1	1	3.8	2	2.4	1	1.3	0	0	11	2.6
jar	0	0	0	0	0	0	0	0	1	3.8	0	0	1	1.3	0	0	2	0.5
jug	12	21.1	0	0	0	0	3	8.1	4	15.4	5	6	6	7.5	5	8.3	35	8.1
bottle	2	3.5	0	0	3	3.8	0	0	1	3.8	1	1.2	1	1.3	0	0	8	1.9
pitcher	2	3.5	0	0	3	3.8	0	0	0	0	1	1.2	0	0	2	3.3	8	1.9
mug	1	1.8	0	0	0	0	1	2.7	0	0	0	0	0	0	0	0	2	0.5
teapot	0	0	0	0	2	2.5	1	2.7	0	0	3	3.6	1	1.3	1	1.7	8	1.9
other	0	0	0	0	2	2.5	0	0	1	3.8	3	3.6	4	5	3	5	13	3.0
unidentified	4	7.02	0	0	6	7.6	2	5.4	3	11.5	2	2.4	5	6.3	3	5	25	5.8
Total vessels	57		8		79		37		26		83		80		60		430	

Table 3.3
Mean Ceramic Date for Each Lighthouse Structure

	MEAN CERAMIC DATE
Structures	
1	1831
2	1827
3	1832
4	1818
5	1836
6	1841
7	1825
8	1814

Smoking Pipes

Another common artifact recovered at the Lighthouse were fragments of kaolin smoking pipes. These commonplace long-stemmed white pipes are familiar to any visitor to a colonial restoration. These pipes were very cheap, expendable items; Noël Hume (1969:296) estimates that pipes were sold by manufacturers for as little as two shillings for a gross in the first decade of the eighteenth century. The average pipe, Noël Hume suggests, was manufactured, sold, smoked, broken, and discarded all within a matter of a year or two (Figure 3.3).

Certainly the pipes were quite inexpensive, and even quite poor people could afford them. It nevertheless is surprising that people so far out at the geographical and social margins of the eighteenth and nineteenth centuries had access to the pipes or even the small disposable income necessary to obtain them. Nevertheless, the pipes are quite abundant at the site. The presence of such a large number of fragments indicates, quite obviously, that smoking tobacco was common at the site. It also indicates that, at least after a time, the inhabitants of the Lighthouse had access to manufactured items like pipes, which they could purchase or trade for.

Coins

Rather remarkably, five intact coins were recovered in the site excavation, and all five were found in the same excavation unit located within Structure 3. Four of the five were Indian head cents, and two had decipherable dates: 1859 (the first year Indian head cents were minted) and 1861. The other two were too damaged after years in the wet, acidic soil of southern New England to determine their dates. The fifth, larger coin is a King George III half-penny token with an impression of the British monarch on one face and the British symbol "Britannia" (a seated woman holding a trident) on the other. Although the coin is badly damaged and the date has been de-

Figure 3.3
Fragments of Smoking Pipes

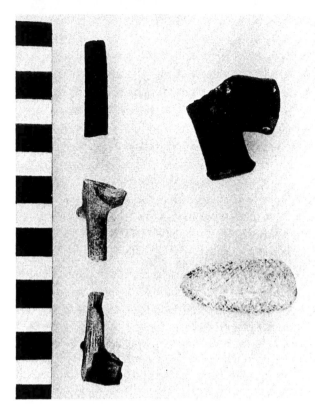

stroyed, enough of the design is visible to place its mint date between 1806 and 1807 (Larry Tallman, personal communication).

Clearly, four of the five coins date to the last years of village occupation in the middle of the nineteenth century. The King George half-penny token suggests that village inhabitants were involved in the larger cash economy at least as early as the first decade of the nineteenth century. We know that the Chaughams had been involved in land purchases as early as 1770, so it is not too surprising to find material evidence to show that this was the case nearly forty years later. The presence of nineteenth-century coins at the Lighthouse is a clear indication that its residents were participants in the broader economic system of surrounding Euro-American communities.

Bricks

Relatively few bricks or brick fragments were found at the site. The sample of 191 pieces of brick constitutes just a bit more than 1.5 percent of the entire artifact assemblage. Although abandoned structures commonly have their bricks appropriated for reuse, the quite small and fragmentary sample at the Lighthouse is a good indication that brick was not a major construction material in the village. Even for chimneys, the residents relied on local fieldstone for their primary raw material; for example, the surface directly adjacent to the southeast corner of Structure 2 is littered with the fieldstones that made up the chimney. Not a single brick was found here. This situation can be compared to a late-eighteenth-century structure located in People's State Forest, northeast of the Lighthouse village. The area around that foundation is littered with the bricks that constituted the structure's chimney.

None of the recovered brick fragments bore any marks that might be used to trace their source or to determine their precise age. Most bricks found on eighteenth- and nineteenth-century sites in America were made here, so it is a good bet that the few bricks that were used at the Lighthouse were American made. Beyond this, though size, color, and coarseness of the clay used to produce bricks do correlate with time, usually one cannot derive an accurate date from such a small, broken-up sample.

Window Glass

The presence of window glass and, hence, windows at the site provides some insight into the kinds of structures that were built there and the degree of contact with the outside world. Certainly window glass was purchased, not manufactured, by site inhabitants.

Bottle Glass

No complete bottles were found at the Lighthouse, and actually a rather small percentage of the entire assemblage consisted of glass bottle fragments (7.12 percent). This conforms well with the data from the free black community of Skunk Hollow, where bottle fragments were relatively infrequently found at the site. As archaeologist Joan Geismar (1982:151) indicates, "Ceramics in the form of creamware were available to the general public beginning in the 1760s . . . whereas bottles were not common until improvements occurred in transportation in the 1830s . . . and in general technology in the 1850s." Bottled items, therefore, became fairly common only by the end of occupation of the Lighthouse village.

There was little in the way of embossing on the bottle glass recovered at the Lighthouse for dating any of the fragments. Beyond this, the fragments tended to be quite small, and many were badly burned or melted. Based on general characteristics that could be assessed—glass color, finishing marks, mold seams, and the method used for neck finishing, all of which changed through time in the bottle industry—we can conclude that bottles were obtained by the inhabitants of the Lighthouse during the early and middle decades of the nineteenth century. This conclusion further supports the inference that with the opening of the Farmington River Turnpike and then the growth of the nearby village of Riverton, manufactured goods became increasingly available to those living at the site.

Gun Parts

During the course of excavation, we recovered five gunflints, seventeen balls of lead shot, five percussion caps, several pieces of lead from shot, and one gun part called a frizzen. Four of the gunflints are English, and one is French. Three of the English as well as the French flint are of a size and shape that conform to nineteenth-century pistols. The other English flint is larger and probably was part of a long gun or rifle. The frizzen is also almost certainly datable to the mid-nineteenth century.

Lithics

Not counting foundation stones or grave markers as individual lithic artifacts and including European gunflints in the separate category "gun parts," we recovered seventy-one stone tools at the site. Most of the lithic artifacts were stone tools manufactured at the site from local raw materials. Most common were quartz and granite-schist cutting and scraping tools. In the presence of stone tools, we have an aspect of the Lighthouse assemblage that distinguishes it absolutely from the material culture of eighteenth- and nineteenth-century Euro-Americans who used metal.

Buttons

Virtually all of the buttons recovered at the Lighthouse were manufactured in the nineteenth century (Figure 3.4). Only four can be ascribed to the eighteenth century, and even these might actually date to the early nineteenth century. Sixty-five of the buttons, a little more than one-third of the assemblage, are brass; some have various designs stamped onto their faces. About an equal number (fifty-seven) are plain glass (primarily white), with assorted bone, shell, soft white metal, faceted glass, iron-backed, and iron-faced buttons making up the remainder of the assemblage.

Miscellaneous Metal

The 1,396 fragments of miscellaneous metal recovered in the excavation are an extremely varied lot. These pieces include a large number of small, very rusted, unidentifiable fragments of iron, pieces of oil lamps, a small

Figure 3.4
Buttons Recovered at the Lighthouse

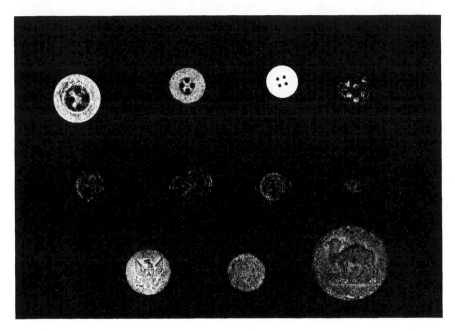

sherd of pewter, horse shoe and bridle buckle fragments, and even a piece of a wood stove.

Nails

Virtually all of the nearly 2,500 nails recovered at the site were cut nails, though a very few appear to have been hand wrought. This is a good indication that much of the nail use at the site occurred in the very late eighteenth and the first half of the nineteenth centuries, the period of site occupation when contact with the outside world was accelerating due to construction and use of the Farmington River Turnpike. Though we are certain that the site was occupied before 1770, the lack of a more substantial portion of hand-wrought nails in the assemblage indicates that these metal fasteners were not being used in early house construction at the site.

Cutlery

We recovered twenty-one complete and fragmentary cutlery items in the site excavation. The assemblage included the fragmentary remains of six spoons, five knives, and two forks. The other fragments could not be assigned a specific function. In some cases the material was too rusted to identify, and in other cases all we recovered were the bone handles of utensils. Two broken but otherwise well-preserved brass utensils also were recovered. One of these was a fork, the other the handle of a fork or a spoon. The items found, not surprisingly, were all quite inexpensive; there was no genuine silverware found at the site.

IMPLICATIONS

Vern Baker (1978) at Black Lucy's Garden and John Otto (1977, 1984) at Cannon's Point Plantation in Georgia have shown that although the material culture of ceramics at both slave and free black communities might look the same as that of local whites at first glance, there are significant differences that betray the nature of nineteenth-century socioeconomic systems in North America.

These researchers found that when compared to the crockery of wealthier whites, the ceramics of poorer blacks—both slave and free—contained a far greater proportion of serving bowls (hollowware) and a lower proportion of dishes (flatware). At Black Lucy's Garden, 51 percent of the tableware recovered in excavation was flatware, and 41 percent consisted of serving bowls (Baker 1978:111). At Cannon's Point Plantation, in slave quarters 49 percent of the excavated tableware was flatware and 44 percent was hollowware (Otto 1977:99). In the plantation owner's house, 84 percent of the tableware consisted of flat dishes, while only 7 percent represented serving bowls (Otto 1977:99).

Serving bowls were used when serving soups, pottages, and stews, and flatware was used when serving cuts of meat like roasts. In the nineteenth century, as well as today, stews, pottages, and soups served in bowls are less expensive dishes to prepare than steaks or roasts served on flat dishes and commonly are served in an attempt to stretch the food budget. Both Baker and Otto conclude that the predominance of serving bowls in the slave and free black sites they excavated is an indication of the poverty of these people. In contrast with the better-off residents of Skunk Hollow in New Jersey, the ceramics recovered are more similar to those recovered at excavations of plantation whites.

A somewhat different explanation for this difference is suggested by Ferguson (1992). He hypothesizes that although black slaves used European glazed ceramics, they incorporated these alien objects into their lives within their own cultural context. In other words, it was a general African and native American practice to treat food in a communal way, with individuals in a family sharing meals from larger serving bowls of earthenware. Ferguson suggests that the abundance of Euro-American glazed ceramic serving bowls shows a persistence, in South Carolina plantations, of an African and/or native American cultural practice of a more communal approach to meals. Interestingly, as Deetz (1977) has pointed out, a similar pattern of a

Figure 3.5
Proportions of Hollowware to Flatware

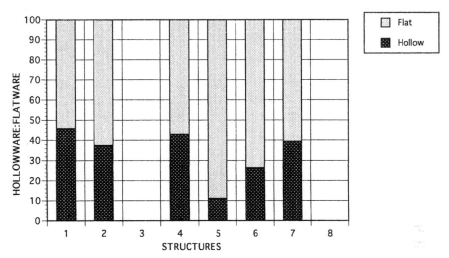

higher proportion of serving bowls and an inferred more communal approach to meals is present in Euro-American sites that date to the seventeenth century.

The proportions of flatware to hollowware in ceramic assemblages of each of the structures at the Lighthouse as well as for the entire site conform quite well to the pattern seen for African-Americans in the nineteenth century (Figure 3.5). Overall at the site, serving bowls constitute a little less than 38 percent of the total of serving ware; two structures exhibited hollowware percentages of well over 50 percent. Although these percentages are generally not as high as the African-American sites noted, people at the Lighthouse fit that general pattern, possibly signifying a fundamentally non-European pattern of food serving and eating—or, at least a non-eighteenth- or -nineteenth-century European pattern.

ECOFACTS: THE FAUNAL ASSEMBLAGE

In his poem, Mills states that the Lighthouse people subsisted in part on the natural resources of the forest, another element substantiated, at least in a general sense, by the archaeological record. An assemblage of more than 1,100 animal bone fragments was recovered in the 1991 excavation of the site. Nearly three-quarters of these remains exhibited evidence of burning, almost certainly resulting from cooking. As a combined result of various food preparation processes, as well as postdepositional deterioration in the acidic, biologically active soil of southern New England, the great majority of the faunal remains are quite fragmentary and unidentifiable as to species.

In fact, only about 3 percent (thirty-four bones) of the entire assemblage could be assigned to a species. The majority of those (twenty-two) are from whitetail deer, and a few are from small mammals (including dog) and fish. A handful of cow bones rounds out the faunal assemblage. Although the numbers are small, the notion that the inhabitants of the Lighthouse subsisted, at least in part, on local game is born out by the archaeological record.

EPILOGUE

When J. E. Mason visited the Lighthouse village in 1855, more than one hundred years after its inception, he ran into Polly Elwell, a granddaughter of James and Molly. Polly was sixty-seven years old at the time and, according to Mason, in robust health and appearing much younger. She took Mason to view the village cemetery, showing him the graves of James and his descendants and noting that only one "foreigner" was buried there. When Mason professed ignorance of Polly's meaning she told him, "He was a foreigner—like you." When Mason disputed this characterization, claiming lineal descent from the Puritans at Plymouth, it became clear that Polly equated "foreigner" with white European: "We were Americans when you foreigners came here," Polly told Mason.

It is an interesting point that Polly considered everyone else in the cemetery to be Indian, though most were of mixed blood, and many of James and Molly's descendants were categorized as white on official documents. Yet Polly Elwell was adamant on this point. She ended her interview intoning the following words: "We Narragansetts, once great, now poor. Pale faces got our corn and hunting grounds—killed us with bad liquor—and the Great Spirit takes us to white man's heaven. Narragansetts all gone— me last one."

Although James Chaugham was almost certainly at least one-half Narragansett, there has always been an undercurrent of doubt among those who have investigated the story about whether the people at the Lighthouse could really be considered Indians. Polly could have been no more explicit about it; the people of the village itself, regardless of the European or African admixture that had certainly occurred, viewed themselves as Narragansett. At least one living resident of western Connecticut who can trace his ancestry back seven generations to James and Molly Chaugham can remember his grandmother—herself a great-great-grandchild of the Chaughams—teaching him words that she told him were Narragansett. The Lighthouse village in northwestern Connecticut truly was, until at least the beginning of the second half of the eighteenth century, an outpost of self-identified native Americans and a testament to the persistence of native culture.

REFERENCES

Baker, V. G. 1978. *Historical Archaeology at Black Lucy's Garden, Andover, Massachusetts: Ceramics from the Site of a Nineteenth Century Afro-American.* Andover, Mass.: Robert S. Peabody Foundation for Archaeology.

"The Barkhamsted Lighthouse." 1854, September 30. *Mountain County Herald,* p. 1.

Bullen, A. K., and R. P. Bullen. 1945. "Black Lucy's Garden." *Bulletin of the Massachusetts Archaeological Society* 6(2):17–28.

Deetz, J. 1977. *In Small Things Forgotten: The Archaeology of Early American Life.* Garden City, N.Y.: Anchor Books.

Feder, K. L. 1993. *A Village of Outcasts: Historical Archaeology and Documentary Research at the Lighthouse.* Mountain View, Calif.: Mayfield Publishing.

Ferguson, L. 1992. *Uncommon Ground: Archaeology and Early African America, 1650–1800.* Washington, D.C.: Smithsonian Institution Press.

Geismar, J. 1982. *The Archaeology of Social Disintegration in Skunk Hollow: A Nineteenth Century Rural Black Community.* New York: Academic Press.

Lehner, L. 1988. *Lehner's Encyclopedia of U.S. Marks on Pottery, Porcelain, and Clay.* Paducah, Ky.: Collector Books.

McBride, K. 1990a. "The Historical Archaeology of the Mashantucket Pequots, 1637–1900." In L. M. Hauptman and J. D. Wherry (eds.), *The Pequots in Southern New England: The Fall and Rise of an American Indian Nation,* 96–116. Norman: University of Oklahoma Press.

———. 1990b. Personal communication.

Mason, J. E. 1855a, June 30. "Barkhamsted Lighthouse." *Mountain County Herald,* p. 1.

———. 1855b, June 23. "Barkhamsted Lighthouse." *Mountain County Herald,* p. 2.

Mills, L. S. 1952. *The Legend of the Barkhamsted Lighthouse.* Hartford: L. S. Mills.

Noël Hume, I. 1969. *A Guide to Artifacts of Colonial America.* New York: Vintage Books.

"The Old Lighthouse." 1900, January 29. *Connecticut Courant,* p. 6.

Otto, J. S. 1977. "Artifacts and Status Differences: A Comparison of Ceramics from Planter, Overseer, and Slave Sites on an Antebellum Plantation." In S. South (Ed.), *Research Strategies in Historical Archaeology,* 91–118. New York: Academic Press.

———. 1984. *Cannon's Point Plantation, 1794–1860: Living Conditions and Status Patterns in the Old South.* New York: Academic Press.

Ripley, K. B. 1942. "Canova pottery." *Hobbies:*58.

Smiley, E. 1934. *History of Riverton, Connecticut.* Riverton: Edmund Smiley.

South, S. 1977. *Method and Theory in Historical Archaeology.* New York: Academic Press.

Tallman, L. 1993. Personal communication.

Wood, F. J. 1919. *The Turnpikes of New England and the Evolution of the Same through England, Virginia, and Maryland.* Boston: Marshall Jones.

4

A Narragansett History from 1000 B.P. to the Present

Paul A. Robinson

This overview of the past 1,000 years of Narragansett history uses archaeological information, late-twentieth-century Narragansett Indian tribal oral history as told to me by two tribal officials, and written sources. One fundamental piece of oral history underlies this overview: that the people representing Narragansett country today are descended from the people who lived around the small coves and estuaries of Narragansett Bay 1,000 (and more) years ago. This is what the Narragansett people tell me, and I see nothing in the archaeological or written records to dispute their assertion. In fact, archaeological data indicate that by 3,000 years ago, certain places around Narragansett Bay were settled and then used repeatedly until European colonization, when these settlements were abandoned or destroyed.

The idea of an enduring Narragansett people is the central construct of this history. Endurance, however, does not imply a history of stasis, made by people who followed unchanging ways of life. Moreover, it is not a history without ambiguity. When viewed from archaeological, written, and oral perspectives, particular elements of Narragansett history that wrap around this construct of an enduring people can be interpreted differently.

Sometimes one source of information contradicts the other, in what are, perhaps, unresolvable differences. In other instances, the use of multiple sources lends welcome complexity to past events that single-source histories have simplified and perhaps misrepresented. Oral history, for example, provides an insight into what some Narragansett people find important to remember and how these remembrances are used to define what it means to be Narragansett now. Archaeological information can be used to question the assertions of both oral and written sources, to guard, for example, against making inaccurate generalizations of the past. In concert all three sources can be used to evaluate the biases inherent in all data gathering and interpretation.

This historical overview is not a confrontational exercise, nor is it an argument for the construction of equally valid, but different, histories. It is, rather, an attempt to include some of the ideas, information, and people that have been omitted, overlooked, or purposefully denied a place in the past. In some cases, the differences and ambiguities may never be resolved, nor need they; in these differences lie subjectively charged views and memories that comprise a living history and define what it means to be Narragansett in the late twentieth century.

The Narragansetts are a federally recognized Indian tribe with approximately 2,400 members and more than 2,500 acres of land. Most of the tribal members live in the state of Rhode Island; tribal land is within the present-day Rhode Island towns of Charlestown and Westerly. In 1985 the Tribal Council established the Narragansett Indian Archaeological-Anthropological Committee (NIAAC) to work with outside scholars and to establish tribal standards for archaeological investigations on tribal lands. NIAAC is chaired by the understudy to the tribal medicine man and includes the tribal medicine man, the tribal genealogist, the tribal historian, a tribal member, a tribal elder, and several honorary members. Members of this committee provided me with the oral history used in this chapter.

This chapter emphasizes four topics to illustrate the interplay of different sources of information: maize agriculture, the idea of Narragansett dominance in the seventeenth century, the death of King Tom Ninigret in the eighteenth century, and detribalization in the nineteenth century.

SUBSISTENCE PRACTICES AND MAIZE AGRICULTURE

One thousand years ago the native American ancestors of the Narragansetts lived in communities located around the small coves and estuaries of Narragansett Bay. Archaeological data suggest that these areas were settled around 3,000 years ago, about the same time that rising sea levels stabilized and the mudflats formed. By 1,000 years ago, these biotically rich coastal areas and the nearby interior—places like Providence, Pawtuxet, Greenwich Cove, and Wickford Cove—were densely settled and seemingly used all the year. Seasonality studies, conducted at two sites, the Greenwich Cove site and the nearby interior Lambert Farm site, indicate year-round use (Bernstein 1993; Jordan Kerber and Alan Leveillee, personal communication).

The Greenwich Cove area has been studied more thoroughly than any other place on the bay. Four site excavations—the Greenwich Cove site (Bernstein 1993), the Sweet-Meadow Brook site (Fowler 1956), the Locust Spring site (Fowler 1962), and the Lambert Farm site (Kerber, Leveillee, and Greenspan—1989) and a survey of Potowomut Neck (Kerber 1984) provide archaeological information regarding the settlement of this area and, especially, its intensive use by native people from 1,000 years ago into the seventeenth century. Bernstein's work is the most comprehensive of these studies, and most of the following discussion about subsistence practices and maize agriculture is based on his findings.

All four sites had complex components dating between 1000 B.P. and European settlement, were located within one mile of each other, and provided strong evidence of sustained and varied use. Collectively these sites contained hearths, human burials, dog burials, ceremonial features, ceramics, stone pipes, bone tools, stone drills, projectile points, knives, and woodworking tools. At the Greenwich Cove site shell midden, Bernstein (1990:110) found "seven species of mollusks, ten species of terrestrial mammals, two species of reptiles, five species of saltwater fish, three species of birds, and two nut species." The environment near the site, he observed, provided excellent habitat for a wide variety of plants and animals:

The site borders a freshwater pond . . . rich in waterfowl and reptile life, and two tidal rivers are located less than a kilometer away. Many of the nutritionally important resources (deer and shellfish) are available most of the year. Tons of refuse . . . were excavated and almost nothing was found that is not available within a few hundred meters of the site. (ibid.)

One of the interesting findings about the archaeological information from sites in the Greenwich Cove area—Lambert Farm, Sweet-Meadow Brook, Locust Spring, Greenwich Cove, and the scores of other sites and features and hundreds of soil samples from these sites and features around Narragansett Bay—is the complete absence of beans, squash, or corn. This absence is in apparent disagreement with Narragansett oral traditions that maintain a vital role for maize agriculture during these centuries and the written record of the sixteenth and seventeenth centuries that clearly indicate corn as an important dietary staple at Narragansett Bay.

Corn has been recovered from features in the lower Connecticut River Valley (Bendremer, Kellogg, and Largy 1991) and on the Boston Harbor Islands (Luedtke 1980) and Martha's Vineyard (Ritchie 1969). People living on Narragansett Bay were undoubtedly familiar with and probably used and consumed these domestic plants, but the archaeological evidence suggests strongly that cultigens were not a major dietary staple. Archaeological evidence of cultigens is found only at a seventeenth-century site (Morenon 1986), corroborating the written record regarding the presence of cultigens at the time of European contact and settlement.

Based on his work at Greenwich Cove and his examination of other published and unpublished studies from the Narragansett Bay area, Bernstein concluded that year-round coastal settlements were common by 2000 B.P., the evidence for "residential stability" is particularly strong by 1000 B.P., sedentism was possible even without agriculture, and by 1000 B.P. there was a "densely packed" coastal population with communities of people living at places like the Greenwich Cove area (1990:110).

THE IDEA OF NARRAGANSETT DOMINANCE

In the seventeenth century, according to the written records, the coves and inlets around Narragansett Bay and nearby interior lands had names like Coweset, Shawomet, Narragansett, Pawtuxet, Touisset, and Sakonnet. Russell Handsman (1991) has used the term *homeland* (from "Council Decisions," a poem by Ron Welburn, a Cherokee) to describe areas such as these: places of long and enduring settlements.

It was into the homelands of Indian people that Europeans came to live in the seventeenth century: Roger Williams settled at Narragansett in 1636, Samuel Gorton at Shawomet, Benedict Arnold at Pawtuxet, and so on. When these Europeans arrived at the western shores of Narragansett Bay, the various west bay native American communities were acting together, under the leadership of the Narragansett sachems. The Narragansetts had represented other western Narragansett Bay communities since at least the end of the great epidemic that killed thousands of Indian people east of Narragansett Bay between 1616 and 1619. These diseases did not penetrate Narragansett country, staying on the eastern side of Narragansett Bay (Salisbury 1982).

The power and dominance of the Narragansetts in the western Narragansett Bay area was based, in part, on the perceived ability of the Narragansett medicine people to keep the European diseases out of their territory (Robinson 1990; Young 1841). During the 1620s and 1630s, this dominance was strengthened, along with that of the Pequots, by their participation in the wampum trade (Salisbury 1982).

Although the Narragansett sachems represented other communities in matters of foreign diplomacy, their authority was not absolute. Rather, it was based in the idea of autonomy in unity (Robinson 1990). This principle was described by Indian and non-Indian people alike: the sachem's authority was based on consensus and persuasion, and people, families, and communities could choose to follow or not. Social organization was based on the authenticity of individuals and communities, and it was the recognition of that authenticity that enabled families and communities to act together. Kinship ties among communities, ties that crossed the bay into Pokonoket and reached west at least as far as Pequot and Mohegan country, enabled this idea to work (ibid.).

Soon after the 1637 English massacre of the Pequots at Mystic, communities at Pawtuxet, Shawomet, Coweset, and some Nipmuc groups separated from Narragansett. Narragansett sachems attempted to prevent and deter this separation. One leader, Pessicus, asserted that he and his ancestors had been the ruling sachems on Narragansett Bay "since time out of mind" (Gorton 1646:90–91). The oral history agrees with Pessicus. The written record, however, suggests that although family lineage was an important factor, leadership was also dependent on circumstance and ability.

Although Pessicus maintained that Narragansett dominance had endured for a long time, "since time out of mind," and was not affected by circumstance, the leaders of some Indian communities disagreed. Their words and actions on this matter were clear. A Nipmuc leader, for example, acknowledged that he had presented gifts to the Narragansett sachems but that the gifts were "a present unto them and not by right or due" (Shurtleff 1854:4, 358). In another instance, some Cowesets and Shawomets pointedly refused a Narragansett demand to mourn the death of an important Narragansett person (Pulsifer 1859:vol. 9, 375). In 1660, Roger Williams wrote, "The Inhabitants of these parts with most of the Cowwesets and Neepmucks have long since forsaken the Narriganset Sachims" (LaFantasie 1988:514).

The leaders of these communities persisted in their denial of Narragansett hegemony and did not act with the Narragansett leaders until the Puritans from Massachusetts and Connecticut invaded their homelands in 1675, drawing the Narragansetts and others into a major and widespread war with Metacom against the Puritans, a war the English named after Metacom's English name: King Philip's War. This regrouping of communities, I suggest, was not a return to normalcy characterized by Narragansett dominance but was, rather, further evidence of a highly fluid political structure, one that was contingent and changeable, now required unification against an English invasion, and probably had been contingent and fluid since "time out of mind."

THE DEATH OF KING TOM NINIGRET

Indian people who survived King Philip's War faced an uncertain and dangerous future. Some people were sold into slavery, others were given terms of indenture with colonial families, and others found relative safety with Ninigret, the Niantic leader, in southwestern Rhode Island. Ninigret had not fought with the Narragansetts during the war and had, on occasion, sided with English from Connecticut. Some people who had decided not to fight with Metacom and the Narragansett sachems stayed with Ninigret during the war. Now they were joined by others to form the largest Indian community in southern New England (Campbell and LaFantasie 1978; Simmons 1978).

In 1709 these various people were declared to be Narragansett in an agreement between the Niantic leader Anquawas, called Ninigret II, and the colony of Rhode Island. From this point on, most native people on the west side of Narragansett Bay would be known to colonial authorities as Narragansett, and what had been composed of many different homelands now was simply Narragansett country (Robinson 1990:256–270).

The Ninigret family, with colonial support, became the established rulers of approximately thirty square miles of reservation land in the present-day town of Charlestown (Boissevain 1975:29) In time they became in many ways like the colonial gentry who kept them in power: they lived in a fine house, had Narragansett people working for them in the fields, were formally educated, and were married in the Anglican church. The Ninigrets sold and rented land, using the proceeds for their personal needs. These practices continued through the eighteenth century, gradually diminishing the reservation lands (Campbell and LaFantasie 1978; Simmons 1989).

In the 1750s a group of Narragansetts complained to the colonial General Assembly that Tom Ninigret, successor to George Ninigret in 1746, had sold their best farms and that they were "in danger of being utterly deprived of the means of procuring a maintenance, and must either starve or become a town charge" (Bartlett 1861: vol. 6, 357). This dissident group, led by Samuel Niles, got no help from the General Assembly: Ninigret's principal creditors and benefactors of land sales were either in the General Assembly or able to influence its members (Simmons and Simmons 1982:38).

King Tom was the last of the influential Ninigrets; his reign ended in 1769 or 1770. A Narragansett tribal council was formed. The recognition of this council by the state of Rhode Island soon after the Revolutionary War marked the formal end of the Ninigret family's rule.

The demise of King Tom is treated differently by written and oral sources. The secondary histories are vague about when and how he died. His grave site is thought, but not known for certain, to be at Indian Burial Hill on Narragansett land in Charlestown. Ethel Boissevain wrote, for example, that "King Tom's life came to an untimely end, undated, but around early 1770" (1975:42). Rhode Island colonial records indicate that in February 1770, a committee was appointed by the assembly "to dispose of the estate of Thomas Ninegret, deceased, late sachem of said tribe" (Bartlett 1862:9).

Narragansett oral history is particularly harsh on these years of Ninigret rule and is less vague, but still uncertain, about how he ended his days as sachem. John Brown, chairman of NIAAC, told me, "King Tom did not die in Narragansett Country. If you think he did, show me where he is buried. What happened is some Narragansett people went into Tom's house in the middle of the night, and put him on a slave boat headed south for Barbados." Another member of NIAAC, Ella Sekatau, did not recall that story precisely but noted that Tom's death was "shrouded in mystery" and that it is generally believed that "his own people got rid of him." Regardless of how Tom left Narragansett country, his departure began the transition to an elected tribal council, a form of government that has persisted into the late twentieth century.

DETRIBALIZATION

In the last half of the nineteenth century, the policy of the federal government toward reservation tribes was based on the idea that reservation life prevented people from becoming self-supporting members of American society. This policy was made law by the Dawes Act in 1887, which ended tribal ownership of land on some reservations and established privately owned allotments for individuals. On these parcels, Indian people were expected to make a living and become fully integrated members of American society.

In Rhode Island, the General Assembly acted on this new idea by declaring that the Narragansett tribe no longer existed. In 1879 a committee was established to oversee the detribalization process, and the state offered to buy tribal land and to sell it at public auction. The land was sold for $5,000. Divided equally, each person received $15.43. Two acres of land, however, were reserved to the tribe. On this land was the stone church, built by Narragansett masons in 1859 to replace the wooden structure that Samuel Niles, leader of the resistance movement against the Ninigret family, had constructed in 1740 (Simmons 1989).

The major secondary historical sources on this period describe detribalization as something the Narragansetts reluctantly agreed to and characterize the proceedings as fair and open. Campbell and LaFantasie, for example, suggested that "most Indians were convinced that the land sale was "fair and equitable" and that detribalization was "a pragmatic decision that made sense in 1880" (1978:78, 79). Ethel Boissevain noted that detribalization enabled Narragansett children to attend district schools and that poor people were thereafter cared for at state expense (1975:73). William Simmons observed that although the tribe was divided on the issue of detribalization, the council agreed to the land sale, and the Rhode Island commissioners and legislature "tried to be honest and fair in terminating the reservation and reimbursing members of the tribe for the sale of their land" (1989:74).

NIAAC members John Brown and Ella Sekatau do not agree that the proceedings were fair and pointed out that a number of Narragansetts refused to collect their share of the land sale money. They say that the council members who agreed to detribalization did so under threats of violence, from people both within and outside the tribe.

A reading of the detribalization proceedings suggests that other scholars have, at best, simplified the record. There were three public hearings between July 30 and October 31, 1879: two at the Indian Meeting House and one at nearby Cross Mills, prior to the decision to detribalize. A fourth closed meeting between the state commissioners and the Tribal Council was held on December 26, 1879, at the office of one of the commissioners, George Carmichael, Jr., in Shannock Mills (Committee 1880:5).

At the public meetings, all but one Narragansett, and some non-Indians, opposed detribalization and the sale of lands, unless the state was willing to recognize past land claims that would have increased Indian lands substantially.

At the first and second hearings, Tribal Council members Joshua Noka, Daniel Sekater, and Benjamin Thomas remarked that detribalization would not make them full American citizens; they would remain second-class citizens in the eyes of most non-Indians. Council leader Gideon Ammons was willing to accept detribalization but only on the condition that the "vacant land" quitclaimed by Ninigret in 1709 be restored first. Ammons also maintained that the tribe had been dispossessed of its shoreline rights—a five-rod strip of land along the state's coast—and requested that it be reimbursed for these lands as well as the vacant lands.

At the third and final public hearing, council president Gideon Ammons repeated the request:

As far as I am concerned, if the State is willing to pay us for our vacant lands and the shore claims . . . then let them make us citizens and raise the guardianship. But until we have what is actually ours, I don't see that it is any use for us to come out citizens for nothing, just for the sake of giving the State what belongs to us. (Committee 1880:82–83)

The commissioners attempted to change the subject, limiting the discussion to the 922 acres of "public lands" within Charlestown. Another Tribal Council member, Joshua Noka, asked the committee to look into the shore claims: "There is one thing I don't want the committee to slip over" (Committee 1880:89). Brister Michael, another council member, observed that it would not "make much difference" if he were made a U.S. citizen, but if the state did sell the land, the money should be paid to "the heads of families" (ibid.:90–91). The hearing ended without resolution and with the Tribal Council still holding to its position that the state would need to settle for the land along the coast and the land quitclaimed by Ninigret in 1709.

On December 26, 1879, however, in a private meeting at the office of state commissioner George Carmichael, Jr., the Tribal Council agreed to sell what was left of the 30 square miles set aside in 1709: 922 acres of tribal land was sold to the state. No minutes were taken at this meeting. The commissioners simply reported that the meeting produced a "satisfactory result to all present" (Committee 1880:5). This seemingly abrupt change in the Tribal Council's position is explained by NIAAC members John Brown and Ella Sekatau as due to threats of violence against some council members.

1890 TO THE PRESENT

Although terminated by the state, the tribe continued to exist. As Joshua Noka said in 1883, "We have the same blood running through our veins that we had before we sold the lands" (Committee 1884). From 1892 into the 1930s, Narragansetts such as Gideon and George Ammons, Daniel Sekater, Joshua Noka, and Abraham Champlin pressed for the state to return land along the Rhode Island shoreline. These shore claims included a five-rod strip of land from Westerly to Pawtucket, land that Ammons said was reserved to the Indians "for the privilege of pitching our tents, and fishing, to procure a living" (Committee 1880:25).

These shore claims were denied by the Rhode Island State Supreme Court in 1898, and subsequent attempts to pursue the matter with the Bureau of Indian Affairs failed (LaFantasie and Campbell 1978). In 1975, led by Eric Thomas and Ella Sekatau, the Narragansetts filed suit in federal court for the return of the detribalization lands. The tribe argued that the state of Rhode Island had violated the federal Non-Intercourse Act of 1790 by disposing of Indian land without federal approval. The suit was settled out of court in 1978; the tribe recovered 1,800 acres of woodland and swamp surrounding the stone meeting house, meeting grounds, and Cocumpaug Pond. Later that year, a fifteen-volume petition for federal tribal recognition was filed. The federal government acknowledged tribal status in 1983. In 1991 a donation of land from Arlene and Irving Crandall increased Narragansett holdings to about 2,500 acres.

The Narragansett homeland endures. At a Rhode Island State House ceremony in 1985 that formally acknowledged the return of lands lost at detribalization, the Narragansett medicine man, Lloyd "Running Wolf" Wilcox, spoke of the feeling this long history evokes:

For this first time in the history of the Tribe we have reversed the process wherein the Indians must always lose the most valuable thing there is, and that's their small portion of the mother earth. It is a sacred thing when you walk the land, and you drink from a spring, and you hunt in a forest, that for a thousand or two thousand years or more your direct ancestors have done this.

NOTE

John Brown and Edward Sanderson provided useful comments on an earlier draft of this chapter. Conversations with Russell Handsman, Robert Goodby, David Bernstein, and Michael Bell were also helpful. I especially acknowledge Ella Sekatau, John Brown, and Lloyd Wilcox for many conversations about Narragansett history. I am grateful to Laurie Weinstein for organizing the original 1993 NEAA symposium and for editing this book. The final responsibility for the contents and conclusions of this chapter is, of course, mine.

REFERENCES

Bartlett, John Russell, ed. 1861. *Records of the Colony of Rhode Island and Providence Plantations, in New England.* Vol. 6: *1757–1769.* Providence: Knowles, Anthony and Company, State Printers.

———. 1862. *Records of the Colony of Rhode Island and Providence Plantations, in New England.* Vol. 7:*1770–1776.* Providence: Knowles, Anthony and Company, State Printers.

Bendremer, Jeffrey C., E. A. Kellogg, and Tonya B. Largy. 1991. "A Grass-Lined Maize Storage Pit and Early Maize Horticulture in Central Connecticut." *North American Archaeologist* 12:325–349.

Bernstein, David A. 1990. "Prehistoric Seasonality Studies in Coastal Southern New England." *American Anthropologist* 92:96–115.

———. 1993. *Prehistoric Subsistence on the Southern New England Coast.* San Diego: Academic Press.

Boissevain, Ethel. 1975. *The Narragansett People.* Phoenix: Indian Tribal Series.

Campbell, Paul R., and Glenn W. LaFantasie. 1978. "Scattered to the Winds of Heaven—Narragansett Indians, 1676–1880." *Rhode Island History* 37:66–83.

Committee of Investigation. 1880. *Narragansett Tribe of Indians. A Historical Sketch and Evidence Taken.* Providence: E. L. Freeman and Company.

———. 1884. *Fourth Annual Report.* Providence: E. L. Freeman and Company.

Fowler, William S. 1956. "Sweet-Meadow Brook: A Pottery Site in Rhode Island." *Bulletin of the Massachusetts Archaeological Society* 18:1–23.

———. 1962. "Locust Spring Site: Its Occupational Activities." Site reports of the Narragansett Archaeological Society of Rhode Island.

Gorton, Samuel. 1646. "Simplicities Defense against Seven-Headed Policy." In Peter Force, ed., *Tracts and other Papers, Relating Principally to the Origin, Settlement, and Progress of the Colonies in North America, from the Discovery of the Country to the Year 1776.* Volume 4, no. 6. New York: Peter Smith.

Handsman, Russell G. 1991. "What Happened to the Heritage of the Weantinock People." *Artifacts* 19(1):3–9.

Kerber, Jordan E. 1984. "Prehistoric Human Ecology and Changing Environment of Potowomut Neck, Warwick, Rhode Island: An Interdisciplinary Approach." Ph.D. dissertation, Brown University.

Kerber, Jordan E., Alan D. Leveillee, and Ruth L. Greenspan. 1989. "An Unusual Dog Burial Feature at the Lambert Farm Site, Warwick, Rhode Island: Preliminary Observations." *Archaeology of Eastern North America* 17:165–174.

LaFantasie, Glenn W., ed. 1988. *The Correspondence of Roger Williams.* 2 vols. Hanover, N.H.: Brown University/University Press of New England for the Rhode Island Historical Society.

LaFantasie, Glenn W., and Paul R. Campbell. 1978. "Land Controversies and the Narragansett Indians, 1880–1938." Unpublished report, Rhode Island Historical Preservation Commission.

Luedtke, Barbara. 1980. "The Calf Island Site and the Late Prehistoric Period in Boston Harbor." *Man in the Northeast* 20:25–76.

Morenon, E. Pierre. 1986. *Archaeological Sites at an Ecotone: Route 4 Extension, East Greenwich and North Kingstown, Rhode Island.* Occasional Papers in Archaeology 14. Providence: Public Archaeology Program, Rhode Island College.

Pulsifer, David, ed. 1859. "Acts of the Commissioners of the United Colonies of New England." In *Records of the Colony of New Plymouth in New England,* edited by Nathaniel B. Shurtleff and David Pulsifer, vols. 9–10. Boston: William White.

Ritchie, William A. 1969. *The Archaeology of Martha's Vineyard.* New York: Natural History Press.

Robinson, Paul A. 1990. "The Struggle Within: The Indian Debate in Seventeenth-Century Narragansett Country." Ph.D. dissertation, State University of New York, Binghamton.

Salisbury, Neal. 1982. *Manitou and Providence: Indians, Europeans and the Making of New England, 1500–1643.* New York: Oxford University Press.

Shurtleff, Nathaniel B., ed. 1854. *Records of the Governor and Company of the Massachusetts Bay in New England.* 5 vols. Boston: William White.

Simmons, William S. 1978. "Narragansett." *The Northeast,* edited by Bruce G. Trigger, 190–197. *Handbook of North American Indians,* Vol. 15. Washington, D.C.: Smithsonian Institution.

———. 1989. *The Narragansett.* New York: Chelsea House Publishers.

Simmons, William S., and Cheryl L. Simmons, eds. 1982. *Old Light on Separate Ways: The Narragansett Diary of Joseph Fish, 1765–1776.* Hanover: University Press of New England.

Young, Alexander. 1841. *Chronicles of the Pilgrim Fathers of the Colony of Plymouth from 1602 to 1625.* Boston: Little and Brown.

5

Samson Occom: A Charismatic Eighteenth-Century Mohegan Leader

Laurie Weinstein

OCCOM'S LIFE AND TIMES

I was Born a Heathen and Brought up In Heathenism, till I was between 16 & 17 years of age, at a Place Called Mohegan, in New London, Connecticut, in New England. My Parents Livd a wandering life, for did all the Indians at Mohegan, they Chiefly Depended upon Hunting, Fishing, & Fowling for their Living and had no Connection with the English, excepting to Traffic with them in their small Trifles; and they Strictly maintained and followed their Heathenish Ways, Customs & Religion, though there was Some Preaching among them. . . . When I was 16 years of age, we heard a Strange Rumor among the English, that there were Extraordinary Ministers Preaching from Place to Place and a Strange Concern among the White People. . . . These Preachers did not only come to us, but we frequently went to their meetings. . . . After I was awakened & converted, I went to all the meetings. . . . I began to Learn the English Letters; got me a Primer, and used to go to my English Neighbours frequently for Assistance in Discovery of the way of Salvation through Jesus Christ. (Occom 1990a:728–729)

So begins Samson Occom's "Short Narrative of My Life." Occom was born in 1723, and by 1743 he had already distinguished himself as an extraordinary man who was wise in the traditions of both native and white societies. He learned English ways, yet he never forgot his people, and he attempted to use the message of Christ to save them.

Occom was very much a product of his environment; the relationships between Indians and whites shaped his mission of salvation. In 1723, the Mohegans had been exposed to white society for over eighty years. During that time, Uncas, sachem of the Mohegan, had befriended the curious foreign settlers who made New London their permanent home. Uncas abetted the English colonists as they destroyed his related yet despised neighbors, the Pequots, in the 1637 Pequot War. Uncas and his successors wooed the colonists with land, which they later quickly snatched up. By alienating lands, the Mohegans gained certain prerogatives with the colonists (for example, the colonists defended Uncas from his other despised neighbors, the Narragansetts), but the strategy failed in the long run for it bargained away the very livelihood of the people—their land. By the turn of the eighteenth century, the Mohegans were restricted to just several thousand acres along the Thames River, above the English settlement of New London. Gone was their acreage, which used to stretch from the Thames River north and east to the present-day borders of Massachusetts and Rhode Island. Deprived of land, many Mohegans were destitute; some purchased English goods from English stores on credit, while others attempted to live a "wandering life" by hunting, gathering, and fowling on the periphery of growing English settlements (Weinstein and Sabo 1993; Weinstein 1991, 1990). Also at the turn of the century, the Mohegans were embroiled in a bitter land suit against the colonists that divided them and forced them to choose between sachems. It also absorbed a lot of Occom's own energies. Despite all the misfortunes the colonists had visited upon their native neighbors, they did bring one new element that Samson Occom seized upon as an instrument of hope: Christianity. Christianity was not new to the New England Indians. During the seventeenth century, missionaries from the colonies of Plymouth, Masssachusetts Bay, and the Providence Plantations had established "praying towns" (organized Indian Christian communities) throughout the region (Brenner 1984). The Mohegans did not initially embrace this new religion; Uncas had remained quite skeptical about it despite the repeated but halfhearted attempts of the colonists to introduce it to him and his Mohegans.

It was Samson Occom who "sold" Christianity to the Mohegans and many other former disbelievers. In order to understand Occom's mission, we must examine the great religious revivalism of the mid-eighteenth century that completely absorbed Occom. The "Extraordinary Preachers" Occom heard were the itinerants, who were a product of the Great Awakening of 1734–1742. They broke with tradition by traveling widely, preaching sermons both day and night, and even preaching in other ministers' parishes.

These New Lights were led by James Davenport, George Whitefield, and Eleazar Wheelock, all of whom held the conviction that New England had fallen into a moral abyss of "religious declension": "The hearts of the people were set on their lands and their cattle rather than on the righteousness and the word of God" (Bushman 1969:3). These preachers were charismatic men who knew how to captivate their audience and prey upon their listeners' worst fears. Such fears arose from the contradictions inherent in Puritanism as illuminated by Morgan (1958:7–8) and Brenner (1984:49): An individual should spend his whole life seeking salvation, but an individual could only do evil. An individual should put all hopes in Christ, but Christ would reject him unless he was foreordained as one of the elect (that is, had received divine grace). An individual should work hard and enjoy the good things in life, but he should focus all his attention on God. An individual should not sin, but he is born with original sin. An individual should transform the world into a holy kingdom, but the depravity of the world is immutable.

Playing upon these contradictions, a charismatic New Light would plunge his listeners

into the blackest despair and then bring him out into light and joy. . . . He told his listeners that they were enemies of God and certain to be damned. When sufficiently crushed by their sinfulness, they learned that good works would never save them but that God's free grace would. This idea lifted men from their misery and restored them to confidence in God's love. (Bushman 1967:187)

Sinners were also told that "impulses beyond their control drove them to resist divine authority" (Bushman 1967:192). It was not their fault that they had these impulses or this "disease." Once this disease had been identified by the New Light revivalist, the path was open for salvation. All the sinner had to do was plainly confront his guilt, repudiate his sins, and then go through a "conversion experience" (ibid.:191–192). Conversion meant that God had directly spoken to an individual and had made that individual an instrument of divine grace. All over New England, new churches were formed by these converted "saints" or New Lights.

Samson Occom's convictions were directly inspired by the New Lights. When he was nineteen, Occom begged his mother to send him off to study with Eleazar Wheelock, who had a reputation for teaching white youth about the ministry (Dankert 1978:3). "Ask him," Occom wrote in his journal, "whether he would take me a little while to Instruct me in Reading" (ibid.). Occom's request was fueled by his desire to teach Indian children to read (ibid.). Wheelock agreed to start working with Occom "as soon as possible," and both Wheelock and his English colleague George Whitefield eventually became Occom's most influential backers and friends (Weinstein and Sabo 1993; Blodgett 1935; Richardson 1933:10–12).

After studying with Wheelock for four years, Occom struck off on his own, first to Niantic, "thinking they may want a School Master," then to Narragansett, then back to Mohegan, and finally off to Montauk, Long Island, in 1749, where he became both a schoolteacher and a minister to the Montauk and Shinecock peoples (Occom 1990a:732; Mohegan Descendants n.d.). Occom was employed by several missionary societies throughout his life. The Society for the Propagation of the Gospel in New England (also called the London Society and the New England Society) supported his work on Long Island. It worked through a Boston Board of Commissioners. The Society in Scotland for Propagating Christian Knowledge supported him next. This society was controlled by the Scotch Presbyterians and went through the Connecticut Board of Correspondents (Blodgett 1935:37, 71; Weiss 1959).

While at Montauk, Occom married one of his pupils, Mary Fowler, and together they produced ten children who "were born . . . as fast as natural law would permit" (Blodgett 1935:44). Occom could barely keep his family fed and clothed. His church suffered too, and his efforts to secure more funding from the missionary societies that employed him almost always ended in disappointment. When Occom asked for additional monies for his work, he learned secondhand that the "gentlemen of Boston [the Boston Commissioners] . . . were much Displeased with him" and blamed him for "being Extravagant." He pointed out the gross inequities in pay between white and Indian missionaries: "These Same Gentlemen gave a young Missionary a Single man, one Hundred Pounds for one year, and fifty Pounds for an Interpreter, and thirty Pounds for an Introducer . . . they gave me 180 Pounds for 12 years of service [on Montauk] . . . . I was my own Interpreter . . . School master and Minister" (Occom 1990a:734–735).

During Occom's Montauk stay, his friend and mentor, Dr. Wheelock, was busy founding his Indian Charity School in Lebanon, Connecticut. It began with two pupils in 1754, but eventually Indian and white students from all over New England began to attend (Szasz 1980), including Occom's brother-in-law, David Fowler, and son-in-law, Joseph Johnson. Both men proved to be influential in Occom's next assignment.

Occom and Fowler were sent to Oneida at the request of the Indians there to set up a ministry. This mission, under the auspices of Wheelock, was sponsored by the Society in Scotland for Propagating Christian Knowledge. Occom traveled to the Six Nations three times between 1761 and 1763. In a 1762 letter he suggested that the Iroquois were "religiously disposed" and that "much good" may be done here among the Indians if "proper methods" were employed. Occom also commented on his instructions from the Scotch Society (Occom: 1762). They asked him to use whatever power necessary to make the Iroquois acknowledge King George and "not suffer any French or Roman Catholick Emmisary's to come amongst them." After all, England was at war with France and Spain at the time, and the English did not want to give those rival nations leverage with powerful Indian tribes, like the Iroquois, in North America.

The Oneida mission was expensive. Wheelock's and Occom's letters often reflect on the costs of fitting out missionaries, interpreters, and schoolmasters to go out into the "wilderness," as the Six Nations was called during the mid-eighteenth century (Wheelock 1765:6–8). These recruits were "cloathed and furnished" with horses, furniture, money, and other necessities (Wheelock 1765:8). Fowler's particular assignment was problematical according to Wheelock. Although the Oneida welcomed Fowler, they were poor and suffering from a famine; they were in need of houses, plows, and carriages, and it was difficult to communicate to them the "things of Religion" due to language problems (ibid.:15).

After Occom's third trip to Oneida, he returned home to Mohegan, where he found himself continually under Wheelock's thumb (Blodgett 1935:54). Occom was appointed missionary to the Niantics and Mohegans by the Boston Commissioners (Mohegan Descendants n.d.). His return brought to a head educational, ministerial, and land problems in Mohegan. Robert Clelland was a belligerent schoolmaster who was afraid that Occom was plotting against him. For his part, Occom charged that Clelland was often absent from school and used Indian houses without asking permission of the occupants (Occom 1727–1808: April 26, 1764). Clelland, along with Reverend David Jewett—a minister to the Mohegans—resented Occom's power and accused him of taking away their converts-students. They also charged Occom with meddling with the all-important land suit that divided Mohegans and whites alike for most of the eighteenth century. Occom sided with the "traditional" faction of the tribe against the colony and Clelland and Jewett.[1]

The traditional faction of the tribe frequently appealed to Occom for help. Not only did this traditional faction support the land suit against the colony, but they also supported certain leaders as sachems. When Occom returned from his last Oneida trip, his tribe was divided between two sachems: Ben Uncas (the pro-colony sachem) and John Uncas (cousin to Ben, and pro-land). The two different factions came to settle two neighboring towns, Johnstown and Benstown, in the present-day area of Mohegan (Stiles 1761). Occom frequently received letters from the Johnstown supporters begging him to "settle the differences" (Occom 1727–1808: August 20, 1764). Another writer told Occom that Ben was a "tool" of the English. The writer charged that the English were meddling with Indian ways despite the fact that the Mohegan had a "law and a Custom to make a sachem without the help of any People or nations in the World" (ibid.).

In 1765 Occom received an opportunity to escape the problems at Mohegan temporarily and travel to England with Reverend Nathaniel Whitaker of Norwich to raise money for Wheelock's charity school in Lebanon. The mission was successful. Occom not only raised a lot of money, but he also preached at the great itinerant, George Whitefield's, tabernacle, as well as at many other churches throughout England and Scotland (Forbes 1934). In 1768, when he returned home, he faced the still unresolved problems at Mohegan, plus new crises over his very work with and support of

Wheelock. Additionally, his family was struggling more than ever to survive. They had been left in Wheelock's care, yet Mary Occom continually had to remind Wheelock of his duties: "I am out of corn and have no money to buy any with" (Love 1899:152). Occom was further enraged with Wheelock's plan to remove the Indian Charity School to New Hampshire. Occom knew of Wheelock's plan, even when Occom was in England raising money for the school. Occom wanted the school to be accessible to Indians. At the very least he thought, Wheelock should move the school to Oneida, in the heart of Indian country. New Hampshire was too far away from Indian communities. Occom also resented Wheelock's plan to educate more white missionaries at the expense of Indian ones, especially since Occom had just collected money in England to educate Indian students (Love 1899:156–158). Occom felt used and neglected. His friendship with Wheelock hung together by the barest of threads.

By 1769 Wheelock's school was chartered in New Hamphsire under the name of Moor's Indian Charity School (after a generous donor; Forbes 1934:55), so Occom returned anew to his missions among the Iroquois. The problems at Mohegan also fueled his desire to move westward. The Ben Uncas faction of the tribe wrote a scathing "memorial" against Occom to the General Assembly: "Ever since he came and lived amongst us he has done a great deal of hurt to our tribe [for] he discourages the Indians from going to hear [Mr. Jewett, whom the Connecticut Assembly sent to Mohegan to preach]" (Mohegan Documents Collection n.d.). Also in the year 1771, the great land suit was brought to a close in favor of the colony. On hearing the court's final decision, Occom sadly noted: "I am afraid the poor Indians will never stand a good chance with the English in their land controversies, because they are very poor, they have no money. . . . The English have all" (Beardsley 1878:223).

Occom received at least one measure of badly needed success in 1772 when he was asked to preach a sermon for an Indian named Moses Paul. Paul was to be hanged for a murder of a white man, a crime Paul committed after a drinking binge. Occom's sermon was a huge success; both Indians and whites came to hear this Mohegan minister deliver a powerful moral lesson about the evils of drinking (Avery 1992). So impressive was Occom's performance that he began receiving requests to preach at churches throughout New England. (Occom's correspondence contains numerous requests from ministers as far away as Boston and New York who asked him to be a guest preacher in their parishes.)

In 1773 Occom and Joseph Johnson gathered the Mohegans together to discuss land problems at Mohegan at the Oneidas' invitation.[2] The two men planned to remove the Christian Indians of the seven towns of Charlestown, Groton, Stonington, Niantic, Farmington, Montauk, and Mohegan to Oneida (Blodgett 1935:149), and each of these towns sent representatives to Oneida to negotiate the removal. The Oneidas granted the New England

Indians over ten square miles, and in 1775 Occom and Johnson led the first contingent of Christian Indians to Oneida.

Although the American Revolution interrupted the trek westward and Joseph Johnson died in the war, it did not dash the Christian Indians' plans for removal.[3] During the early 1780s a huge influx of praying Indians left New England for the Oneida lands, where they joined either Occom's Brothertown community or New Stockbridge.[4] These two nascent towns, which were united for a time under Occom's pastorate, became neighbors of the Oneida's Christian community of New Town (Blodgett 1935:169; Davidson 1900:157).

Occom did not move his family to New Brothertown until 1784, preferring instead to travel back and forth to Mohegan to preach the gospel. In 1789 he left Mohegan for the last time and brought with him more Indian families. The settlement of these communities was not without issue. The original deed of 1774 had given the Brothertown Indians title without reservation. Problems quickly arose over this arrangement (Blodgett 1935:205), and in 1786 the Oneidas attempted to persuade the Brothertown settlers to surrender their land and live at large with them. Occom rejected this agreement (ibid.). The Oneidas made matters worse when they ceded all their lands to the state of New York in the Treaty of Fort Schuyler. This treaty would have reduced the Oneidas' lands to a two-by-three-mile tract (Watson 1986:x). New York rejected this conveyance, in no small part because of Occom's influence and instead passed an Act for the Sale and Disposition of Lands (1789) to secure unalienable lands to the New England Indians (Watson 1986:x). This act was designed to prevent Indians from both selling and leasing their lands to whites, with a stipulation of no leases over ten years; however, it proved to be only a stopgap measure. A land war was brewing at New Brothertown between one faction and a more traditionalist faction (followers of Occom) that wanted to adhere to the act (Watson 1986:xi). This land war was abetted by a growing Indian population that was overloading a shrinking land base. Eventually both the New Brothertown and New Stockbridge groups began leaving New York for the Midwest. Wisconsin became the new promised land for the vagabond New England groups, who eventually established their new utopia in 1832 (Watson 1986:xii).

Besides the issues over land in Oneida, other problems, surrounding the Oneidas themselves, occasioned the Christian Indians' determination to move to the Midwest. Oneida only halfheartedly embraced Christianity and the European cultural model with its emphasis upon plow agriculture and individual ownership of land. The Oneidas followed a strong traditionalist model with authority vested in sachems and chiefs (Mochon 1968:196). Iroquois matriclans controlled the land, and farming was women's work; men did not participate (ibid.:197). In contrast, the New England groups followed the Connecticut town government model (Love 1899:299), as well as European husbandry, land tenure, and division of labor. Families were landowners. Both men and women worked the land, and women learned European technologies such as weaving woolen cloth and the manufacture of clothing (Mochon 1968:197). Wheelock's missionaries like David Fowler and Occom had early noted the problems among Oneida; nevertheless, they were optimistic that a mission would effect positive change.

OCCOM'S VISION

Why did Samson Occom embrace Christianity—a product of the alien culture he often resented—as a model of salvation for the New England Indians? Why didn't Occom simply move the Indians away from Europeans? The answer is that Occom never completely rejected Europeans, despite his disillusions. He wanted what whites had to offer: frame houses, education, farms, livestock, and new technologies. His sermons and letters make this desire very clear. In his sermon at the execution of Moses Paul, Occom boldly stated:

By this sin [of drunkenness] *we can't have comfortable houses, nor any thing comfortable in our houses, neither food nor raiment, nor decent utensils.* We are obliged to put up with any sort of shelter just to screen us from the severity of the weather, and we go about with very mean, ragged and dirty clothes, almost naked. And we are half-starved. . . . And our poor children are suffering every day for want of the necessaries of life. . . . When we are intoxicated with strong drink we drown our rational powers. (Occom 1990b:749)

Occom similarly chastized his son Benoni for "carousing" and "drinking" and for rejecting the European-like trappings that Occom had worked so hard to achieve for his family: "You know, I have a pretty good foundation for you and your little brother to begin with . . . [a] building . . . some good land brought under good improvement . . . sufficient husbandry tools" (Occom 1728–1808: June 24, 1780).

European goods had an intrinsic value to Occom, apart from their utilitarian one: they represented salvation. Material goods were proof of God's grace (Avery 1992). Herein lies the heart of the issue. For God-fearing, Calvinistic Christians in seventeenth- and eighteenth-century New England, there were two paths: one led to divine grace and the other to hell. Individuals fearfully charted their progress; they perceived worldly possessions as positive signs of both individual industry and divine acceptance. A "chosen" person had more things.

Not only was material wealth linked to salvation, but so was learning. Learning meant reading and writing and studying the New Testament (Occom 1990a:730–735; Avery 1992:3). "European learning is not merely a catalyst of the gift of Chrisitian salvation but a necessary cause" (Avery 1992:3). Occom understood this connection, for early in his life he reported how, after he learned the "English letters" and discovered Christ, the "Burden of my mind was removed and I found serenity and Pleasure of Soul in serving God" (Occom 1990:730).

Salvation was open to all who chose the path; it did not discriminate between Indian and white. All had equal footing. All were born into sin, and all were judged by the same creator. In his sermon to Moses Paul, Occom preached:

Them be who they will, great or small, honorable or ignoble, rich or poor, bond or free. Negroes, Indians, English, or of what nation soever; all die in their sins must go to hell together; for the wages of sin is death. (Occom 1990b:743)

Christianity promised a way out to Occom and his followers. The land problems, the poverty, and the dissension were all minimized by his larger vision of eventually receiving God's grace and the Kingdom of Christ.

NOTES

I thank Sheila Sabo, an undergraduate in anthropology at Western Connecticut State University, for her help in collecting and transcribing most of the Papers of Samson Occom from the Connecticut Historical Society. I also thank David Detzer, Department of History, Western Connecticut State University, for reviewing and critiquing the manuscript. I am indebted to the Connecticut Historical Society, which allowed me to use its collections—in particular, the Papers of Samson Occom (which are on microfilm)—plus many of the Eleazar Wheelock Narratives. The New Haven Colony Historical Society provided materials on Ezra Stiles, such as the Itineraries and Letters. The Huntington Free Library, Museum of the American Indian, gave me Watson's Family History of the Brothertown Indians, and Mary Davis of the library was kind enough to send me copies of the Mohegan Documents Collection. The Beinecke Rare Book and Manuscript Library at Yale University had copies of the Ezra Stiles Papers. The American Philosophical Society gave me a small grant with which to pursue my initial investigations on Samson Occom. The article by Davidson is from their library. Both the Huntington Library and the American Philosophical Society have a number of materials on the removal of the New England Indians to both New York and Wisconsin.

1. This long and complicated land suit really began in the seventeenth century when the deputy governor, John Mason, handled a land deed given to him by Uncas in 1659. Mason, his heirs, and the Mohegans claimed that Mason was acting on behalf of the Indians and that the title to the soil was vested in the Mason family on behalf of the Indians. The colony claimed otherwise and said that the land in question belonged to it, not to the Indians. The Masons and the Mohegans took the colony to court by saying that the Mohegans were fraudulently deprived of thousands of acres of land. A royal commission was established to review the case, and the court decided against the colony in 1705. Connecticut protested the deci-

sion, and the whole affair was kept in agitation until 1743 when the king determined that title to the lands belonged to the colony. The case was not officially settled until 1771 (Trumbull 1898:248–361; Weinstein 1991). Occom's involvement cost him the support of the Connecticut Board of Correspondents, and he had to "beg Forgiveness of God" for not soliciting the board's advice (Richardson 1933:29).

2. Joseph Johnson was a Mohegan and a son-in-law to Occom (he was married to Occom's daughter Tabitha). Johnson, who was educated by Wheelock, was first a school master to Farmington Indians. He then received a certification from Wheelock that he was "licensed to preach the gospel among the Indians." Johnson was instrumental in the removal of the New England Indians to Oneida (see Occom 1729–1808: January 29, 1776; Love 1899:202–203).

3. A number of Stockbridge and "Mohickans" were recruited to fight in the war by George Washington (Occom 1729–1808: June 24, August 2, 1776). For the most part, the Christian Indians followed a policy of neutrality, and Occom, Fowler, and Johnson were instrumental in carrying this message to the Iroquois (Love 1899:225–231). Occom saw the conflict as a dispute "betwixt a father and a son"; consequently, he urged that the Indians not get involved (Occom 1729–1808:1775 May 4, 1775).

4. New Stockbridge was established by white missionary John Sargent and based on the original community of Stockbridge in Massachusetts (Mochon 1968).

REFERENCES

Avery, Brian. 1992. "Preaching to Glorify and Empower Samson Occom's Sermon on the Execution of Moses Paul." Paper presented at the Northeastern Anthropology Association annual meetings, Bridgewater, Massachusetts, March.

Beardsley, E. Edwards. 1878. "The Mohegan Land Controversy." *New Haven Historical Society Papers* 3:205–225.

Blodgett, Harold. 1935. *Samson Occom*. MS Series 3. Hanover, N.H.: Dartmouth College.

Brenner, Elise. 1984. "Strategies for Autonomy: An Analysis of Ethnic Mobilization in 17th Century Southern New England." Ph. D. dissertation, University of Massachusetts.

Bushman, Richard L. 1967. *From Puritan to Yankee: Character and Social Order in Connecticut, 1690–1765*. Cambridge: Harvard University Press.

———. 1969. *The Great Awakening: Documents on the Revival of Religion 1640–1745*. Chapel Hill: University of North Carolina Press.

Chandler, John. 1705. "A Map of the Mohegan Sachems Hereditary Country Plotted Aug. 1st 1705. By John Chandler, Surveyor." State Library, Hartford, Conn.

Dankert, Clyde. 1978. *Samson Occom and Eleazar Wheelock*. Dartmouth Essays Hanover, N.H.: Dartmouth Essays Hanover, N.H.: Dartmouth University Press.

Davidson, John N. 1900. "The Coming of the New York Indians to Wisconsin." In *Proceedings of the State Historical Society of Wisconsin*. Madison: The Society.

Forbes, Allan. 1934. *Some Indian Events of New England*. Boston: State Street Trust and Company.

Lauter, Paul, ed. 1990. "Samson Occom (Mohegan) 1723–1792." In *The Heath Anthology of American Literature*. Vol. 1. Lexington, Mass.: D. C. Heath.

Love, Deloss. 1899. *Samson Occom and the Christian Indians of New England.* Boston: The Pilgrim Press.

McCallum, James D. 1932 *Letters of Eleazar Wheelock's Indians.* Manuscript Series 1. Hanover, N.H. Dartmouth College.

Mochon, Marion. 1968. "Stockbridge-Munsee Cultural Adaptations: Assimilated Indians." In *Proceedings of the American Philosophical Association* 112, no. 3:182–219.

Mohegan Descendants. n.d. "Residing at Mohegan, Connecticut (Chronology of Some Important Events in Connection with Samson Occom 1723–1792)." Unpublished manuscript, New London Historical Society.

Mohegan Documents Collections. n.d. "Memorial of the Mohegan Indians to the Honorable the General Assembly of Connecticut." May 28, 1771. Huntington Free Library, Heye Foundation, Museum of the American Indian.

Morgan, Edward. 1958. *The Puritan Dilemma: The Story of John Winthrop.* Boston: Little, Brown & Co.

Occom, Samson. 1727–1808. Papers of Samson Occom. Correspondence 1727–1808. Collections of the Connecticut Historical Society, Hartford, Conn.

———. 1990a. "A Short Narrative of My Life." In *The Heath Anthology of American Literature,* edited by P. Lauter, 730–735. Lexington, Mass.: D. C. Heath.

——— 1990b. "A Sermon Preached by Samson Occom." In *The Heath Anthology of American Literature,* edited by P. Lauter, 1:736–751. Lexington, Mass.: D. C. Heath.

n.d. Diary. Unpublished manuscript. New London Historical Society. [This diary is incomplete.].

Richardson, Leon B. 1933. *An Indian Preacher in England.* MS. Series 2. Hanover, N.H.: Dartmouth College.

Stiles, Ezra. 1761. Itineraries, July 25, 1761. Map of Johnstown and Benstown on Thames River in New London. Ezra Stiles Papers, Beinecke Rare Book and Manuscript Library, Yale University.

Szasz, Margaret. 1980. " 'Poor Richard' Meets the Native American: Schooling for Young Indian Women in Eighteenth Century Connecticut." *Pacific Historical Review* 69:215–235.

Trumbull, Benjamin. 1898. *A Complete History of Connecticut, Civil and Ecclesiastical, from the Emigration of Its First Planters, from England, in the Year 1630, to the Year 1764; and to the Close of the Indian Wars.* Vol. 1. New London: H. D. Utley.

Watson, L. S. 1986. *Family History of the Brothertown Indians.* Laguna Hills, Calif.: Histree.

Weinstein, Laurie. 1990. "The Promised Land: The Interplay of Land Rights and Christianity in 18th Century Mohegan." Paper presented at the Northeastern Anthropological Association meetings, Burlington, Vermont, March.

———. 1991. "Land, Politics and Power: The Mohegan Indians in the 17th and 18th Centuries." *Man in Northeast* (Fall).

Weinstein, Laurie, and Sheila Sabo. 1993. "Samson Occom: An 18th Century Mohegan Indian Leader." *In Proceedings of the New Age of Exploration: The Next 500 Years.* Danbury: Western Connecticut State University.

Weiss, Frederick. 1959. "The New England Company of 1649 and Its Missionary Enterprises." *Colonial Society of Massachusetts* 38:134–218.

Wheelock, Eleazer. 1762–1765. *A Continuation of the Narrative of the Indian Charity School at Lebanon, in Connecticut 1762–1765.* Boston: Richard & Samuel Draper.

———. 1763. *A Plain and Faithful Narrative of the Original Design, Rise, Progress and Present State of the Indian Charity School at Lebanon, in Connecticut.* Boston: Richard and Samuel Draper.

———. 1767. *A Brief Narrative of the Indian Charity School in Lebanon in Connecticut, New England.* 2d ed. London: J. & W. Oliver 1767.

———. 1771. *A Continuation of the Narrative of the Indian Charity School in Lebanon in Connecticut from the Year 1768 to the Incorporation of It with Dartmouth College and Removal and Settlement of It in Hanover in the Province of New Hampshire.* Printed by Ebenezer Watson.

6

A Native Perspective of History: The Schaghticoke Nation, Resistance and Survival

Trudie Lamb Richmond

When we were young it was our grandmother who gathered us around to tell us of many things; of how the world began; of where we came from; why we must respect all living things; of the wonders of the universe. She always told us of the old ways. And when we were told these things, these truths, we searched her face of many wrinkles and believed she must have been there, way back then, in the beginning, so vivid were her words and the pictures she created in our mind's eye. It was only when we were much older that we realized that this was the way of the elders. Their words were the traditions being passed down from their grandmothers and grandfathers. The hypnotic quality of grandmother's carefully selected words healed us, cured us, strengthened and enriched our lives—which we were committed to pass on.

—Trudie Ray Lamb

Native people's histories and stories have been told by others—rather dispassionately at times and not always with accuracy. Something is missing when we cannot or do not know our true past. Something is terribly wrong when our past is not accurately recounted. It should not be unreasonable to expect that whose history is told is as important as how history is told. I value this opportunity to present a native perspective of what happened to the native peoples of the lower Housatonic River Valley and the choices they made in an effort to survive. I live on the Schaghticoke Reservation, a

Map 6.1
Native Communities of the Housatonic River

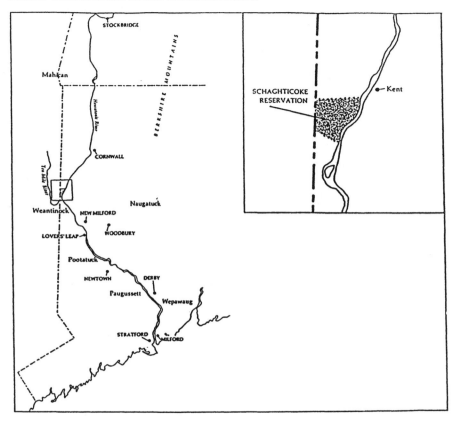

Source: "Spirituality and Survival in Schaghticoke Basketmaking." In *A Key into the Language of Woodsplint Baskets,* edited by A. McMullen and R. G. Handsman, 126–143. Washington, Conn.: American Archaeological Institute, 1987.

reservation that has existed for nearly 250 years, situated on homelands of ancestors whose existence dates back at least 8,000 years (Map 6.1).

Historical silences have largely contributed to the invisibility of the indigenous peoples of southern New England. Local histories have reduced our existence to a few short paragraphs in their writings. We are more often discussed in the past tense and seldom in the present. But we have endured and survived, in spite of being fragmented, factionalized, Christianized, and Americanized. Our tenacity, our resilience, our stubbornness, and our beliefs enable us to continue and work toward rebuilding who we are: the indigenous people of this land.

It is these survival techniques and paths of resistance that I wish to explore and interpret here. The native communities along the Housatonic, from the coast up to the Mahican village at Stockbridge, were all related. Movement up and down the Housatonic River had been common for centuries. Following the impact of colonization, those trading relationships and personal bonds were continually tested and strained as native people made individual or collective choices.

HISTORICAL BACKGROUND

The Housatonic River, in volume smaller than the Connecticut River or the Hudson River, was a source of great power and majesty to its native inhabitants. Chard Smith (1946) wrote,

The value of a river as a symbol of eternal truth is increased if the valley through which it flows likewise suggest permanence beyond change; if the hills are wide and gracious under the sky, especially if man's cupidity has violated them little, so that the forest retains its seeming timeless rest, while within it the trees turn their cycle of seed and growth and decay . . . part of a truce which man has long reached of nature, by which each serves the other and both survive.

For centuries native people had settled along the Housatonic River, fishing, planting, and hunting. The sound was filled with great varieties of shellfish—oysters, clams, mussels, and lobster—and the rivers with shad, herring, and salmon. In the spring, while the women planted, the men fished. In late summer, when the first corn was harvested, the people prepared for their annual Green Corn Ceremony. In the fall, when crops were harvested, another Thanksgiving was offered. A good portion of the harvest was stored in grass-lined pits. In the winter months, the people shared with the young important stories of what could happen in times of gluttony and waste. Village life was one of cooperation and sharing. A large extended family was necessary for survival. Emphasis was on the group rather than the individual, although one always had the freedom of choice.

The native communities settling along the Housatonic, which they called the Great River, had a true partnership with the land, and their subsistence cycle was regulated by centuries of spiritual tradition. That belief system was challenged again and again in the sixteenth and seventeenth centuries by European technology, Christianity, and disease. The steady increase of the English from the east and Dutch from the west contributed to weakening native social and political systems. As a result, native people were faced with difficult choices for survival. Some, like the Pequots, chose the path of opposition, while the Mohegans decided to join forces with the English colonists. On the other hand, the Quinnipiacs, who signed away great portions of their homelands after the Pequot massacre of 1637, supported the English during King Philip's War in 1675 yet refused to convert to Christianity. Eventually the majority of Quinnipiacs gradually left the reserved lands set aside for them and joined the great exodus of native people leaving Connecticut during the early 1700s.

The first hundred years of colonization were devastating and shattering; subsistence activities were seriously curtailed, and native people found themselves faced with damning decisions as to whether they would accommodate and adapt or boldly resist. Whatever the decision, their foremost desire was always to maintain their identity. One factor that native communities along the Housatonic River had in their favor was that they were all related. There were major village settlements such as those of the Paugussett people, who had several sites along the mouth of the river and inland as far as what is now Derby and Shelton. The Pootatucks were located in the Southbury/Woodbury area, and the Weantinocks, who held the major Council Fire, were in New Milford. There were also relations who chose to congregate in small hamlets along both the Great River and its tributaries. The Housatonic was well populated, and there was a great deal of movement along its extensive shores.

The time following the destruction and subjugation of the Pequots, from 1640 to approximately 1660, is often described by historians as a fairly stable period in Indian-white relations. But from whose perspective? The massacre of 400 Pequots at Mystic and the killing of at least another 600 in the Great Swamp within Paugussett territory had to create great emotional turmoil in the hearts of native people in the area. There was fear, anger, and remorse. Quinneticut lands were being auctioned off at a rapid pace as English settlers moved to create their own townships and gain control of Long Island Sound. At the same time, there was constant trade in furs, wampum, and European goods. Competition between the Dutch and English for furs and lands took its toll on the native inhabitants. In addition, Puritan missionaries sought to convert Indian people not just to Christianity but to a way of life dependent upon English resources and an explicit renunciation of native traditions and beliefs.

The Reverend John Eliot created a series of praying villages in eastern Massachusetts. Roger Williams looked to convert the Narragansetts in Rhode Island, and Thomas Mayhew was at Martha's Vineyard on the Cape. John Sargent in 1736 traveled all the way up the Housatonic to establish a praying village with the Mahicans at Stockbridge. He intended to build a boarding school for Indians, but the Indian people in western Connecticut resisted Christianity until the Moravian missionaries arrived at Schaghticoke in 1740.

The Housatonic native settlements in 1680 were fortunate to come under the leadership of a young Pootatuck sagamore or subchief by the name of Waramaug. The period after King Philip's War in 1675 was a time of great confusion and migration of native peoples from the coast. Many Paugussett people elected to settle with relatives in the Derby/Shelton area, while others chose to go to Pootatuck in Southbury. Waramaug was named grand sachem of the entire lower valley—the chief of all chiefs, from Paugussett on the shore to the native villages situated as far as Litchfield and Bantam. He moved to the seat of the Grand Council at Weantinock, "where the water swirls around," named because of the Great Falls, an excellent fishing place that provided an abundance of shad, herring, and lamprey eels.

The people looked to Waramaug as a gifted leader who was able to keep them together in a time of such turmoil. They respected his decisions. There were those who described him as a man of "uncommon powers." Not much else is written about Waramaug except for the description of his lodge, which offers an important glimpse into Pootatuck life-style. His lodge, built some two miles below the Weantinock village on the western precipice of the Housatonic, was 100 feet long and 20 feet wide. It was thatched with huge slabs of specially selected bark. Sachems and sagamores sent their best artists to work on the interior decorations. The main council room had portraits of Waramaug and his family. In the smaller rooms, the walls were painted with "beasts, birds, reptiles and insects." The Reverend Daniel Boardman, who had become friendly with the chief, was so impressed that he wrote about the lodge and Waramaug to a friend.

The northwestern corner of Connecticut was the last to be settled by the English. Waramaug had been grand sachem for nearly twenty-five years when he and his subchiefs agreed to sign over great tracts of land. In these agreements, Waramaug believed that his people had reserved for their use the right to their planting fields and privileges for fishing at the Great Falls of Metichawon ("because of big rapids"). The planting fields of Weantinock, Waramaug's people, stretched along the floodplain of the Housatonic for several hundred acres. These communal fields had been worked for generations by the Weantinock women and were the mainstay of the people (Handsman 1991) But the town of New Milford was incorporated in 1712, and families had soon moved in.

Waramaug died in 1735, but many of his people had already begun moving farther north to a place they called Pishgoch-ti-goch, later known as Schaghticoke. And with them they took the memory of the reserved use of planting fields and fishing rights. Once again, they built their wigwams and remained undisturbed for a brief period without a leader.

SCHAGHTICOKE AND CHRISTIANITY

The people were fortunate, because a new leader did emerge. His name was Mauwee or Hungry Bear. Like Waramaug he had been a sagamore, a subchief. Leadership is generally hereditary and leaders' powers are absolute, but the actual use of power depends upon one's ability as a diplomat. Mauwee was greatly respected and a man of many skills. He was a canoemaker as well as skilled at building sweatlodges. He was the one who told the people when and where to plant and when to harvest. For a long

Waramaug's Monument
Source: John Deforest, *History of the Indians of Connecticut, from the Earliest Known Period to 1851.* Hartford, CT: William James Hamersley, 1851.

time, it was Mauwee's vision and leadership abilities that enabled the people to come together. He welcomed other native people as they traveled upriver looking for new homes and called out to relatives and friends to join him in this new place called Schaghticoke. By 1740, Schaghticoke's population had peaked, with over 500 native people moving into the area.

It was also about this time that Moravian missionaries visited Schaghticoke. Mauwee and his people had established a trading relationship with the Mahican village of Shekomeko located on the New York State side. When the Moravians approached the Mahicans, Mauwee became interested and invited them to Schaghticoke. He was drawn to their friendliness,

Figure 6.1
Moravian Mission at Schaghticoke

Photo by Richard Wryley Birch. Used by permission of Alison Wryley Birch.

which was in great contrast to the hostile attitude of the townspeople of Kent, who had rejected requests for teachers and a school. The Moravians were willing not only to work among the native people but live with them and assume a native life-style. The arrival of the Moravians was timely. The Schaghticoke people had become very disillusioned. Many often traded furs and baskets for rum, a habit frequently encouraged by the tavern owners.

The Moravians lived at Schaghticoke for nearly twenty years. A stone mission was built as a place of worship, and many Schaghticokes, including Mauwee, were converted and baptized (Figure 6.1). During this period, the Schaghticoke people flourished. They built canoes, made baskets, carved bowls and spoons, braided cornhusk mats, and planted their gardens. For a time, things looked good. The Moravians had renewed their confidence and strength. Although everyone did not convert or believe, Christianity provided the balance Schaghticoke needed. Basket making became an important industry, and it was a communal effort.

Some of the townspeople and town leaders were not too pleased with the Moravians' being such a positive influence on the Schaghticokes and believed that the Moravians posed a threat. The minister of Kent was curious and rather upset by the situation. He sent his church elder to confront

Mauwee and announce to the Indians that they should search for a minister
and schoolmaster from New England. The Kent minister and Reverend
Boardman, a minister from New Milford, said they would procure the sal-
ary for this new minister to the Schaghticoke from the governor of Connecticut. Gideon Mauwee responded, "Thank you very much, but I need
neither minister nor school master, because we already have one and two
won't be necessary. The Governor wouldn't need to pay for our teachers as
we [the Indians] would come to terms with this." The church elder said,
"Why do you take on such strangers, who come so far as from Old England
and nobody knows who or what they are?" And Mauwee answered,

And where are you from? Didn't you come yourself across the same way from Old
England, too? As for us, we are natives. We don't come from there. Now you want
to give us a teacher. Why don't you leave us the one we have? You say they don't
teach properly. But why does that matter to you? Usually you let people walk in
their evil ways. Why don't you let us walk our ways? Leave us at liberty. In your
towns there are many churches . . . and everyone says that he is right and not the
other. And yet you grant each one their freedom. Therefore, let me and mine also
believe what we want to. If you think we are wrong. What concern is that to you?
(Moravian Diaries)

It was apparent that Mauwee made the decision to Christianize his people
to Moravian beliefs in an effort to keep his people together and provide
them with some of the strengths they needed to survive and endure. This
conclusion is substantiated by the fact that although many Schaghticokes
converted to the Moravian faith, periodically they would announce that
they would be absent from vespers on a given evening because they were
going to the sweatlodge. The Moravians kept a daily diary, and sandwiched
between lengthy descriptions of vespers and the Lamb of God are descriptions of the daily life of the people. But for those diaries, a great deal of
information would be lost.

Survival became a constant struggle as the colonial population increased
in Kent. The Moravian diaries report the scarcity of firewood and the rapid
depletion of timber. In addition, there were frequent food shortages. Native
hunters complained that on many occasions they would meet at least twenty
white hunters in the woods and return with no game. There were periods
of great suffering and extreme poverty. At one point, some of the families
reported that they were returning to Pootatuck because they had no food.
Others left to join Moravian missions in Ohio, while others fled to Canada.
But there was a small core of Schaghticokes who refused to leave their
homelands at any cost. Mauwee was one of them. He died in 1760 on
Schaghticoke Mountain at the age of seventy-three. My ancestors, the Cot-
shures (Cogswell), who rejected Christianity, also refused to leave.

The present Schaghticoke Reservation, located on the western bank of

Basket maker Sarah Mauwee Cotsure (Cogswell) with son, Will, 1865.

the Housatonic River, near the town of Kent, is approximately 400 acres, of which 385 are rocky ledges and mountainous terrain. With most of the reservation squeezed against a mountainside, only five families insist on remaining on their homelands. The reservation continues along Schaghticoke Road for a two-mile stretch. *Pishgoch-ti-goch* is an Algonkian word meaning "where the waters meet," in this case, where the Ten Mile River empties into the Housatonic River.

This glimpse into history from the native perspective, brief as it may be, seeks to illustrate one of many of the historical silences that needs to be told.

NOTES

Funds from the Connecticut Humanities Council made possible the translations from the Moravian diaries.

Daniel Boardman's 1836 letter, written to John Warner Barber of New Haven,

Connecticut, on August 1, 1836, is in the collection of the Connecticut Historical Society, Hartford, Connecticut. A portion is also published in Orcutt (1882).

Moravian diary translations were from the Moravian Archives B.111.F.2. 8-1-1743. Index to the Records of the Moravian Mission, Box 115, Folder 8; Box 114, Folders 4, 5, 8. Moravian Library, Bethlehem, Pennsylvania.

REFERENCES

Andrews, William G. 1904. *The Moravians at Scatacook; Historical Records of the Town of Cornwall, Litchfield County, Connecticut by T. S. Gold,* 361–364. Hartford, Conn.: Case, Lockwood and Brainard Company.

Handsman, Russell G. 1991. "What Happened to the Heritage of the Weantinock People." *Artifacts* 19, no. 1.

Orcutt, Samuel. 1882. *History of the Towns of New Milford and Bridgewater, Connecticut, 1703-1882.* Reprint ed., 1976. New Milford, Conn.: New Milford Historical Society.

Smith, Chard Powers. 1946. *The Housatonic: Puritan River.* New York: Rinehart and Company.

Part III

Current Issues

The twentieth century ushered in enormous changes in native culture. Most important, native peoples became more visible, in large part because of a variety of cultural activities. The spark for these actions goes back to the beginning of the century and the pan-Indian movement that was sweeping across the country:

This movement, a counteraction to the dominant culture of the United States, was a means for Indians to reinforce their "Indianness." Before the arrival of Europeans, most Indian tribes had kept to themselves, interacting on occasion with similar neighboring tribes to form loose alliances. . . . By the early 20th century, several Indian leaders and tribes had come to see the value in working together to press for their rights against the government bureaucracy—and to assert their unique Indian identity, which they realized they were losing.

The customs and traditions of the Great Plains Indians came to symbolize the new identity of all Indians. In every section of the United States and Canada, Indians adopted Plains Indian dress along with some of that culture's rich ceremonialism as symbols of Indianness. (Weinstein 1989:75)

Tribes became revitalized as they celebrated their identities as native peoples. (Revitalization is the concept most commonly used to discuss the visibility of Indian ethnicity. See Chapter 7 for a critique of this concept.) In public pageants and parades, groups, like the Gay Head Wampanoags and the Mohegans, dressed in a combination of Plains Indian headdresses and northeastern traditional regalia and paraded through town on decorated floats. Besides the pageants were other symbols of ethnicity such as the powwows. Twentieth-century powwows are both public events and homecomings for the native peoples. The two- to three-day events are filled with dancing and drumming, plus the sale of Indian arts and foods. The powwows begin with a prayer from the medicine man of the hosting tribe. In the procession that follows, native peoples dressed in ceremonial regalia move into the center of the dance area and begin to dance in a circle to the drumming and chanting of the native men. The dances, chants, and drumming represent individual prayers to the spirit world. Thousands of tourists may attend a powwow (the Mashpees' July 4 weekend powwow is one of the largest in New England); however, native people representing many different tribes also attend. For the natives who come, the powwow represents an expression of common ethnicity. It is also a homecoming—a time to return home to renew kinship ties.

The pageants and the powwows are just one expression of Indian identity in the twentieth century. Other, more powerful expressions can be found in the myriad of political actions. The pan-Indian movement spawned native organizations such as the Wampanoag Nation, which was founded in the 1920s as a confederacy of Wampanoag people in the southeastern Massachusetts and Cape areas. The Indian Council of New England was another political and social group which was also founded during the 1920s (see Chapter 7). During the 1960s, the Boston Indian Council was established as a fraternal organization for urban Indians who had left their reservations (mostly in northern New England) to move into the cities in search of wage labor. All of these organizations had numerous goals, but foremost was the education of members and the sharing of native identities. Education of whites about native peoples (the Wampanoag Nation initiated the first Wampanoag powwow) was equally important. Other goals included recreation, agency referrals, legal aid, and learning native languages and arts (Kehoe 1992:277).

Since the 1970s, a new arena has opened for the expression of Indian identity: land claims. Numerous New England groups have filed suit against landowners (usually municipalities and/or agencies for the state) for the illegal alienation of lands (Campisi 1993). Most of these suits go back to the Trade and Intercourse Acts of the 1790s when the newly created United States passed a series of laws stating that only the federal government could deal with Indian tribes. Any state that sold Indian lands without the consent of the federal government was in violation of the laws. (See Campisi 1985 for information about the legality and history of land claims.)

The Passamaquoddies were one of the first New England groups to file suit in 1972. The tribe claimed they had been defrauded of over 12 million acres of land by the Commonwealth of Massachusetts in 1794. (The borders of Massachusetts extended north into present-day Maine until 1820, when Maine became a state.) After eight years of complicated and drawn-out hearings, the Passamaquoddies, along with the Penobscots and the Houlton band of Maliseets, won $81.5 million, to be held in trust by the federal government. Some of this money has been used to buy back lands to add to the reservations (Campisi 1985; Brodeur 1985). The Passamaquoddy case was unique in the history of eastern land claims, for it represented the first (and thus far only) time when the federal government interceded on the tribe's behalf and ordered a suit to be filed against a state (Campisi 1993).

Since the 1970s, other groups have filed land suits: the Mashpee Wampanoags, the Gay Head Wampanoags, the Narragansetts, the Mashantucket Pequots, and the Mohegans, among others. In many cases, the award of land has been contingent upon the achievement of federal recognition status, thanks to the Mashpees' unsuccessful battle. Federal recognition status means that the petitioning group is indeed a bona-fide Indian tribe. Recognition carries with it a variety of benefits: it strengthens land suits and provides monies for the development of tribal businesses, health care, welfare, and other services.

The Mashpee Wampanoags' battle began in the 1960s when the Indians watched with growing alarm as more and more tourists flooded into their Cape Cod town to purchase summer resorts. In 1976 the Mashpees filed a federal suit to recover the entire town of Mashpee. After lengthy deliberations and testimonies from anthropologists and historians representing both sides, the judge ruled that the Mashpees were not a tribe on certain key dates in their history. This 1978 ruling sent shock waves throughout New England: how could an Indian community with a long and uncontested cultural presence in the region be denied its very ethnicity (Campisi 1985, 1990; Brodeur 1985; Peters 1987)?

The Mashantucket Pequots learned from the Mashpee case and prepared both a petition for federal recognition and a land claim for the return of over 800 acres of land. In 1983 the Pequots received monies to buy back land and achieved recognition, despite near disaster after President Reagan vetoed the initial settlement (Campisi 1990).

The Narragansetts won their land settlement in 1978 with the passage of the Rhode Island Claims Settlement Act, whereby the tribe received 1,800 acres of land (half of it cedar swamp). In addition, the tribe prepared a petition for recognition. Recognition was granted in 1983 (Campisi 1985).

The Mohegans filed a petition for recognition in 1984 after submitting an earlier land suit. Recognition was denied in 1989; however, the Mohegans appealed the decision, and in March 1994 they received recognition.

Successful land and recognition battles translate into money for tribal enterprises. Because of a variety of grants, the Pequots, Gay Head Wampanoags, and Narragansetts have been able to develop a variety of projects, such as reservation housing, community centers, schools, and new businesses.

The Pequots are probably best known for their large bingo and gambling operations, which draw millions of visitors yearly. This enterprise is guided by the federal Indian Gaming and Regulatory Act of 1988, which establishes conditions and restrictions under which various kinds

of games can occur. There are three types of classes of operations: Class
I, unregulated traditional gaming activities; Class II, bingo; and Class
III, casinos. Casinos are permitted only if the tribe secures a compact
from the state in which the casino is to be built. The Pequots took the
state of Connecticut to court to secure the right to build their casino
because Connecticut initially refused to negotiate with the Pequots on
their proposed Class III operations. The Pequots won. Their operations
have been so successful that they have begun work on a resort hotel to
house all the visitors. In economically depressed Connecticut, the
Pequots' game is the only game in town; consequently, white entrepreneurs are attempting to find ways to cash in on their success. The Narragansetts, Mohegans, and Paugussetts are also considering plans for
opening a casino.

Contemporary tribes are involved in a wealth of other activities too.
Native arts are still manufactured and sold for profit. Art for sale has
become another way in which native New Englanders can both maintain their identities and reap a profit (Chapter 8). Beautiful basketry,
a variety of ceramic wares, beaded jewelry, t-shirts, ribbon shirts, and
woodworking are just some of the items that can be purchased at powwows and museums and in local stores. More and more museums are
dedicating exhibit space to native artwork and native histories. For example, the Haffenreffer Museum at Brown University, the Institute of
American Indian Studies, and the Wampanoag Indian Program at Plimoth Plantation continually host new exhibits, many of which are cu-
rated by native people. Further, many Indian tribes, like the Pequots,
the Mohegans, the Mashpee Wampanoags, and the Penobscots, are either planning or have already opened their own museums.

Tribal newsletters and pan-Indian newspapers, such as the *Eagle
Wing Press,* help keep contemporary native peoples abreast of current
political developments, powwows, museum openings, craft fairs, and
other events in the region.

Today's native groups endure because they have refused to disappear.
They have learned the court system and have used white man's law to
fight back for their lands and their dignity. They are opening successful
businesses; they are relearning native languages; they are opening museums and taking a role in their future. They have set aside ancient tribal
animosities and are working together in recognition of their proud heritage as native peoples.

The chapters that follow address some of these twentieth-century developments. Ann McMullen looks at the establishment of an early fraternal pan-Indian organization, the Indian Council of New England,
and she relates this council to regional expressions of Indian ethnicity.
Next, Joan Lester and also Laurie Weinstein, Delinda Passas, and Anabela Marque discuss artwork and demonstrate how contemporary arts
are continuous with the past. The photos in Lester's essay illustrate
both the beauty and utility of native design.

REFERENCES

Brodeur, Paul. 1985. *Restitution: The Land Claims of the Mashpee, Passama-quoddy, and Penobscot Indians of New England*. Boston: Northeastern University Press.

Campisi, Jack. 1985. "The Trade and Intercourse Acts." In *Irredeemable America,* edited by Imre Sutton, 337–362. Albuquerque: University of New Mexico Press.

———. 1990. "The New England Tribes and Their Quest for Justice." In *The Pequots in Southern New England,* edited by L. Hauptman and J. Wherry. 179–193. Norman: University of Oklahoma Press.

———. 1993. Personal communication.

Kehoe, Alice. 1992. *North American Indians: A Comprehensive Account*. 2d ed. Englewood Cliffs, N.J.: Prentice-Hall.

Peters, Russell. 1987. *The Wampanoags of Mashpee: An Indian Perspective on American History*. Indian Spiritual and Cultural Training Council. Boston: Nimrod Press.

Weinstein-Farson, Laurie. 1989. *The Wampanoag*. New York: Chelsea House.

David Richmond (Mohawk), Melissa Fawcett (Mohegan tribal historian), Ralph Sturges (chief of Mohegan), and Trudie Lamb Richmond (Schaghticoke) at the Mohegan Church. (Photo: Barrie Kavasch)

Gladys Tantaquidgeon (Mohegan medicine woman) and David Richmond at the Tantaquidgeon Indian Museum. (Photo: Barrie Kavasch)

Gladys Tantaquidgeon with Laurie Weinstein at the Tantaquidgeon Indian Museum. (Photo: Barrie Kavasch)

Paula Peters talking to unidentified man wearing feather roach at a Mashpee powwow. (Photo: Marie Pelletier)

Food stands at a Mashpee powwow. (Photo: Marie Pelletier)

7

What's Wrong with This Picture? Context, Coversion, Survival, and the Development of Regional Native Cultures and Pan-Indianism in Southeastern New England

Ann McMullen

The cultural history of native southeastern New England has focused heavily on cultural disintegration after King Philip's War, nineteenth-century factionalism, and revitalization in the twentieth century. Tribal culture, tribal history, and visible cultural expressions have been explained to the near exclusion of "covert" cultures, regional cultural networks, native pan-Indian organizations, and the contextualization of native histories and cultures within New England's social milieu (Brasser 1971; Conkey, Boissevain, and Goddard 1978). This chapter seeks to remedy these deficiencies by focusing on the importance of regional culture, covert cultures (those whose expressions are invisible or unrecognizable to non-natives), and pan-Indianism in interpreting the culture history of southeastern New England.

Rather than solely emphasizing tribal culture histories, we should rethink the importance of regional perspectives, aiming toward the broader perspectives of the "new Indian history" (cf. White 1991 and others). After discussing the difference between local and regional cultures and regionalization as an integrative process, I outline the shortcomings of tribal histories—often poorly contextualized—and interpret anthropological and native neglect of regional cultures and movements. With the growing importance of incorporating native versions of the past into current interpretations, regional histories may be problematic for native people because they depart from their own interpretations of the past. Generally, anthropologists and ethnohistorians have also ignored mixed-heritage communities, interaction networks important to regional cultures, and the development of regional organizations and pan-Indianism. However, reinterpreting the development of regionalism and regional cultures as survival rather than cultural disinte- gration (Brasser 1971) refocuses attention on the importance of regional perspectives to understanding larger cultural contexts.

As Americans and New Englanders, native people were cognizant of their position within different social frameworks and understood the ideological messages, both implicit and explicit, communicating that position. Non- native attitudes were (and are) important to the way native people expressed their ethnicity. Thus, I review the larger context of American assimilation policies and native reactions to them, attitudes about Indians and the mean- ing of "Indian" to non-natives, and race and race terminology with regard to native people. I also discuss reformers' work to acculturate native Ameri- cans and how these and other groups—fraternal and pan-Indian organiza- tions—manipulated stereotypical symbols to express ideas about native peo- ple and their cultures. Within the context of New England, I explore how social and race ideologies were worked out, including the role of the Ameri- can Pageantry Movement, and how national trends in the treatment of na- tive people affected local populations.

While much has been written about historic Indian-white relations and federal Indian policies, few policies had significant effects in southeastern New England. However, generalized attitudes toward native Americans played an important role in defining their social position in New England; thus, the local situation is quite different from situations in the West. Com- paratively little has been written on native cultures of New England: what exists generally focuses on cultural "disintegration" resulting from centuries of contact and massive acculturation. Following a brief review of the cul- tural-historical literature on southeastern New England, I examine how em- phasizing local rather than regional contexts hampers understanding and how stressing visible aspects of culture leads to simplistic interpretations of cultural disintegration rather than survival.

Rather than explain New England native revitalizations of the late nine- teenth and early twentieth centuries as rising out of intratribal racial con- flicts and tourism (Brasser 1971; Conkey, Boissevain, and Goddard 1978), I interpret the reemergence of native cultures within the racial context of New England society. There, native people formed a social and economic subclass but were seldom recognized as native because of the relative invisi- bility of the covert cultures they maintained and the lack of a recognizable Indian phenotype. Following Brasser (1971), I suggest that reactions to white America's notions of class and race (Vogt 1957) resulted in native cultural resurgence in the early twentieth century. Furthermore, I suggest native people consciously adopted pan-Indian symbols to be recognized by non-natives and later abandoned these for internally defined symbols, using personal research into their own cultures to augment surviving traditions.

Finally, I will use the development of the Indian Council of New England, a fraternal pan-Indian organization founded in Providence, Rhode Island, in 1923, as a case study of the importance of regional culture studies and a view into mechanisms of cultural resurgence. Through a brief history of the Indian Council, its organization and activities, I illustrate how New England's native people reacted to dominant society, including race consciousness, using regional culture and pan-Indian symbols to gain local recognition. I will also briefly discuss the role of research in native efforts reconstructing coherent cultural wholes and eliminating pan-Indianism following recognition.

THE IMPORTANCE OF REGIONAL PERSPECTIVES

The importance of regional native histories has been neglected, in part because the concept of tribe has long driven our concept of culture: a culture is what a group or tribe has that is specifically its own (Rosenthal 1968:86). *Culture* has not been used to define what groups share within a region, except with regard to the culture area concept. While local or tribal cultural traditions are those confined to specific cultural groups or communities, I suggest we examine regional cultures as well.

I use *regional culture* to describe cultural similarities allowing interaction between tribal groups, for instance, social relations and the importance and meaning of interaction. Within regional cultures, emphasizing similarities among groups becomes more important than articulating differences. Within these situations, cultural leveling—loss or deemphasis of cultural differences due to acculturation or intermarriage with neighboring peoples and subsequent accentuation of shared characteristics—may occur.

Regional patterns are both founded on and foster frequent intermarriage, gatherings, and sharing of ideas and traditions. However, not all people within a region shared the same culture. As any culture is differentially held by its members, regional cultures have variants, including communities or individuals who do not participate. In addition, regional cultures can overlap, and communities may participate in different regional cultures within specific situations.

Regionalization and cultural leveling have been important for many periods and situations. For instance, Brasser's Northeastern "gypsy" basketmaker culture (1971:84) is an example of regional networks and cultural developments. However, regionalization is not solely a postcontact process. In New England, earlier trade and kin relationships—forms of regional culture—continued, and interaction networks formed between communities coalesced from diverse groups after epidemic decimation and native-white wars. Regionalization was a constant integrative process both before and after the artificial horizon of European contact, and regional cultures were constantly created as social situations and interaction changed. Despite changes in native cultures, cultural processes guaranteeing reproduction of society remained constant.

While the development of historic regional cultures in New England has been characterized as disintegrative (Brasser 1971), regionalization is analogous to the diverse processes that create similarities within culture areas. In fact, the "culture area process" and regionalization are simultaneously integrative and disintegrative, and differ from one another in terms of scale. Similarly, the culture area process and regionalization also differ in their relative rates of cultural change. Because culture areas are based on the ethnographic present, regionalization is more visible in acculturative situations where we depend on written records to identify change.

With the growing importance of incorporating native versions of the past into current interpretations, regional histories may be problematic because they depart from native interpretations of the past. However, reinterpreting development of regionalism and regional cultures as a means of survival rather than cultural disintegration (Brasser 1971) may refocus attention on the importance of regional views to understanding larger cultural contexts.

Neglect of regional perspectives results from Federal Acknowledgment, which is specific to the tribe, not the region: the history of a specific tribe, group, or community is reconstructed rather than a regional synthesis. Tribal histories of Northeastern native cultures (Trigger 1978) cannot treat their respective situations comprehensively since by their very nature they focus on the history of a single group. Native groups were not isolated in the precontact past nor were they isolated from one another or the larger context of American society after Euro-American contact. Despite this, few studies attempt to move beyond the narrow perspective of tribal histories. Proper study of individual tribes demands that we also look beyond tribal boundaries and take into account communities with mixed tribal heritages and larger networks of native interaction that developed and drew on regional cultures.

Examination of New England native communities composed of members from different tribes has seldom been attempted. However, recent work on the Lighthouse community in Barkhamsted, Connecticut—composed of Narragansetts, whites, and others (Feder 1993; Chapter 3 in this book)—suggests its "native culture" was not exclusively Narragansett, but rather a combination of cultural influences.[1] Elsewhere, I have suggested that many mixed-heritage native communities and interaction networks existed in southeastern New England. In some cases, their material culture suggests synthesis of styles and cultures rather than separate maintenance of tribal cultural traditions (McMullen in press).

Besides neglecting the roles of mixed-heritage communities and regional networks in creating regional cultures, anthropologists, ethnohistorians, and native people have ignored the importance of pan-Indian movements and organizations to survival of late nineteenth- and early twentieth-century native cultures. As "the expression of a new identity and the institutions and symbols which are both an expression of that new identity and a fostering of it" (Thomas 1968:128–129), pan-Indianism exemplifies the growth of regional cultures. In many areas, including New England, crowding and amalgamation of small groups fostered cultural exchange and regional pan-Indianism (Hagan 1961:150). Growth of pan-Indianism in many situations may illustrate that native people were willing to adopt new traits—from western groups and other groups nearby—and change their cultural expressions (ibid.:170).

Pan-Indianism, American fraternalism,[2] and the advent of fraternal pan-Indian organizations all affected native cultural expressions in the early twentieth century. Fraternal pan-Indianism and fraternal pan-Indian organizations existed largely in cities, helping members of diverse groups retain Indian identity through contact, ceremonies, and public performances (Hertzberg 1971:213). The Tepee Order, the Grand Council Fire of the American Indians, and the Wigwam Club all encouraged cultural celebrations and sharing in cities (ibid.:213–236). Smaller organizations, such as the Indian Council of New England, were equally common and brought together members of diverse groups.

Anthropologists' disregard of fraternal pan-Indian organizations stems from their general neglect of the effects of social reform and fraternal movements on native people (Hertzberg 1971:298). While educated Indians often acted as informants and translators for anthropologists or trained as anthropologists themselves (ibid.:81), many anthropologists objected to reform and did not promote education and change among native people. In fact, reformers accused anthropologists of hindering assimilation by encouraging performance of traditional dances and ceremonies (Hagan 1988:214) and generally trying to preserve native cultures—as anthropological subjects—intact (Hertzberg 1971:23).[3] In their search for aboriginal cultures and survivals, anthropologists also recognized manipulation of Plains and other symbols as inappropriate to local native cultures. They discouraged pan-Indianism because it obscured or eliminated aspects of surviving native cultures.

The reasons why today's native people downplay the roles of fraternal or pan-Indian organizations are more complex. Passage of the Indian Reorganization Act in 1934 reemphasized native self-government on a tribal basis and local contacts and organizations over earlier regional links and organizations (Hertzberg 1971:305). Although this may be a factor in native neglect of fraternal pan-Indian organizations like the Indian Council of New England, the ways that modern native people talk about this period are affected more by the formats in which they must discuss that history. Native efforts to achieve Federal Acknowledgment necessitate emphasizing their own efforts to create and preserve their cultures rather than showing that intertribal organizations stimulated cultural preservation.

Native people may also minimize the role of fraternal organizations because they were often organized by whites, or with the assistance of whites, rather than by native people themselves. Regional native organizations in New England, such as the sachems' councils of the 1880s organized entirely by native people, are discussed proudly as evidence of regional contacts and cultural survivals (McMullen fieldnotes 1990–1993).

Besides Federal Acknowledgment's effect on the ways native people talk about their pasts, the role of pan-Indianism in regional and fraternal organizations may also be revealing. Because native people today acknowledge the inappropriateness of pan-Plains symbols to New England native cultures, admission of participation in pan-Indian events in the early twentieth century may be slightly embarrassing. Although pan-Indianism was a national trend, it also had regional forms (Thomas 1968) that took aspects of pan-Plains culture and combined them with local traditions. While native Americans in other regions took on Plains traits because local traits had disappeared (ibid.:129), adopting pan-Indian symbols to assert native identity was acceptable in early twentieth-century New England. Today these have given way to a greater focus on New England traditions (McMullen 1993).

Besides examining the roles of regional cultures and organizations, regional perspectives also necessitate setting native history within the contexts of New England society and the rest of America. Such contexts include how native people were perceived by non-natives, and how this affected their actions. Local non-natives' perceptions and attitudes greatly influenced native cultural expressions and symbols; thus, analysis of regional organizations and movements like pan-Indianism informs discussions of native-white relations and the expression of native identity in the early twentieth century.

THE CONTEXTS OF AMERICA AND NEW ENGLAND

Understanding the contexts of native Americans' lives is vital to interpreting their actions during historic times. With regard to the nineteenth and twentieth centuries, we must outline American attitudes toward native people, how these were worked out in New England, and how they were affected by changing race relations after the Civil War. To set up appropriate contexts for exploring attitudes about native people and their cultures, I will briefly review attitudes and policies concerning American Indians leading up to this period.

Assimilation Policies and Native Reactions

Assumptions of eventual assimilation of native Americans and immigrant populations are a fundamental part of the U.S. Constitution (Higham 1963:234; Gordon 1964:4; Deloria and Lytle 1984:3). The melting pot concept was based on the assimilation of diverse populations, bringing the strengths of ethnic characters together to yield a superior hybrid American race (Higham 1963; Gordon 1964).

Despite assumptions of voluntary assimilation, the tremendous flood of immigrants and subsequent formation of communities retaining ethnic characteristics brought about a nativist, anti-immigrant trend in the later nineteenth century, intended to break down separations and speed complete assimilation of European immigrants (Higham 1955:24):

Our task is to break up these groups or settlements, to assimilate or amalgamate these people of our American race, and to implant in their children, so far as can be done, the Anglo-Saxon conception of righteousness, law and order, and popular government, and to awaken in them a reverence for our democratic institutions and for those things in our national life which we as a people hold to be of abiding worth. (quoted in Gordon 1964:98)

Despite rhetorical similarities to federal Indian policies, the author was discussing Italians in New York City. Obviously, assimilation was not limited to native people. However, policies toward them were different. Native people were under the control of the federal government rather than being represented by it. In this regard, only native cultural differences were unacceptable; it was unnecessary to break up the Amish and other groups adhering to white standards of behavior (La Farge 1957:42).[4]

Attitudes and Policies about Indians

Early missionization among eastern native groups gave way to the attitudes of the 1840s and 1850s: Indians were thought incapable of improvement (Horsman 1988:32). Pushed west and segregated to delay contact with whites, native people were given more time to assimilate (Philp 1977:ix). Seizure of eastern native lands and removal of native peoples to Oklahoma and the Great Lakes region were explained as philanthropically motivated because Indians could not live close to the corrupting influences of whites (Nichols 1986:129).

During the nineteenth century, *Indian* had different meanings, at some times implying a racial classification and at others a cultural description (Hertzberg 1971:306). Those who saw native Americans as culturally different from whites felt they could be transformed by acculturative efforts and that no physical or genetic capacities limited their incorporation in American society. Those who saw native people as a race implied native people were all similar to one another, had definite genetic predispositions, and could be placed above or below other races and explicitly compared with blacks.[5] Although federal censuses after the Civil War labeled most off-reservation Indians "colored"—meaning people of color or mixed heritage separate from blacks—and implied racial difference (Forbes 1993:250), native Americans generally were considered racially equal to whites but culturally different (Hertzberg 1971:20–21; Hoxie 1988:208). As a category, *Indian* was usually reserved for those living on reservations (Forbes 1993:250) and those who required federal stewardship (Baca 1988:230).[6]

Because native people were seen as culturally rather than racially different from whites, they were admitted to white society, especially schools. However, their classification in New England as colored would put them at a definite disadvantage. Nineteenth-century transformation of *colored* to a term equivalent to *Negro* or *black* (Forbes 1993:262) disallowed recognition as Indian and, in some settings, fostered native reaction against being classed as colored.[7]

Although phenotype became the basis for racial classification (Blu 1980; Forbes 1993), intermarriage and racial admixture were relatively common between segments of New England society, and all "brown" people were problematic for race classification by the lay public. In the absence of recognizable phenotype, non-natives looked to visible cultural differences to determine race, ignoring nonmaterial aspects of culture, such as kinship and oral tradition.

Those who were recognized as native Americans, by either phenotype or visible cultural difference, were often subject to federal Indian policies or the actions of social reformers. Following the federal government's failure to assimilate native people rapidly and growing criticism of the reservation system, numerous Christian reform organizations rose in the 1870s and 1880s to help the "plight" of the Indian (Hoxie 1984), influence public opinion, and gain political and civil rights for native people (Hertzberg 1971, 1988:305; Hagan 1988:207).[8]

Most reformers were white easterners (Lurie 1968:70), whose limited contact with native people allowed them to believe Northeastern Indians were extinct. These reformers thus romanticized native Americans (Hagan 1961:70, 123, 1988:207; Edmunds 1988:174; Hoxie 1988:205) and believed assimilation immeasurably aided native salvation and survival. They did not comprehend native desires to maintain their cultures (Levine 1968:12).

Native people themselves were divided over federal assimilation policies. While some actively resisted, the Society of American Indians—organized in 1911 by Fayette McKenzie, a non-native (Hertzberg 1971:178)—included a number of "Red Progressives" (Hoxie 1988:219), held up by reformers as examples of successful assimilation (Hagan 1988:212). Later, many became active in reform, urging education and assimilation while remaining proud but somewhat detached from their heritage. Red Progressives stressed assimilation of individuals rather than tribes and were said to be "more sentimental about Indian life and less closely in touch with it" (Hertzberg 1971:31). The work of the Red Progressives suggests many native people understood white attitudes toward them and acted accordingly to shape native assimilation.[9]

Federal Indian policies like the Dawes Act, supported by reformers, brought about new criticism of government action. For instance, the American Indian Defense Association, founded in the 1920s by John Collier, tried to restore native societies (Deloria and Lytle 1984:41). In 1924, Indians were made citizens by a congressional decree as a reward for their service in World War I (Lurie 1968:74). However, citizenship was intended for those abandoning tribal ties: native people were not expected to be U.S. citizens and tribal members (Smith 1986:234). Thus, the federal government continued indirect assimilation and absorption of native people.

Reformers, anti-reformers like Collier, fraternal organizations, and pan-Indian groups all used stereotypical images of native Americans and pan-Indian symbols differently. Fraternal pan-Indian groups, such as the Indian Council of New England, used western Indian dress and public ceremonies to express native culture. Fraternal organizations, both white and native, used these symbols to emulate Indian values consistent with white ideas of native cultures. Simultaneously, white reformers used pan-Indian symbols to exemplify aspects of native cultures they felt should disappear.

These uses of Indian symbols suggest multiple perceptions of native people in the late nineteenth and early twentieth centuries. Thus, native people reacted to attitudes and stereotypes consistent with their situations. As I have suggested, native Americans understood ideological messages used by nonwhites to establish and reify the social order. However, such messages were not always directed at native people but could be the way whites defined themselves and their place in American history.

For instance, growth of the American Pageantry Movement (1905–1925) stressed celebratory reenactments and involved cooperation among segments of American society to eliminate ethnic and class divisions (Prevots 1990). Themes emphasized American values and the growth of America, including takeover of Indian lands, granting of royal charters, or signing Indian deeds (ibid.). Like the contemporaneous scouting movement, pageant organizers saw native cultures as noble but absent (Powers 1988:558). Thus both scouting and pageantry excluded native Americans from participation, since the America that pageants were intended to unify did not include native Americans. In New England pageants, Indian roles were played by Iroquois or Maine Indians brought in for that purpose or by creatively dressed and made-up whites (Prevots 1990:31). Local native people, descendants of historic figures portrayed in pageants, were not involved because they failed to meet white expectations and were not recognized as Indians.

Although Collier's work and citizenship had little impact on eastern native groups, nostalgia and interest in native cultures and history in New England simultaneously grew. This nostalgia was accompanied by the growth of pan-Indian organizations. Although New England's native people were to some extent assimilated and their cultures transformed, the early twentieth century brought reemphasis of native cultures, and specific individuals became important as culture bearers and keepers of traditional knowledge.

EARLIER VIEWS OF CULTURAL DISINTEGRATION AND REVITALIZATION

Federal policies and the work of social reformers had little effect on native people in southeastern New England. Nevertheless, nonwhite attitudes toward native Americans and blacks played an important role in defining their social position. In this regard, New England differs from native situations in the West. Literature about late nineteenth- and early twentieth-century Indian policy and Indian-white relations focuses on western situations, and New England is usually dismissed based on naive assumptions about extinction of local native people (Champagne 1989:34). Since federal Indian policies were designed to deal almost exclusively with western reservations and postallotment situations, they often failed to affect northeastern native people. Most families lived off-reservation among non-natives and "remained almost defiantly Indian, even where government experiments in granting stubborn 'returnees' homesteads scattered among White neighbors did not automatically result in Indian assimilation or break-down of a sense of community" (Lurie 1968:71).

Relatively little has been written on New England's native cultures. Although Frank Speck worked tirelessly to document traditional survivals, ensuing research focused more on cultural disintegration resulting from centuries of contact. Native culture histories dwell on dwindling land bases and language survivals, and cultural summaries include population decline, native occupations, and descriptions of material culture as if these embody culture (Brasser 1971; Conkey, Boissevain, and Goddard 1971:185). Anthropologists and historians have interpreted 1676 as the effective end of native cultures in southeastern New England (Brasser 1971; Conkey, Boissevain, and Goddard 1978). Population declines, combined with seventeenth- and eighteenth-century conversions to Christianity, were said to result in simplified native ceremonies, with religious changes affecting all aspects of culture (Brasser 1971:83).

Native dispossession and population movements began in the seventeenth century (Conkey, Boissevain, and Goddard 1978). Remnant populations withdrew from white settlements and coalesced. High male mortality resulting from the Pequot War, King Philip's War, the Revolutionary War, whaling, and other sea pursuits resulted in unequal native sex ratios. Subsequent intermarriage with whites and blacks yielded dispersed mixed-heritage populations, many remaining close to their homelands. Individuals disappeared by leaving to fight in the Revolutionary War, take up whaling, or join native communities to the west and north to escape white encroachment. Remaining communities and individuals were spatially, socially, and economically marginalized. Native people are often invisible historically, except in terms of craft production, which augmented subsistence farming and wage labor until the late nineteenth century (McMullen and Handsman 1987). Invisibility may also be explained by native movements away from homelands and settlement in New England cities (O'Connell 1992).

After removal of a significant portion of southeastern New England's native population to Brothertown, New York, in the 1780s (Love 1899), small communities remained in marginal areas. Except by their own choice, native people probably were not segregated (Wax 1971). These racially mixed populations seldom "looked Indian" to non-natives, were rarely recognized as such (Brasser 1971:89), and were usually seen as part of the colored underclass.

Brasser states these communities were divided into relatively pure-blood groups and mixed groups and that racial factionalism arose around 1800. Pure factions were relatively endogamous and "the mission culture and aboriginal crafts and customs lived on and died off with this faction, and after that no population increase could restore what had been lost" (Brasser 1971:86). He characterizes native populations of this period as "detribalized tramps," referring to participation in regional craft production networks (ibid.). After about 1860, racial factionalism was said to increase, yielding cultural revivals:

Both the resultant status struggles and the development of tourism gave rise to the birth of a neo-Indian culture and intertribal activities that are currently characteristic of the coastal groups. This modern Indianism is at best remotely connected with the aboriginal culture. The immaterial world of ancient times was lost together with the language; traditions preserved among the present older generations mainly consist of some hunting, fishing, and weather lore of colonial derivation. The new development was clearly a revitalization after a period of cultural distortion. Neo-Indianism made use of intertribal relations developed by the Indian whalers and wandering basket vendors and of hazy memories romanticized by literary fashions of the period. The urban Whites, creators of this romanticism, now came as tourists, more than willing to believe in the survival of the heroic Indians of the first frontiers. (ibid.)[10]

Indian names, long hair, and dress, influenced by St. Regis and Brothertown Indians in the 1880s, were the recognizable symbols used in public displays. Brasser suggests little native culture remained, and the "means by which the coastal Indians assert their identity are of foreign origin" (1971:88). No matter what its source, this "emphasis on Indianism did much to reestablish a self-respect and group pride long subdued by the racial attitudes of local Whites" (Conkey, Boissevain, and Goddard

1978:185). Speaking about Indians of the mid-Atlantic region, Brasser states:

Their recent history is one of slow and painful emergence of racial consciousness as a reaction to the attitude of the dominant whites, of the birth of a race as a hybrid and as assured of its historical myths as any other race. The significant difference, however, is provided by the skepticism of the others about the ancestry claimed by this new group. . . . In view of the racist attitudes of the local whites, there is no denying that this Indianism has done much good to the individuals and to the social life of these Indians. Self-respect and group spirit have reasserted themselves, and the relations between the Indian and mestizo factions have, among many groups, lost much of their old bitterness. (1971:84, 88) [11]

Failure to contextualize native histories adequately within New England and emphasis on disappearance of visible aspects of culture have led to interpretations of regionalization as disintegrative. A closer look at native motivations for regionalization and later cultural resurgence illustrates the extent of native cultural survival through historic times.

A NEW WAY OF LOOKING AT "DISINTEGRATION" AND "REVITALIZATION"

While Brasser and others recognized the importance of regional craft networks in the eighteenth and nineteenth centuries, the focus of cultural histories is usually material culture, language, and native land bases and their gradual demise, ignoring resistant native enclaves and less visible aspects of culture. Regionalism and regional cultures have been seen as disintegrative, although coalescence of communities, regionalization, and reorganization of native cultures after epidemic decimation and Indian-white wars occurred to maintain coherent traditions and cultures. Rather than interpreting regionalism as disintegrative, we should recognize native efforts to preserve aspects of culture under pressure of rapid change. And because regionalization is a continuous process, we must also realize that distinct networks of interaction and cooperation evolved for different periods and areas. Here, I will discuss two such phases: the invisibility of native cultures after King Philip's War and late nineteenth- and early twentieth-century resurgence of native culture in southeastern New England.

Anthropologists and historians have referred to nineteenth- and twentieth-century reemergence of native people as "revitalization." However, this suggests native cultures disintegrated after King Philip's War rather than simply becoming less visible. Such interpretations also ignore the impact of non-native attitudes on native self-perception, subsequent reactions, and defenses of their identity.

Public perceptions of native people in New England were part of the larger ideological framework of local society. While native and non-native individuals interacted as relative equals, social relationships among native people, whites, and blacks as *segments of society* were acted out in ways native people understood as representing non-native attitudes. As exclusion from twentieth-century pageants indicated white rejection of native identity, colonial policies and attitudes of the seventeenth and eighteenth centuries identified native people and their cultures as dangerous and their elimination, via extermination or assimilation, as critical to American colonial success.

Because of these attitudes, I suggest, native identity became a stigmatized category in southern New England after King Philip's War. Native people reacted to the stigmatization of their identity by covering (Goffman 1963) its recognizable symbols to give the impression of assimilation (Braroe 1975:121, 132–135). This strategy has been documented in other parts of North America and is analogous to denials of native religion (Rountree 1990:153) or traditional craftwork (Braroe 1975). In trying to manage information about themselves (Goffman 1963:102), New England's native people restricted use of identifying symbols to avoid recognition and appear, superficially, to be like non-natives, a process I call "coversion."

While King Philip's War probably caused stigmatization and coversion of native cultures in southeastern New England, different events apply for each group or situation. For instance, the Pequot War had a greater impact on the Pequots and others in southeastern Connecticut, since the Pequots were declared exterminated and none could profess that identity. However, events that brought about "covering" or stigmatization need not be events we recognize but processes, nonevents, imagined events, or epitomizing events—"narratives that condense, encapsulate, and dramatize longer-term historical processes" (Fogelson 1989:143). In this way, native people developed oral traditions and ideologies rationalizing invisibility. Recognition of white intolerance may also explain voluntary native removals during this period. For the Wampanoags, Narragansetts, and Nipmucs who fought against the colonists in King Philip's War, this is particularly significant. Having forfeited their lands as spoils of war and with populations reduced by war deaths, enslavement, or indenture, native people left the region or disguised their identity as enemies of the emerging American nation.

Those who remained in southeastern New England appeared to assimilate. Many converted to Christianity while retaining significant aspects of their worldview. Native people hid their languages and ceremonies and altered material aspects of culture to appear similar to non-native neighbors. For those living close to whites, all visible evidence of native culture may have disappeared. Families in more marginal areas maintained traditional wigwams but created new social relations with non-natives based on wage labor and craft production, similar to other poor people in their areas. However, basket makers decorated baskets with traditional designs to maintain identity and communicate internal political concerns (McMullen and

Handsman 1987; McMullen 1987). Native dress disappeared, although traditional ornaments that could be hidden under European clothing may have continued (McBride 1991).

Despite subversion of visible symbols, native people maintained significant covert cultures unrecognizable to non-natives. Frank Speck, along with later anthropologists, documented many traditions, but the categories of survivals described would have escaped non-native notice. Kinship and kin relations, seasonal native observances and celebrations, oral tradition and oral history, traditional worldviews, native foodways and planting rituals, herbal medicines and remedies, place names and the significance of place, ideas about time, weather lore, and the like have all remained viable traditions up to the present (Speck 1909, 1928; Tantaquidgeon 1928, 1972; Simmons 1986; Crosby 1991; McMullen fieldnotes 1990–1993). While some traditions show evidence of non-native influence, native people regarded them as native and consciously maintained them as such. While individuals may have been recognized as Indian, invisibility of covert native cultures continued until the late nineteenth century.

At that time, New England's native American cultures began to become more visible; native people emphasized aspects of culture they had maintained, augmenting them with traditions borrowed from native people involved in traveling Wild West shows, neighboring groups, and research on their own pasts. While individual Indians had been identified earlier, native groups and communities sought recognition and encouraged expressions of native identity. Public native celebrations included demonstrations of traditional practices and the wearing of traditional dress influenced by contacts with Plains Indians.

Participation in regional pan-Indian events is another form of covering since New England native people adopted western symbols recognizable to non-natives, such as feather bonnets and western Indian dress, rather than emphasizing the invisible, preserved aspects of their own cultures such as kinship and oral tradition. Although traditional dress was a cultural category widely identified by non-natives as specifically Indian, New England native people probably realized that centuries of covering had left them with few material traditions—hence, their adoption of western Indian dress. Like the Lumbee (Blu 1980:5) and other groups (Rountree 1990) who might not be readily recognizable, New England's native people attempted to redefine non-natives' ideas about Indians by combining selected adoptions from western traditions with their own survivals. Public displays became the focus for New England Indians' expressions of ethnicity and a way to express differences between natives and non-natives.

The "revitalization" of native culture in southeastern New England has been interpreted by Brasser (1971) and others as the result of racial factions vying for recognition by non-native tourists. However, such an interpretation suggests native people were economically rather than culturally motivated in their desires to make their cultures more visible. Similarly, it neglects the effects of non-native views on Indian self-presentation.

As a counter to explanations of revitalization in New England stressing tourism or internal racial factionalism, I suggest instead that native people recognized changing social attitudes and altered their actions accordingly. The problem of agency is important here because native efforts to gain recognition in southeastern New England may have resulted from an amelioration of their stigmatized condition or the realization that being labeled colored could result in a greater stigma than being Indian. I suspect a combination of factors explains the end of covert native cultures in southeastern New England and renewed efforts to make native identity and culture more visible. Despite centuries of covering their cultures and heritages, native people desired recognition as Indian: new pride in being Indian and a reduction in the stigmatization of their position encouraged recognition, although some individuals may have been motivated more by the desire not to be classed as colored.

Reactions against being labeled colored, denials of African heritage, and recourse to racial arguments about their identity do not make New England's native people themselves racists. Rather, it suggests they understood fully the attitudes of non-native society, the reasoning behind whites' insistence they were colored, the symbols used to make such identifications, and the risks involved. During the seventeenth through early nineteenth centuries, native people and their cultures survived despite an ideological system that identified them as a marginal underclass based on phenotype and/or visible cultural differences. Within this milieu they altered the use of cultural symbols to coexist with non-natives and maintain invisibility of their covert cultures. Concern for the integrity of their communities, not recognition as Indians, was the primary concern for native people in New England, especially during the eighteenth and nineteenth centuries (Russell G. Handsman, personal communication, 1993). With erosion of their communal lands in the latter half of the nineteenth century, native people were left with their cultures and their future yet were confronted by a changing social environment that increasingly emphasized phenotype and a language of racial identification and hierarchy that subsequently denied their existence. Their shift from covert tactics to dialogues about identity, including symbols of racial ideology, illustrates the necessity of flexibility in defining themselves to non-natives and of maintaining cultural and identity differences between themselves and other segments of society.

Native people in southeastern New England worked toward achieving recognition as Indian through adoption of pan-Indian symbols and traditions. While the rise of pan-Indianism in some contexts has been explained by native awareness of cultural loss (Thomas 1968), it can also result from desires to gain social recognition (ibid.; Blu 1980). In New England the latter appears to have been the case: native people understood that Plains and other western symbols were inappropriate but realized that centuries of coversion had left them only traditions that whites could not identify as Indian. Therefore, local native people adopted pan-Indianism for a brief time and abandoned most practices after non-natives began to acknowledge them as Indians. Having perceived the losses wrought by coversion, native people in southeastern New England began to research their cultures, adopting traditions from their own pasts and those of nearby groups, yielding a new regional culture. As a fraternal pan-Indian organization composed of individuals from many different groups, the Indian Council of New England exemplifies the importance of pan-Indianism and personal research in the development of regional Native culture.

THE INDIAN COUNCIL OF NEW ENGLAND

The Indian Council of New England, whose motto was "Algonquin 'I still live!'" was a fraternal pan-Indian organization based in Providence, Rhode Island. Founded in 1923, it continued as an intertribal organization into the 1930s. Through a brief history of the origins and organization of the council, I will demonstrate the value of regional approaches in native culture histories and how native people used regional organizations and pan-Indianism to gain recognition.

In the 1920s, a number of nonacademics were involved in researching native New England history: Mathias Speiss (Connecticut), Thomas Bicknell (Rhode Island), Eva Butler (Connecticut), Fannie Eckstorm (Maine), and others. Some were interested in cultural survivals; others held more romantic notions about local native people and their past. For instance, Thomas Bicknell, an amateur historian, began to organize a series of fifty to one hundred monuments to the Narragansetts in 1923, enlisting the aid of local native people in public dedications (Figure 7.1). In their correspondence, Mathias Speiss forwarded Bicknell a letter he received from a young Mohegan woman, Gladys Tantaquidgeon, suggesting that a living memorial to help New England's native people would be more appropriate than memorials to past Narragansetts (Indian Council of New England 1923–1925).

Struck by the idea, Bicknell immediately organized "an Indian committee" to create a New England Indian Council and sought advice from Frank Speck. Having engineered cultural revivals among native people in the South (Rountree 1990:216–218), Speck saw the goals of the Indian Council as revitalizing native cultures, documenting survivals, and encouraging public performances and ceremonies to regain recognition by non-natives:

The New England Indians can accomplish a great deal toward bringing back their past and preserve what remains to them. They still have to a great extent their splendid native languages which are a testimony to the modern world of the depth

Figure 7.1

Dedication of the first of Thomas Bicknell's monuments to the Narragansetts, October 28, 1923, Exeter Hill, Rhode Island. Standing in the foreground: Chief Occum (Lemuel Fielding), Mohegan, and Mathias Speiss. Bicknell is the tall, elderly man with the white beard. From the Indian Council of New England Scrapbook. Courtesy of the Haffenreffer Museum of Anthropology, Brown University.

of thought and expression, and the type of mind of the original New England native. They have their historical traditions and their homeland still left to them in part. They have their native type of government and the wonderful poise and carriage of their ancestors. The Indian character of generosity, sympathy and other standard virtues so much admired by their friends everywhere, and so much needed in the world of the white man today. So we pray to see them prosper, increase and expand to show the revival of the real and original American spirit. Would that there were two million of their number in old New England instead of two thousand! . . . A great day seems to be dawning for the eastern tribes. (Indian Council of New England 1923–1925; Frank G. Speck to Thomas Bicknell, December 11, 1923)

Although Speck supported Bicknell's work, he did not approve of Bicknell's choices for the committee: "I am a trifle disappointed to see that the individuals whom you have chosen to speak as representatives of their tribes are in some cases not the best qualified to do their people justice in the matter of speaking ability, education, and ideals" (ibid., December 4, 1923). Speck recommended instead a number of his students and informants rather than individuals Bicknell had chosen, including Gladys Tantaquidgeon, then in her twenties, to replace Lemuel Fielding (Chief Occum) as representative of the Mohegan.[12]

Bicknell called the first meeting of the Indian Council of New England in December 1923 in Providence. Having granted himself the title of Paleface Honorary Sachem, he had already written a constitution and set up goals for the council:

The Council of the Indian Tribes of New England is formed to promote acquaintance, friendship, business cooperation, education, finance, protection of civil rights, benefits of aged, sick and helpless, social and moral reforms, the preservation of Indian language, folk-lore, traditions, history, the record of achievement of great chiefs and tribesmen and the erection of monuments, memorials, tablets to perpetuate the memories of the events and the braves. (Ibid., December 1923)

According to his own criteria, Bicknell also defined membership in the council:

Any person who is a lineal descendant of a family of any one of the ancient Indian tribes of New England of good moral character may be a member of the Council. . . . Any pale-face interested in the Indian Council may be a member by vote of the Council. Any tribe of Indians or any one a descendant of any one of the other tribes of the Algonquin Nation, not of New England descent, may become an Associate member of this Council; such member may have all the privileges of the Council. (Ibid.)

The structure of council offices included two honorary sachems (one white—Bicknell—and one native—Penobscot Governor Nicholas Sockbeson), a chief sachem (Alfred C. A. Perry, Narragansett), a sachem from each tribe, a secretary, a treasurer, an executive committee composed of one member from each tribe, and several other offices (ibid.).[13]

Although native people with African heritage were not excluded from the council, it was a point of contention for many members, who questioned whether "typical Negroes" should be granted membership on the basis of claims to native blood. Many individuals otherwise engaged in native ceremonies and tribal organizations refused to participate in council activities because of "mixed blood." At one point Chief Occum refused to host an Indian Council meeting at Mohegan because he did not approve of some council members (Indian Council of New England 1923–1925:Sciota Nonsuch to Thomas Bicknell, May 3, 1923). While this suggests only a segment of southeastern New England's native population was involved in the council, it also illustrates that members and nonmembers used racial classification and phenotype to exclude others and to perpetuate the self-images they presented to non-natives.

Although discussions of blood and the appropriateness of particular indi-

viduals for membership dominate much of the correspondence in the Indian
Council papers, some members felt these discussions prevented the council
from doing the social work it intended:

Too many of our leaders are wrangling over full-bloods, half-bloods, etc. instead of
lining up on the side of the progressives and non-progressives. We need the progres-
sive Indian today; the silly sentimentalist who would reserve the Indian for the
Museum, the shows etc. has passed, and the Indian with all the qualities handed
down from his fathers, who were able in the wilderness to meet the trials and overcome, is needed on the trail today (Indian Council of New England 1923–
1925:Wild Pigeon, Sachem of Montauk [James Waters] to Thomas Bicknell, n.d.,
1925)

During its early years, the council was also associated with the American
Indian (Tipi) Association, a national fraternal organization of native people.
Some members of the national organization served as master of ceremonies
and in other offices for the council (Hertzberg 1971:226). Later, the Indian
Council broke away from the national organization, and local individuals
recognized as cultural carriers or active in researching their cultures took
over influential roles in the council, setting examples in traditional dress,
knowledge, and ceremonies.[14]

One explicit message of the national order that members of the Indian
Council of New England took to heart was the importance of personal
research rather than relying on misinformation, and many New England
Indians began studying the past with an eye toward reconstructing lost aspects of their own cultures. This research often took the form of extensive
reading of historical and ethnographic accounts of native people and cultures, beginning with the earliest explorers' and travelers' accounts. In many
cases, native people looked to nearby groups for information to reconstruct
cultural wholes, including studying written accounts and learning directly
from knowledgeable individuals from other tribes.

Council activities centered around events, powwows, the dedication of
monuments, and the like rather than education, health care, and social good
as laid out in the council's charter. By 1925, council members were prominent in tribal celebrations, as well as in their own powwows and meetings.
At the Narragansett August meeting of 1925, services were held in the
Narragansett church by LeRoy C. Perry, a Wampanoag who was a council
officer and pastor of the Narragansett church, and a mock wedding of two
Council members (Figure 7.2). Bicknell also gave a speech on the future
purposes of Narragansetts and their meetings, which he felt included

a true recognition and appreciation of the Indian character and ideals . . . an absorption of all Indians into American citizenship and ideals . . . a restoration and
preservation of ancient Indian rites, ceremonies and the religious observation of the
Narragansetts . . . erection of memorials to perpetuate the great names and events

Figure 7.2

Mock marriage ceremony conducted at Narragansett August Meeting, August 9, 1925, Charlestown, Rhode Island. Participants include LeRoy C. Perry, Wampanoag (wearing the dark-colored feather bonnet), the "bride," Miss Doris Steele, and the "groom," Edward Michael, both Narragansett. From the Indian Council of New England Scrapbook. Courtesy of the Haffenreffer Museum of Anthropology, Brown University.

of Indian history and especially of the Narragansetts . . . the holding of an annual powwow in August with Indian rites and dances to perpetuate the Narragansetts, the most powerful of the New England Indians. (Indian Council of New England 1923–1925:"Narragansett Indians Meet at Charlestown," *Providence Sunday Journal,* August 9, 1925)

Thomas Bicknell died in 1925, but the council he founded continued after his death. Many individuals prominent in the council's early years broke away and devoted their time to their own tribal councils and activities, strengthened by the knowledge that other native people in New England had similar goals in awakening interest and recognition of New England's native people. LeRoy Perry, the Council's Prophet, became the first Supreme Sachem of the Wampanoag Nation in 1928 (Campisi 1991:131); James L. Ciscoe and his daughter, Sarah M. Ciscoe, among the most active Nipmuc members of the council, created a branch in the Worcester area and led Nipmuc cultural preservation and activities. Gladys Tantaquidgeon,

Figure 7.3

Meeting of the Indian Council of New England held at Roger Williams Park, Providence, Rhode Island, October 8, 1924. From the Indian Council of New England Scrapbook. Courtesy of the Haffenreffer Museum of Anthropology, Brown University.

the council's first secretary, and members of the Fielding family of Mohegan continued their long-standing traditions of the Mohegan Wigwam Festival and other activities.

The Indian Council of New England was not the beginning of regional native consciousness in New England, but native involvement in the council and its activities made its members realize other native people in New England were fighting the same problems. Involvement in the council also allowed members to learn from each other, become aware of the national native scene, and sympathize and work with native Americans in other parts of the country. This work was carried on by Princess Red Wing, whose *Narragansett Dawn* continued to keep local native people apprised of Indian affairs in the West during the 1930s (Simmons 1989:78).

Evidence that southern New England's native people used activities of the Indian council to increase their visibility and public awareness comes from photos of council meetings, which show a marked increase in regalia onward from the time the council was founded (Figure 7.3). Letters between non-native members of the council suggest native people had to adopt "authentic native dress" in order to be regarded seriously (Indian Council of New England 1923–1925). Similarly, strong influences from Frank Speck and native people outside New England affected public events and ceremonies carried out by council members. For example, early in the council's history, Speck recommended the involvement of his student Joseph Strong Wolf (variously identified as an Abenaki and an Ojibwa), suggesting he conduct the pipe ceremony—now a standard fixture of many native ceremonies and powwows—saying no New England Indian knew how to perform it properly (Indian Council of New England 1923–1925: Frank G. Speck to Thomas Bicknell, December 4, 1923). Later, Strong Wolf was installed as "Chief of Powwows" for the Indian Council of New England and organized their public events in the 1920s.

The strong influences of Thomas Bicknell, Frank Speck, and Mathias Speiss on the Indian Council of New England suggest non-natives concerned over the welfare of New England's native people encouraged regionalism. Their insistence on public displays, regalia, and other visible markers of Indian culture suggests that they too were cognizant of white attitudes about native people and sought to reverse them by creating regional cultures. However, subsequent disavowal of pan-Indianism and withdrawal from regional patterns demonstrates that native people regained confidence in their own ideas about their cultures and how they should be expressed.

Today, native people throughout North America maintain that they take from white culture what they want and leave the rest, but the same can be said for what they take from other native cultures. This willingness to adopt aspects of other cultures selectively contributed in large part to localized pan-Indianism in New England: native people took what they needed for a time in order to be recognized. Later, as their own research and increased knowledge gave way to more coherent cultural wholes and they had achieved the recognition they so badly wanted, they abandoned these practices in favor of their own traditions.

NOTES

Funding for research on native historiography in southeastern New England was provided by the Wenner-Gren Foundation for Anthropological Research and the Haffenreffer Museum of Anthropology, Brown University and is gratefully acknowledged.

Earlier versions of this chapter, originally titled "The Algonquin Council and the Elders of Yesterday: Forging a Unified Identity," were presented at the Third Annual Conference of the New England Native American Institute, Boxborough, Massachusetts, April 1992, and the Annual Meeting of the Northeast Anthropological Association, Danbury, Connecticut, March 1993.

I thank Russell G. Handsman, Shepard Krech III, Daniel P. Odess, and Rochelle K. Rosen for their insightful comments on earlier versions of this essay. To Dan especially, I owe much for long and insightful discussions on the concept of regionalism and many other aspects of this essay.

1. While regionalism includes development of broader cultural similarities, populations of mixed-heritage communities may have participated in a form of regional culture or may have developed polysynthetic cultures drawing on their constituent parts, such as diverse native cultures, "poor white" culture, and free black or slave culture. While such communities are better documented for the mid-Atlantic region and the Southeast, they probably also existed in New England. I am indebted to Dan Odess for reminding me of the necessity of considering the non-native heritages of these communities.

2. During the 1920s, white fraternal organizations grew on a massive scale, especially those emphasizing national origin, such as the Knights of Columbus and Sons of Italy (Hertzberg 1971:209). In addition to these, a number of other groups with largely white membership with "Indian" names existed, such as the Improved Order of Red Men (ibid.:215–216). Despite their names, these organizations seldom involved native people. Other non-native fraternal organizations excluded those with African heritage (Hertzberg 1971:215), making it impossible for many native Americans to join. While Hertzberg suggests native people were barred from the IORM (1971:216), there were exceptions: Len Bayrd, a Narragansett, was a member of the order (Joan Lester, personal communication, 1991).

3. In the same vein, some anthropologists, such as Frank Speck, felt intermarriage with non-natives lead to "deculturation," and native Americans should attempt to maintain their cultures while being educated (Hertzberg 1971:121–122). Unlike Speck, Arthur Parker, the Seneca anthropologist, felt native people should be educated and fully integrated into American society, with the eventual disappearance of native cultures. Parker and Frank Speck were said to have parted company on "differing views on the relationship of Indians to larger society" (ibid.:51), while other anthropologists disagreed with the idea of allowing native cultures and reservations to remain as "zoological parks" (Kluckhohn 1962:338).

4. Native cultural differences were probably less acceptable than those represented by the Amish or other groups because native people generally did not conform to American ideals of education, success, and so forth. Without these basic values, assimilation of native people was seen as impossible.

At this point, it was not understood that people assimilate as individuals rather than groups (Dozier, Simpson, and Yinger 1957), and despite the complete assimilation of some individuals, both immigrants and native people resisted assimilation. By the 1890s, American policies to assimilate immigrant populations forcefully gave way to greater tolerance for separate European traditions (Higham 1963:119–121), and efforts were made to maintain cultural traditions by setting up "settlements" and community centers in cities (ibid.; Philp 1977).

5. In western reservation schools, Indian children were taught that the "red race" came after white, yellow, and black races in its capabilities and accomplishments (Adams 1988:227).

6. This policy is illustrated by a court decision of the 1870s, which stated that Pueblo people need not be treated or regarded as Indians because they were Christian and agricultural (Baca 1988:230; Philp 1977:28).

7. Early twentieth-century native letters and writings illustrate that race consciousness and racism were part of the way native people in southeastern New En-

gland defined themselves and that many avoided being linked with blacks or being identified as colored (Indian Council of New England 1923–1925). This situation is analogous to those described by Blu (1980) and Rountree (1990).

Within this discussion I intend to use the term *colored* as it was used during the late nineteenth and early twentieth centuries. From today's perspective, *Negro, colored, black, Afro-American,* and *African-American* are seen as synonyms that have supplanted one other because of articulations by Black Power rhetoricians and audiences wanting to be politically correct in their terminology. However, these terms are not synonymous because they represent changing social positions of these segments of society, with each term referring to a particular group and their social position for a different period and context.

Use of the term *colored* lumped together all people of color and ignored any distinctions. After about 1790, *colored* supplanted *mulatto* as a cover term for all nonwhites (Forbes 1993:250): census takers separated "Black" and "M" peoples—mulatto, mixed, or "brown"—hence, almost all native people were classed as "M." Only Indians living on reservations, and thus exempt from taxation, were usually classed as Indians, a category separate from whites (ibid.). *Colored* did not necessarily imply mixture with black, just mixture (ibid.:260; Blu 1980). After the Civil War, *colored* and *Negro* became synonymous (Forbes 1993:262); this is borne out in legislative changes during Reconstruction equalizing the way native Americans and blacks were treated as citizens and voters (Plane and Button 1993). Racial attitudes of the period implied the "colored" race was limited in its potential and demanded segregation from whites in society.

8. These included the Women's National Indian Organization (1879), the Indian Rights Association (1882), and the Lake Mohonk Conference (1883), among others. For more on these organizations, their aims, and work, see Hertzberg (1971, 1988), Hagan (1988), and Hoxie (1984, 1988). Social reforms and help for native people were rationalized via reference to native poverty, poor health, and lack of education rather than inherent rights to their own lands or constitutional or treaty guarantees (Wax 1971:66). One of the most important results of social reformers' work in the late nineteenth century was the passage of the General Allotment Act of 1887 (variously called the Dawes Act or Indian Emancipation Act), which tried to make native people independent farmers but only resulted in massive land loss (Hertzberg 1971:21; Philp 1977:x).

9. Some educated Indians were familiar with immigrant assimilation policies and saw them as ideal models for Indian assimilation (Hertzberg 1971:23). Members of the Society of American Indians felt native people should eliminate aspects of their cultures contrary to progress but maintain those characteristics denoting cultural advancement, such as bravery, values, personality, and ecological philosophy (ibid.). At the same time, the Red Progressives were proud of their heritage but resented that they often had to "play Indian" and dress up to be recognized as such (Hertzberg 1971:57).

10. Brasser (1971) also suggests that the presence of anthropologists, such as Frank Speck and James Mooney, encouraged cultural displays and ceremonies around 1900.

11. While I agree with Brasser's general conclusions about the social and racial climate of the Northeast for this period, his work unfortunately covers too great a region—Cape Hatteras to Maine—to be of much practical use. In addition, it generally lacks documentation.

12. Speck's statement that individuals chosen by Bicknell were inadequate suggests that the "racial conflicts" dividing native groups during this period may not always have been internally generated. Speck appears to have occasionally created such conflicts when he insisted on engaging informants from only the "purest families" and made his own research funds a focus of competition among tribal members. Speck's disapproval also suggests native people were affected not only by the beliefs of the general public but also by the attitudes and actions of anthropologists and others knowledgeable about their cultures. Speck was widely regarded as the single person—native or non-native—with the greatest knowledge of Northeastern native cultures.

13. According to the original council letterhead, the tribal sachems included Hamilton Creighton (Narragansett), Julian A. Harris (Mohegan), John W. Braxton (Nipmuc), LeRoy C. Perry (Wampanoag), Mrs. Mary M. Chappelle (Massachuset), Benjamin W. Dailey (Pequot), Charles D. Mitchell (Penobscot), Joseph Neptune (Passamaquoddy), Sciota A. Nonsuch (Western Niantic), Lemuel M. Fielding (Mohegan), James L. Ciscoe (Hassanimisco Nipmuc), and Joseph Strong Wolf (Abenaki). Gladys Tantaquidgeon (Mohegan) acted as secretary, while Mrs. Minnie B. Steele (Narragansett) was treasurer. The following offices were also named: Monuments, Thomas W. Bicknell; Education, William B. Cabot; Historian, Frank G. Speck; Sports and Games, Charles D. Mitchell; Laws, Cyrus E. Dallin; Chief of Powwows, Joseph Strong Wolf; and Prophet, LeRoy C. Perry.

14. The Indian Council of New England broke away from the American Indian Order as a result of a disagreement between Gladys Tantaquidgeon, then secretary of the council, and Flying Eagle, executive secretary of the American Indian Association, over an article by "the Wolf" on the New England Indians published in the *Indian Tepee*. Drawing on nineteenth-century histories of New England, "the Wolf" suggested "of the Mohegan tribe, a few miserable drunken families survive," a statement repudiated by Gladys Tantaquidgeon and defended in a later *Indian Tepee* by Flying Eagle, who stated that no more histories of the New England Indians would be printed in the *Indian Tepee* (Indian Council of New England 1923–1925; *Indian Tepee*, 1925).

REFERENCES

Adams, David Wallace. 1988. "From Bullets to Boarding Schools: The Educational Assault on the American Indian." In *The American Indian Experience: A Profile, 1524 to the Present,* edited by Philip Weeks, 218–239. Arlington Heights, Ill.: Forum Press.

Baca, Lawrence R. 1988. "The Legal Status of American Indians." In *History of Indian-White Relations,* edited by Wilcomb E. Washburn, 230–237. Handbook of North American Indians, Vol. 4. Washington, D.C.: Smithsonian Institution Press.

Blu, Karen I. 1980. *The Lumbee Problem: The Making of an American Indian People.* Cambridge: Cambridge University Press.

Braroe, Niels Winthur. 1975. *Indian and White: Self-Image and Interaction in a Canadian Plains Community.* Stanford: Stanford University Press.

Brasser, Ted J. C. 1971. "The Coastal Algonkians: People of the First Frontiers." In *North American Indians in Historical Perspective,* edited Eleanor Burke Leacock and Nancy Oestreich Lurie, 64–91. Prospect Heights, Ill.: Waveland Press.

Campisi, Jack. 1991. *The Mashpee Indians: Tribe on Trial*. Syracuse, N.Y.: Syracuse University Press.

Champagne, Duane. 1989. *American Indian Societies: Strategies and Conditions of Political and Cultural Survival*. Colonial Survival Report 32. Cambridge: Cultural Survival.

Conkey, Laura, Ethel Boissevain, and Ives Goddard. 1978. "Indians of Southern New England and Long Island: Late Period." *The Northeast*, edited by Bruce G. Trigger, 177–189. Handbook of North American Indians, Vol. 15, Washington, D.C.: Smithsonian Institution Press.

Crosby, Constance A. 1991. "Myth, Folklore, History, and the Algonkian Spiritual Landscape." Paper presented at the Dublin Seminar for New England Folklife, Deerfield, Massachusetts, June.

Deloria, Vine, and Clifford M. Lytle. 1984. *The Nations Within: The Past and Future of American Indian Sovereignty*. New York: Pantheon Books.

Dozier, Edward P., George E. Simpson, and J. Milton Yinger. 1957. "The Integration of Americans of Indian Descent." In *American Indians and American Life*, edited by George E. Simpson and J. Milton Yinger, 158–165. Annals of the American Academy of Political and Social Science 3.

Edmunds, R. David. 1988. "National Expansion from the Indian Perspective." In *Indians in American History*, edited by Frederick E. Hoxie, 159–178. Arlington Heights, Ill.: Harlan Davidson.

Feder, Kenneth L. 1993. "Material Culture at the Lighthouse Village: The Legend and the Evidence." Paper presented at the Annual Meeting of the Northeastern Anthropological Association, Danbury, Connecticut, March.

Fogelson, Raymond D. 1989. "The Ethnohistory of Events and Nonevents." *Ethnohistory* 36(2):133–147.

Forbes, Jack D. 1993. *Africans and Native Americans: The Language and Race and the Evolution of Red-Black Peoples*. Urbana: University of Illinois Press.

Goffman, Irving. 1963. *Stigma: Notes on the Management of Spoiled Identity*. Englewood Cliffs, N.J.: Prentice-Hall.

Gordon, Milton. 1964. *Assimilation and American Life: The Role of Race, Religion, and National Origins*. New York: Oxford University Press.

Hagan, William T. 1961. *American Indians*. Chicago: University of Chicago Press.

———. 1988. "Reformers' Images of the Native Americans: The Late Nineteenth Century." In *The American Indian Experience*, edited by Philip Weeks, 207–217. Arlington Heights, Ill.: Forum Press.

Hertzberg, Hazel W. 1971. *The Search for an American Indian Identity: Modern Pan-Indian Movements*. Syracuse: Syracuse University Press.

———. 1988. "Indian Rights Movements, 1887–1973." In *History of Indian-White Relations*, edited by Wilcomb E. Washburn, 305–323. Handbook of North American Indians, Vol. 4. Washington, D.C.: Smithsonian Institution Press.

Higham, John. 1963. *Strangers in the Land: Patterns of American Nativism, 1860–1925*. New York: Atheneum.

Horsman, Reginald. 1988. "United States Indian Policies, 1776–1815." In *History of Indian-White Relations*, edited by Wilcomb E. Washburn, 29–39. Handbook of North American Indians, Vol. 4. Washington, D.C.: Smithsonian Institution Press.

Hoxie, Frederick E. 1984. *A Final Promise: The Campaign to Assimilate the Indians, 1880–1920*. Lincoln: University of Nebraska Press.

————. 1988. "The Curious Story of Reformers and the American Indians." In *Indians in American History*, edited by Frederick E. Hoxie, 205–230. Arlington Heights, Ill.: Harlan Davidson.

Indian Council of New England. 1923–1925. Scrapbook of Thomas Bicknell's correspondence, newspaper clippings, photographs, etc. Haffenreffer Museum of Anthropology, Brown University, Bristol, Rhode Island.

Kelly, Lawrence C. 1988. "United States Indian Policies, 1900–1980." In *History of Indian-White Relations*, edited by Wilcomb E. Washburn, 66–80. Handbook of North American Indians, Vol. 4. Washington, D.C.: Smithsonian Institution Press.

Kluckhohn, Clyde. 1962. "Indian Americans in a White Man's World." In *Culture and Behavior: Collected Essays of Clyde Kluckhohn*, 336–342. New York: Free Press.

La Farge, Oliver. 1857. "Termination of Federal Supervision: Disintegration and the American Indian." In *American Indians and American Life*, edited by George E. Simpson and J. Milton Yinger, 41–46. Annals of the American Academy of Political and Social Science 3.

Levine, Stuart. 1968. "The Survival of Indian Identity." In *The American Indian Today*, edited by Stuart Levine and Nancy Oestreich Lurie, 9–48. Baltimore: Penguin Books.

Love, William De Loss. 1899. *Samson Occum, and the Christian Indians of New England*. Boston and Chicago: Pilgrim Press.

Lurie, Nancy Oestreich. 1968. "Historical Background." In *The American Indian Today*, edited by Stuart Levine and Nancy Oestreich Lurie, 49–81. Baltimore: Penguin Books.

McBride, Kevin A. 1991. " 'Ancient and Crazie': Pequot Lifeways during the Historic Period." Paper presented at the Dublin Seminar for New England Folklife, Deerfield, Massachusetts, June.

McMullen, Ann. 1987. "Looking for People in Woodsplint Basketry Decoration." In *A Key into the Language of Woodsplint Baskets*, edited by Ann McMullen and Russell G. Handsman, 102–123. Washington, Conn.: American Indian Archaeological Institute.

————. 1990–1993. Fieldnotes on the Mohegan, Pequot, Nipmuc, Narragansett, and Wampanoag concerning native culture, traditions, cultural expression, and historiography.

————. 1993. "Blood and Culture: Ethnic Symbols in Native Southern New England." Unpublished Manuscript.

————. In press. "Native Basketry, Basket Styles, and Changing Group Identity in Southern New England." In *Proceedings of the Dublin Seminar for New England Folklife*, edited by Peter Benes. Boston: Boston University.

McMullen, Ann, and Russell G. Handsman, eds. 1987. *A Key into the Language of Woodsplint Baskets*. Washington, Conn.: American Indian Archaeological Institute.

Nichols, Roger L. 1986. "The Indian in Nineteenth-Century America: A Unique Minority." In *The American Indian: Past and Present*, edited by Roger L. Nichols, 127–136. New York: Alfred A. Knopf.

O'Connell, Barry, ed. 1992. *On Our Own Ground: The Complete Writings of William Apess, A Pequot*. Amherst: University of Massachusetts Press.

Philp, Kenneth R. 1977. *John Collier's Crusade for Indian Reform: 1920–1954*. Tucson: University of Tucson Press.

Plane, Ann Marie, and Gregory Button. 1993. "The Massachusetts Indian Enfranchisement Act: Ethnic Contest in Historical Context, 1849–1869." *Ethnohistory* 40(4):587–618.

Powers, William K. 1988. "The Indian Hobbyist Movement in North America." In *History of Indian-White Relations,* edited by Wilcomb E. Washburn, 557–561. Handbook of North American Indians, Vol. 4. Washington, D.C.: Smithsonian Institution Press.

Prevots, Naima. 1990. *American Pageantry: A Movement for Art and Democracy.* Ann Arbor: UMI Research Press.

Rosenthal, Elizabeth Clark. 1968. " 'Culture' and the American Indian Community." In *The American Indian Today,* edited by Stuart Levine and Nancy Oestreich Lurie, 82–92. Baltimore: Penguin Books.

Rountree, Helen C. 1990. *Pocahontas's People: The Powhatan Indians of Virginia through Four Centuries.* Norman: University of Oklahoma Press.

Simmons, William S. 1986. *Spirit of the New England Tribes: Indian History and Folklore, 1620–1984.* Hanover N.H.: University Press of New England.

————. 1989. *The Narragansett.* New York: Chelsea House Publishers.

Smith, Michael T. 1986. "The History of Indian Citizenship." In *The American Indian: Past and Present,* edited by Roger L. Nichols, 232–241. New York: Alfred A. Knopf.

Speck, Frank G. 1909. "Notes on the Mohegan and Niantic Indians." In *The Indians of Greater New York and the Lower Hudson,* edited by Clark Wissler, 183–210. Anthropological Papers of the American Museum of Natural History, vol. 3.

————. 1928. "Native Tribes and Dialects of Connecticut: A Mohegan-Pequot Diary." *43rd Annual Report of the Bureau of American Ethnology, 1925–26:*199–287.

Tantaquidgeon, Gladys. 1928. "Mohegan Medicinal Practices, Weather-Lore and Superstition." In "Native Tribes and Dialects of Connecticut: A Mohegan-Pequot Diary." *43rd Annual Report of the Bureau of American Ethnology,* 1925–26:264–279.

————. 1972. *Folk Medicine of the Delaware and Related Algonkian Indians.* Anthropological Series Number 3. Harrisburg, Pa.: Pennsylvania Historical and Museum Commission.

Thomas, Robert K. 1968. "Pan-Indianism." In *The American Indian Today,* edited by Stuart Levine and Nancy Oestreich Lurie, 128–142. Baltimore: Penguin Books.

Trigger, Bruce G., ed. 1978. *The Northeast.* Handbook of North American Indians, Vol. 15. Washington, D.C.: Smithsonian Institution Press.

Vogt, Evon Z. 1957. "The Acculturation of American Indians." In *American Indians and American Life,* edited by George E. Simpson and J. Milton Yinger, 137–146. Annals of the American Academy of Political and Social Science 3.

Wax, Murray. 1971. *Indian Americans: Unity and Diversity.* Englewood Cliffs, N.J.: Prentice-Hall.

White, Richard. 1991. *The Middle Ground: Indians, Empires, and Republics in the Great Lakes Region, 1650–1815.* Cambridge: Cambridge University Press.

8

Art for Sale: Cultural and Economic Survival

Joan Lester

A surprising number of non-native people assume that native Americans in New England have either vanished or been fully assimilated into mainstream society. In fact, native people have been here for at least 12,000 years, and they are still here.

Like all other living cultures, native cultures have changed significantly over time. Personal and community life-styles have been painfully disrupted by the New England history that began with the arrival of European fisherman more than 400 years ago. But many of the more than 10,000 native Americans who live in New England today still actively participate in their cultures. People who appear to have incorporated mainstream culture into their lives are, at a deeper level, still strongly connected to their tribal and communal identities. Native people express their identity in different ways. For the past 250 years, some have chosen to sell works of art to non-native people, for economic survival and to affirm their native traditions.

There was no word for art within native cultures. The beautiful objects that people created were part of the integral fabric of their lives. While fine work was recognized and appreciated, art for art's sake was unknown. Although the creation of art was not an end in itself, the look of cultural objects did change over time as people experimented with new shapes or materials and absorbed ideas from other native nations. Often the sources of these new ideas came from the objects given as gifts or in trade. In the seventeenth century, art continued to evolve as artists also began to incorpo-

Figure 8.1

Women's blue tradecloth leggings, glass bead embroidery, Northern New England, nineteenth century. L: 18″ W: 14″.

rate forms, materials, and technology from non-Indian sources. Trade cloth and glass beads provide the most dramatic examples of this integration. Native people translated their own cuts of leather clothing into cloth and ornamented them with European glass beads (Figure 8.1). These glass beads have become such an essential part of Indian decoration that many non-natives think that they were Indian in origin.

The idea of creating art for sale may have originated as European domination of native homelands increased and people were less able to rely on traditional sources of food and clothing for their survival. To purchase essentials, they began to sell objects that they had originally made only for their own culture. In selling their Indian work,[1] artists applied their native skills and knowledge to creating objects for non-native buyers. In New England, woven splint baskets, birchbark containers, carved wooden clubs, and multicolored pottery all serve as examples of this Indian art.[2]

UTILITARIAN BASKETS

For centuries, native New Englanders had used strips of wood (referred to as splints) to weave large baskets, which they used to store dried foods,

Figure 8.2

Covered storage basket, wood splint, stamped designs. Mohegan (?), nineteenth century. D: 12″ H: 7″.

gather wild foods, and harvest and transport their crops. By the 1750s, native peddlers, with quantities of such baskets strung on their backs, were traveling from house to house and town to town selling their wares. Because they were inexpensive and well suited to farm and household tasks, such baskets were eagerly acquired by non-native consumers. Often native weavers modified their forms to meet the needs and tastes of their new buyers. For example, they added covers to round and rectangular baskets, creating hat boxes (Figure 8.2), and trunks.[3]

TOURISM

By the late 1800s, the era of the great summer resorts had begun. Non-native tourists began to travel in great numbers to seashore and mountain areas, such as Bar Harbor, Poland Springs, Old Orchard Beach, and Kennebunk in Maine; the White Mountains of New Hampshire; and Campobello Island in New Brunswick, Canada. These tourists were eager to buy souvenirs of their stay, as well as furnishings for summer cottages. The Victorians embellished their homes with lavish decoration. Sometimes they created curio corners where they displayed Indian and other "exotic" mementos. Native artists responded to this new market by increasing their production and expanding the variety and types of work that they created for sale. Many artists traveled to a resort and set up camp for the summer; others sold work from their homes or in native-owned shops in their community. Some filled orders from stores in other parts of New England.

FANCY BASKETS

In addition to large, utilitarian baskets, native weavers began to create "fancy baskets," smaller, elaborately decorated, and colored baskets that appealed to the Victorian fondness for embellishment and elaboration. Artists added sweetgrass, brightly colored splints, and decorative weaves and often based the forms of these fancy baskets on non-native objects, such as sewing, glove, and handkerchief boxes, knitting baskets (Figure 8.3), napkin rings, and pocketbooks. Whether an item was made of cloth, china, or glass, a skilled weaver could transform it into basketry, creating a functional and appealing souvenir. During this era, native people devised new tools to increase basket production and assure uniformity. These included wooden molds around which to weave a basket and multitoothed gauges, to cut the splints into strips for weaving.

BIRCHBARK SOUVENIRS

While some people wove baskets, others formed and shaped souvenir containers of birchbark. For centuries, native people in Maine and Canada had used birchbark as a writing surface and to make canoes, wigwam coverings, and a multitude of utensils and containers. In the late nineteenth century, they began to cut, fold, and stitch birchbark into picture frames, wastebaskets, wall pockets, and other objects whose forms were again appropriated from Victorian America. Some artists incised the surfaces of their containers with floral and geometric motifs; others chose to decorate work with scenes from their own lives. Tomah Joseph, a Passamaquoddy artist,[4] decorated his birchbark objects with illustrations of origin stories, scenes of past and present life, and the animals and plants of his homeland (Figure 8.4).

CLUBS

In the mid-nineteenth century, carved wooden clubs, originally used in warfare and carried as part of a man's formal dress, also began to be made for sale to tourists. When people made clubs for themselves, they usually shaped the head of the club into a ball and sculpted carvings that may have represented a person's clan or guardian spirit on the head and grip. The clubs made for non-native buyers were more elaborately carved and painted,

Figure 8.3

A type of knitting basket popular since the late nineteenth century. Ash, dyed blue splints and paper cord, northern New England, c. 1930. D: 6″   H: 12 ½″.

often with human faces on the club head (Figure 8.5), and were sold to tourists as "war clubs."[5] The root tips were left on these clubs, providing more surface for decorative carvings.

GAY HEAD POTTERY

For centuries, the Wampanoag Indian people of Gay Head on Martha's Vineyard had gathered and used the multicolored clays from the Gay Head cliffs and other island clay pits for making cooking pots and storage jars. In the late nineteenth century, Gay Headers, like the basket makers and root

Figure 8.4

Double picture frame, birchbark, with plants, animals, and
scenes of native life. L: 8½″ W: 6¾″. Box, birchbark, with
scenes of native life. L: 4¼″ W: 3¼″ H: 3″ (both by Tomah Joseph, Passamaquoddy).

club carvers, began to produce pottery work to sell to tourists who had
come by steamboat to visit the Gay Head lighthouse, the Indian settlement,
and the colorful cliffs. The souvenirs developed especially for these new
buyers were different from the pottery once made for household use. In
addition to pots, vases (Figure 8.6), and bowls, people also modeled small
sculptures of rabbits, Bibles, tepees, and canoes. Since firing the clay eliminated most of its color, these mementos were now baked only in the sun to
preserve the multicolored appearance important to tourists.

Figure 8.5

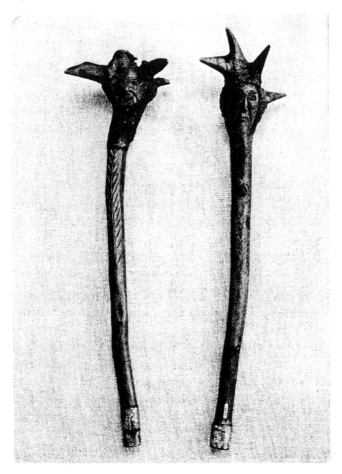

Root club, birch, with human face and wolf carved into root mass. Northern New England, late nineteenth century. L: 28″ W: 8″ (at head). Root club, birch, with human face, feathers carved into root mass. Northern New England, late nineteenth century. L: 29″ W: 7″ (at head).

CULTURAL SURVIVAL

Although the sale of baskets, birchbark, clubs, and pottery souvenirs is directly related to economic survival, creating and selling Indian work also supports cultural survival. When native artists gather their traditional materials or travel to summer resort areas to sell what they have created, they follow the seasons, as did their ancestors. When they use materials or processes that are centuries old, they again follow and retain the ways of their

Figure 8.6

Vase, wheel-turned, sun dried, Gay Head clay. Van der Hoop family, Gay Head Wampanaog, late nineteenth century. D: 4½″ H: 9½″.

ancestors. When they choose to create Indian work rather than work in a mainstream occupation, they express their resistance to total assimilation and again affirm their native identity.

LIVING TRADITIONS

Art made for sale also reveals the changing nature of living traditions. In the late nineteenth century, native artists successfully integrated new ideas into their Indian work. They introduced new forms, such as picture frames and sewing baskets; used new tools for carving and weaving; changed processes, such as firing pots in the sun to retain their colors; and selected new images for their clubs and birchbark souvenirs. The art that resulted from this meeting of cultures satisfied both tourist and native needs.[6] The selection and integration of new ideas increased the appeal of the art for tourists without negating its native content. Images and forms catered to tourist expectations and still expressed a native view of the world. In exchange for their creativity, native artists received economic support and cultural affirmation, while non-native buyers received vacation souvenirs that served as useful household objects and, often, as mementos of meetings with native people.

Woven splint baskets, carved clubs, and Gay Head pottery continue to be made in New England today. This art is part of the same ongoing and evolving relationship between the native past and the native present. The objects that people create today may not look exactly like those made in previous centuries, but they are still part of a long period of development that combines the strength of tradition with the resources and experiences of the present.[7]

Like the objects made in the late nineteenth century, contemporary artists may integrate new forms, new materials, and new technology. As in the past, these innovations keep the art alive. For example, John Francis, Passamaquoddy (Figure 8.7), burns designs into his clubs and walking sticks with a wood-burning tool and then colors in the outlines with felt-tipped markers. A human head, carved in high relief, usually dominates the head of John's clubs, and abstract designs, floral motifs, and scenes of Passamaquoddy life decorate the handles (Figure 8.8). Gladys Widdiss, Gay Head Wampanoag (Figure 8.9), combines tradition with innovation. Like her mother, Heath Hen, she hand-models jars, bowls, and canoes. She also experiments with the clay, varying the amount and patterning of colors, carving pot rims and shoulders (Figure 8.10), and inventing new forms such as necklaces and earrings. Until his recent death, Billy Altvater wove rugged, utilitarian backpacks and laundry, market, shopping, half-bushel, and bushel baskets similar to ones that have been created for hundreds of years. He also designed and built a new mold to increase production of his popular hiker's backpack and added manufactured nylon straps for carrying it (Figure 8.11). Leslie Ranco, Penobscot, is one of the few men who makes fancy baskets. He weaves basket types from previous eras and also creates new designs. After coloring his splints with fuscia and other brightly colored commercial dyes, he may twist them into ornamental ribbons on a jewelry box (Figure 8.12), weave them into a bold design on a barrel basket, or use them to create a new shape based on a form found in nature, such as a sea anemone basket.

Today, native artists sell their work in their own shops and homes, at powwows, and in non-native galleries and stores across America. Their art is purchased by museums, art collectors, native people, and tourists from many parts of the world. Utilitarian and fancy ash splint baskets, elaborately

Figure 8.7

John Francis, Passamaquoddy, with one of his walking
sticks, 1977.

carved and painted root clubs, and pottery from the multicolored cliffs of
Gay Head are all art forms from New England that demonstrate the ongoing connections between earlier cultural traditions and contemporary life.
Through their Indian work, artists augment their economic resources and
retain and affirm their native identity.

Figure 8.8

Root club, poplar, with man wearing feathered headdress, 1976. L: 23″ W: 7½″ (at head). Root club, poplar, with eagle and snake, 1985. L: 25″ W: 8″ (at head). Both by John Francis, Passamaquoddy.

Figure 8.9

Gladys Widdiss, Gay Head Wampanoag, wearing one of her own necklaces, 1977. L: 18″.

Figure 8.10

Pottery jars, hand-modeled, Gay Head clay, signed "Wild Cranberry." Gladys Widdiss, Gay Head Wampanoag, late twentieth century.

Figure 8.11

Backpack, ash splint, nylon straps. Billy Altvater, Passamaquoddy, 1977. L: 12″   W: 9″   H: 15″.

Figure 8.12

Jewelry Box, four-legged, braided sweet grass and ash splint, magenta splint ribbon weave. Leslie Ranco, Penobscot, 1983. L: 7″   W: 6″   H: 7″. Square handkerchief basket, braided sweet grass and ash splint. Josephine Bailey, Passamaquoddy, 1977. L: 4″   W: 2½″   D: 4″. Pocketbook, ash splint, braided sweet grass, braided paper cord. Passamaquoddy Basketry Co-op, 1977 L: 5″   W: 4″   H: 6″.

NOTES

All of the objects illustrated in this chapter are part of the Boston Children's Museum collection. They may be seen in the Northeast Native American Study-Storage area, by appointment or during posted open hours. Photographs by Rob Cooper, Cambridge, Massachusetts. Used by permission.

1. Tom McFeat (1987) uses the term *Indian work* for certain activities including basket making, guiding fishermen and hunters, and manufacturing snowshoes, paddles, and a variety of toy and miniature objects.

2. The photographs that follow present only a brief overview of native American art in New England. For a fuller, more detailed description of these and other art forms, see Lester (1987b).

3. For an in-depth, multivoiced description of woodsplint baskets, see Ann McMullen and Russell G. Handsman, *A Key into the Language of Woodsplint Baskets* (Washington, Conn.: American Indian Archaeological Institute, 1987).

4. At the turn of the century, Tomah Joseph, Passamaquoddy, changed the style of birchbark art by introducing figurative scenes into an abstract, floral tradition. For an in-depth description of his life and work, see Lester (1993).

5. Gabriel Tomah, Passamaquoddy, kept a journal describing events on the reservation, his travels, interactions with tourists, and the prices of work sold. In his journal, he used the term *war club* to describe a carved, wooden club.

6. Dr. Ruth Phillips is studying art for sale and the nature of native-tourist interactions. Consult her writings for further explanations of the cross-cultural exchanges and modifications that occur.

7. Rick Hill fully explains and expands upon these ideas in his catalog, *Creativity Is Our Tradition* (1992).

REFERENCES

Hill, Rick. 1992. *Creativity Is Our Tradition: Three Decades of Contemporary Indian Art at the Institute of American Indian Arts*. Santa Fe, N.M.

Lester, Joan. 1987a. "We Didn't Make Fancy Baskets Until We Were Discovered." In *A Key into the Language of Woodsplint Basketry*, edited by Ann McMullen and Russell G. Handsman, pp. 38–59. Washington, Conn.: American Indian Archaeological Institute.

———. 1987b. *We're Still Here: Art of Indian New England: The Children's Museum Collection*. Boston: Children's Museum.

———. 1993. *History on Birchbark: The Art of Tomah Joseph, Passamaquoddy*. Haffenreffer Museum of Anthropology, Brown University, Bristol, Rhode Island.

McFeat, Tom. 1987. "Space and Work in Maliseet Basket-Making," In *A Key into the Language of Woodsplint Baskets*, edited by Ann McMullen and Russell G. Handsman, pp. 61–73. Washington, Conn.: American Indian Archaeological Institute.

Phillips, Ruth B. 1991. "Glimpses of Eden: Iconographic Themes in Huron Pictorial Tourist Art." *Native American Studies* 5(2):19–28.

———. 1993. "Why Not Tourist Art? Significant Silences in Native American Museum Representations." In *After Colonialism: Imperialism and the Colonial Af-*

termath, edited by Gyran Prakash. Princeton, N.J.: Princeton University Press.

Walker, Willard. 1973. "Gabriel Tomah's Journal, a Report." Unpublished. Wesleyan University, Middletown, Conn.

9

The Use of Feathers in Native New England

Laurie Weinstein, Delinda Passas, and Anabela Marques

Our stereotypes indelibly link feathers to Indians. Ask anyone on the street what an Indian looks like, and he or she will invariably mention that the Indian wears a feather headdress (see also Nanepashemet 1990:1). It is imperative that we go beyond our simplistic stereotypes, however, and examine the important symbolism that feathers play in Indian identity. Indians throughout North America traditionally used feathers in headdresses, clothing, and jewelry and as embellishments on a variety of utilitarian items. Feathers are still an important symbol to native Americans.

This chapter examines past and present featherwork in native New England. We draw upon historical records of the sixteenth- and seventeenth-century explorers, traders, and colonists to document the use of feathers in New England. We then compare this historical featherwork with that of contemporary New England Indians. We discuss the kinds of feathers used in native manufactures and show how the choice of feathers reflects pervasive symbolic value systems. Traditional featherworking is still important to New England Indians who have incorporated this meaningful art into their everyday lives.

SIXTEENTH- AND SEVENTEENTH-CENTURY MATERIAL

The earliest mention of featherworking comes from Giovanni da Verrazano, who explored the coast of New England from the Carolinas to Nova

Scotia in the spring of 1524 (Howe 1941:19). Along the Carolina coast, Verrazano said that "some wear garlands similar to birds' feathers" (Winship 1905:5). More information is known about the seventeenth century when Indians were noted for using feathers in a variety of ways, including as hair knot ornaments and marks of status, for coats or mantles, and as fletching for arrows.

Indians used feathers in their hair knots, as almost all the seventeenth-century observers reported. Men gathered and tied their hair into a long, round knot at the back of the head, "like a horse's tail bound with a fillet." A twist of feathers of either eagle or turkey was then fastened in this knot (Willoughby 1935:248). Feather ornaments represented more than just decorative items, however, and may have also implied status. Wearing either a crown of feathers or the wearing of particular feathers seemed to indicate superiority. Johan de Laet, a Dutch West Indian Company representative, said that the Indians in Boothbay Harbor "shave their heads to the crown . . . but suffer the hair to grow on the back part, confining it in knots, interweaving feathers of various plumage" (Sewall 1859:39). Confirmation for this kind of hair style comes from *Mourt's Relation* (1622) about the Indians in the Plymouth area: "On their heads long hair to their shoulders, only cut before, some trussed up before with a feather, broadwise, like a fan, another a fox tail hanging out (Heath 1986:53)

Feathers could also signify status. Sagamores in northern New England were observed to wear a "kinde of Coronet . . . made very cunningly, of a substance like stiffe haire coloured red, broad, and more than a handfull in depth, [which was] some ensigne of . . . superioritie," observed George Weymouth, who went on a fur trading mission to Maine (Winship 1905:93–94). The more common people wore "white feathered skins of some fowle round about their head" (ibid.). Feathers from the "Tassell gent" (probably the marsh hawk; see Adams 1967:197) were saved for a "person of estimation among the Indians to weare in the knot of his lock, with traine upright, the body dried and stretched out" (ibid.).

Feather coats were also woven by New England Indians. According to Thomas Morton, a colorful seventeenth-century Puritan, Indians made "some Coates of the Feathers of turkies, which they weave together with twine of owne makinge, very prittily; these garments they weare like mantels knit over their shoulders and put under their arme" (Adams 1967:142). His observation was supported by others. This turkey mantle coat might have been made by elder men (Williams 1973:186) and worn principally by the children (Josselyn 1833:298).

A contemporary Wampanoag Indian, Nanepashemet (1990:4–5), summarizes these early references to feathered mantles in New England:

In the northeast, mantles seem to have been made primarily of the feathers of the wild bronze turkey. . . . The feathers used were not the long tail or wing feathers, but were from the necks, backs, and breasts of large fowl. If one examines these feathers of the wild turkey, one can easily see their beauty. One can also see how Native People could envision the appearance of their mantles by seeing how the feathers lay on the bird's skin, in overlapping rows of iridescent colors. It is possible that in ancient times whole bird skins may have been sewn into garments. The use of mallard and goose head skins, as cited above, may have been a survival of this technique.

Feathers were used for fletching on the arrow shafts, as indicated by most of these early explorers and colonists. George Weymouth discussed how Indians along the St. Georges River in early seventeenth-century Maine made arrows of "ash, big and long, with three feathers tied on, and nocked very artificiallie: headed with the long shanke bone of a Deere, made very sharpe with two fangs in manner of a harping iron" (Winship 1905:119). Martin Pring, an Englishman who traveled to the Massachusetts coast in 1603, thought that the natives used a "fine light wood" and attached "three long and deepe blacke feathers of some Eagle, Vulture or Kite" (Howe 1943:71).

Feathers had a number of other uses: as soft, warm bedding, according to Morton (Adams 1967:189); as whole feathered skin caps, according to Weymouth (Winship 1908:132); and as identity markers, according to Lechford (1867:116), that is, tribes could distinguish each other on the basis of how the feathers were worn.

That feathers were prized items can also be gleaned from the historical records. In at least two cases, colonists gave Indians exotic feathers (peacock? and ostrich) as desirable trade items (Weymouth quoted in Sewall 1859:62; Altham quoted in James 1963:29; Nanepashemet 1991b).

CONTEMPORARY FEATHERWORKING

It is easier to identify contemporary uses of feathers since you can use your own eyes to verify uses without relying upon ancient accounts. The problem for the contemporary observer is to identify the hundreds of ways in which feathers or feather motifs are now used. A partial list of contemporary uses includes the incorporation of feathers in shields, silver pendants, earrings, and other kinds of jewelry, hairties, fans, headdresses, jackets, pipes, rattles, bonnets, bolo ties, letter openers, walking sticks, birchbark baskets, roaches (hair ornaments), crowns, caps, arrows, t-shirts, and sweatshirts. Indeed, feathers by themselves ornament offices and cars as well.

Some of the most exquisite examples of this contemporary feather artwork come from the Northeast Native American Study-Storage at the Boston Children's Museum and the Wampanoag Indian Program at Plimoth Plantation. Readers will appreciate the beauty of the following items from

Bolo tie by Len Bayrd (Eagle Claw), Narragansett, Boston Children's Museum. Beaded bolo on a leather strip; red and black crow beads, and cream colored pipe bones ornament both ends of the leather strip. Beaded piece that slides up and down the leather strip depicts an Indian wearing a full feather headdress. (Photo: Laurie Weinstein)

Feather hairtie by Nogeeshi K. Aquash, Red Lake Chippewa, Boston Children's Museum. Hairtie with two main feathers, feather shafts wrapped with deerhide; red feather fluffs decorate the two main feathers; an abalone button placed centrally over tips of feathers as decoration. (Photo: Laurie Weinstein)

Birchbark box (with etchings of Indians wearing feathers) by Tomah Joseph, Passamaquoddy, 1902, Boston Children's Museum. Oblong birchbark box with drawings
of Native Americans engaged in scenes of daily life.

Paula Jennings from the Boston Children's Museum indicated that the figures on
the box tell a story of Passamaquoddy Indians going moose hunting; the side depicts how the Indians ran down the moose in the water, and the top view shows
them bringing the moose back to camp. (Photo: Laurie Weinstein)

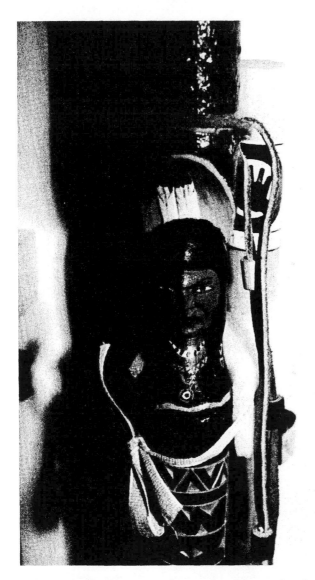

Walking stick (with carved figure of Indian wearing feather head-dress) by Senabeh Francis, Penobscot, Boston Children's Museum. Elaborately carved and painted walking stick with carved Indian face in high relief. (Photo: Laurie Weinstein)

Silver necklace (with feather ornaments) by Tony Chin, Narragansett
and Blackfoot, Boston Children's Museum. The silver necklace is a silver shield with a large turquoise stone and two silver feather motif ornaments. (Photo: Laurie Weinstein)

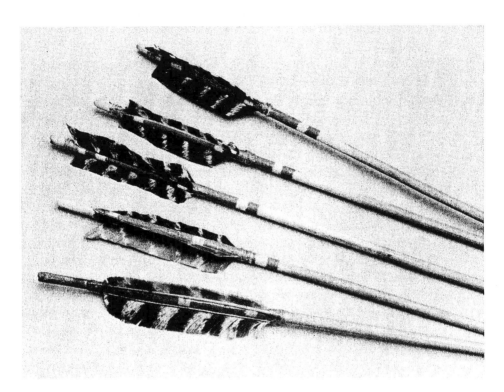

Arrows by Brian Bartibogue, Micmac; quiver by Nanepashemet, Wampanoag, Wampanoag Indian Program at Plimoth Plantation (hereafter cited as Plimoth Plantation). Split turkey feather fletching with otter skin quiver. (Photo: Ted Curtin. Used by permission of Plimoth Plantation.)

Feather crown by Nanepashemet, Wampanoag, Plimoth Plantation. Deer headband with turkey feathers. (Photo: Ted Curtin. Used by permission of Plimoth Plantation.)

Roach (head piece) purchased by Plimoth Plantation; spreader (the deer bone hair holder on top of the roach) by Nanepashemet, Wampanoag, Plimoth Plantation. Porcupine and deer hair, brass, leather, deer bone, and turkey feather. (Photo: Ted Curtin. Used by permission of Plimoth Plantation.)

Hairtie by Darrel Dunn, Wampanoag, Plimoth Plantation. Hair ornament of turkey and partridge feathers with leather tie on. (Photo: Ted Curtin. Used by permission of Plimoth Plantation.)

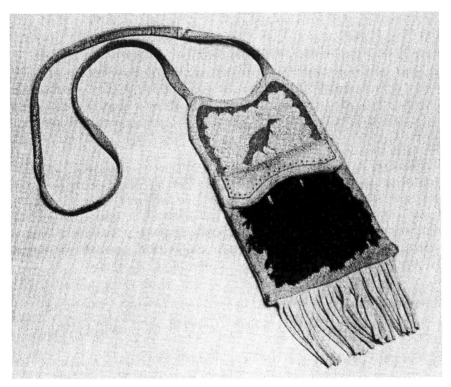

Deerskin pouch by Debra Pollard (non-Indian) and Nanepashemet, Wampanoag, Plimoth Plantation. Pouch of deerskin with a mallard duck head skin sewn on front. Painted turkey design. (Photo: Ted Curtin. Used by permission of Plimoth Plantation.)

these two museums. The photographs are accompanied by descriptions of the artwork that were researched by the two museums.

COMPARISON OF CONTEMPORARY AND HISTORIC FEATHERWORKING

How does contemporary featherworking differ from that of the seventeenth-century artistry? First, many more kinds of feathers are worn now. Besides the traditional eagle, hawk, turkey, partridge, and geese feathers are feathers from cardinals, hackles (roosters), ostrich, peacock, and "anything really" (Nanepashemet 1991a). Second, Indians use feather motifs in the various artforms. Such motifs are made out of silver, beads, wood, and fabric.

Third, some previously used feathers are almost impossible to obtain. Eagles are now an endangered species; consequently, Indians must obtain Department of the Interior federal fish and wildlife permits to allow them to "receive and possess" eagle feathers and other parts of the bird "for ceremonial purposes." Indians also improvise by dying turkey feathers to look like eagle feathers.

A fourth way in which featherworking has changed is that it has greatly expanded, as indicated by a comparison of historic and contemporary uses. Native New Englanders still make the traditional crowns of feathers and put feathers in their hair; however, now they also carve feathers on a variety of items from walking sticks to birchbark boxes to painted pictures on t-shirts.

In spite of these changes, feathers have continued to represent Indianness and have been an important part of Indians' symbolic systems.

SYMBOLISM

Feathers represent just one of the many "gifts" from animals to humans:

Animals gifted them [Micmac] with more than meat. Fur and hides were used for clothing, animal sinew for sewing, and animal bones for awls and painting tools. The people incorporated into their costume animal hair, feathers, shells, and bone, teeth, claws, dew-claws, quills, beaks, tail, horns—even the entire skins of stuffed bodies of small animals. (Whitehead 1987:24–25).

In order to understand this gift, we must also understand that everything in the universe has a power that is both particulate and conscious (Whitehead 1988:4). According to Ruth Whitehead, curator of the Nova Scotia Museum, all living things in the Micmac world contain this power until they die; then another animate being emerges (Whitehead 1991). The old power is not lost; it is merely transformed (Whitehead 1991): "A tree is spoken of as animate until it dies, yet its dead wood, shaped into something, lives again. Suffused in the Power of the shaper, and the Power of the function it will assume, it once more takes the animate case ending" (Whitehead 1988:11).

A slightly different interpretation of this power comes from Nanepashemet, a Wampanoag. He says that when an animate thing dies, its power merely lies "dormant" until someone else uses it again (1991a).

Power can be collective too, as when a variety of materials are used to make an object. Ruth Whitehead (1988:11) offers this insight: "What happens is that the . . . formerly parts of living things, combine their disjointed inanimacies into a new being—a hair ornament. . . . They are manifestations of Power which can wake to consciousness. And yet they are formed—recreated from dead matter."

By analogy, then, feathers are powerful objects. When the bird dies, it loses its power until the feathers, or skins, or both, are reused in some way. Once reused, the formerly inanimate or dormant materials become animated with power again.

Just what kind of power does a feather possess? Many of the historical references to New England featherwork concern turkey feathers. The turkey was a prized bird because it had the powers of quickness and cleverness (Richmond 1990). The seventeenth-century Dutchman Isaack de Rasiere certainly understood these attributes of the wild New England turkey: "There are also very large turkeys living wild; they have very long legs, and can run extraordinarily fast, so that we generally take savages with us when we go to hunt them; for even when one has deprived them of the power of flying, they yet run so fast that we cannot catch them unless their legs are hit also" (James 1963:79–80). By putting turkey feathers in a hair knot or coat, the individual is incorporating the turkey's keen abilities.

The turkey mantle of southern New England may serve as a protective item from malevolent spirits in much the same way that clothing protects Indians of northern New England:

By this same law (possession of part confers Power over the whole and Power of the whole), clothing is a protective mechanism, one which was used by the Micmac throughout their early history. . . . For clothing, adornment and even tattooing or body painting is armour: the cumulative Power fields of all the materials and symbols used . . . are Power locked into dress. (Whitehead 1988:13)

The eagle is considered to be the most powerful, and certainly the strongest, of all birds; it flies the highest and closest to the sun (Richmond 1990). When an individual wears an eagle feather, he or she is incorporating that strength, power, and ability.

Feathers have an important symbolic ceremonial use. Both the very movement of powerful items, as well as the noise created by this movement, are significant to Indians. One of the best examples of feathers' ceremonial use comes from contemporary powwows, a twentieth-century phenomenon that owes its popularity to the pan-Indianism that swept across North America during the early part of this century. Powwows are celebrations of dancing, singing, drumming, and feasting to which the public is invited. Indians dance in a ceremonial circle while wearing their fancy dresses. The woshing of the feathers during the dances creates a pleasing noise, which heightens the feathers' powerful effects (Lamb Richmond 1990; see also Whitehead 1987:25, 1988).

New England powwows reflect a mix of both northern (North and central Plains) and southern (South and central Plains) influences in terms of dress and dance styles. New Englanders also have a style that is distinctly their own. This "eastern style" might include eastern buckskin leggings, finger woven sashes, shellwork (particularly quahog), moccasins, and beaded motifs (Nanepashemet 1991b). Eastern male traditional dancers wear eagle, hawk, and turkey feathers in their hair, using hairties, roaches, bonnets, or plains' style headdresses (Nanepashemet 1991a). Female traditional dancers might also wear feathers—a barrette of eagle feathers in their hair perhaps (Nanepashemet 1991a).

If anyone should drop an eagle feather in the course of the dance, everyone stops the performance. A prayer is then said, and the individual who dropped it is admonished by an elder (Nanepashemet 1991a). Nanepashemet (1991a) told us of an occasion when an individual kept dropping his eagle feather; an elder took it away until he could handle it with proper respect.

We cannot finish our discussion of feathers and ceremonial use without making reference to the feather dance, occasionally practiced in southern New England. Competition is the object of this nonsacred dance: dancers attempt to pick up a feather stuck in the ground by bending low and using nothing more than their teeth to pluck it out (Nanepashemet 1991a, 1991b).

CONCLUSIONS

Non-Indians stereotypically view feathers as representative of Indians. Indians themselves, however, see feathers as an important part of their shared identity. Moreover, feathers play an important part of the larger natural symbolic system. The feathers link the wearer with the wider world of power relations.

NOTES

We are indebted to many individuals and institutions. We first thank the anonymous donor for the faculty-student collaborative grant from Western Connecticut State University that made our research possible. Special thanks also go to both Trudie Lamb Richmond (Institute for American Indian Studies) and Ruth Whitehead (Nova Scotia Museum) for their help. We are extremely grateful to

Nanepashemet and Linda Jeffers Combs (Plimoth Plantation) and Joan Lester and Paula Jennings (The Boston Children's Museum) for allowing us to use their materials and giving us important insights on this project. Finally, we thank Marianne Stoller (Colorado College) for suggesting that we research this topic on featherworking.

REFERENCES

Adams, C. F. Jr., ed. 1967. *The New English Canaan of Thomas Morton.* New York: Burt Franklin.

Forbes, Allen. 1941. *Other Indian Events of New England.* Boston: State Street Trust Company.

Heath, D., ed. 1986. *Mourt's Relation: A Journal of the Pilgrims at Plimoth.* Cambridge/Boston: Applewood Books.

Howe, Henry F. 1941. "The Sources of New England Indian History Prior to 1620." *Bulletin of Massachusetts Archeological Society* 3, no. 2:19–24.

———. 1943. *Prologue to New England.* New York: Farrar & Rinehart.

James, S. V. Jr., ed. 1963. *Three Visitors to Early Plymouth.* Introduction by Samuel Eliot Morison. Plymouth, Mass.: Plimoth Plantation.

Josselyn, John. 1833. "An Account of Two Voyages to New England." *Massachusetts Historical Society Collections,* ser. III, vol. III.

Lechford, Thomas. 1867. *Plain Dealing or News from New England.* Boston: J. K. Wiggin and William Parson Lunt.

Marten, Catherine. 1970. "The Wampanoags in the 17th Century." *Occasional Papers in Old Colony Studies* 2:3–40.

Nanepashemet. 1990. "Native Featherwork." Unpublished report for the Wampanoag Training Program, Plimoth Plantation.

———. 1991a. Personal communication.

———. 1991b. Letter, January 25.

Richmond, Trudie Lamb. 1990. Personal communication.

Sewall, Rufus King. 1859. *Ancient Dominions of Maine.* Bath: Elisha Clark and Company.

Williams, Roger. 1973. *A Key into the Language of America.* Detroit: Wayne State University Press.

Whitehead, Ruth Holmes. 1987. "I Have Lived There since the World Began: Atlantic Coast Artistic Traditions." In *The Spirit Sings,* 19–49. Toronto: McClelland and Stewart.

———. 1988. *Stories from the Six Worlds: Micmac Legends.* Canada: Nimbus Publishing Ltd.

———. 1991. Letter, April 24.

———. In press. "Everything They Make and Wear." In *12000 Years of Maine Native History,* edited by Bruce Bourque.

Willoughby, Charles C. 1905. "Dress and Ornaments of the New England Indians." *American Anthropologist* 7:499–505.

———. 1935. *Antiquities of the New England Indians.* Cambridge: Peabody Museum of American Archaeology and Ethnology, Harvard University.

Winship, G. P., ed. 1905. *Sailors' Narratives of Voyages along the New England Coast, 1524–1624.* New York: Burt Franklin.

Appendix: Regional Resources

NATIVE PEOPLE

Connecticut

Golden Hill Paugussett
95 Stanavage Rd.
Trumbull, CT 06415
(203) 537-0390

Mashantucket Pequot Tribal Council
P.O. Box 160
Ledyard, CT 06339
(203) 536-2681; fax 572-0421

Mohegan Tribe
1814 Norwich–New London Turnpike
Uncasville, CT 06832

Paucatuck Eastern Pequot
North Stonington, CT 06359

Schaghticoke Indian Reservation
Schaghticoke Rd.
Kent, CT 06757

Maine

Aroostook Band of Micmac Indians
P.O. Box 772
Presque Island, ME 04769
(207) 764-1972

Houlton Band of Maliseet Indians
Route 3, Box 450
Houlton, ME 04730
(207) 532-4273

Indian Township Passamaquoddy
    Tribal Council
P.O. Box 301
Princeton, ME 04668
(207) 796-2301; fax 796-5256

Penobscot Tribal Council
Community Bldg., Indian Island
6 River Rd.
Old Town, ME 04468
(207) 827-7776; fax 827-6042

Pleasant Point Passamaquoddy Tribal
Council
P.O. Box 343
Perry, ME 04667
(207) 853-2551; fax 853-6039

Massachusetts

Mashpee Wampanoag Tribal Council
P.O. Box 1048
Great Neck Rd.
Mashpee, MA 02649
(508) 477-0208

Wampanoag Tribal Council of Gay
Head
State Rd.
RFD Box 137
Gay Head, MA 02535
(508) 645-9265; fax 645-3790

New Jersey

American Indian Council of New Jersey
P.O. Box 553
18A East Commerce Street
Bridgeton, NJ 08302
(609) 455-6910

Rhode Island

Narragansett Indian Tribal Council
P.O. Box 268
Charleston, RI 02813
(401) 364-1100 Fax 364-1104

STATE AND REGIONAL ORGANIZATIONS, MUSEUMS, AND PARKS

Connecticut

Connecticut Historical Society Museum
1 Elizabeth St. at Asylum Ave.
Hartford, CT 06105
(203) 236-5621

Connecticut Indian Affairs Council
Department of Environmental Protection
165 Capitol Ave., Room 240
Hartford, CT 06106

Historical Museum of the Gunn Memo-
rial Library
Wykeham Rd. at the Green
Washington, CT 06793

The Institute for American Indian
Studies
38 Curtis Rd.
P.O. Box 1260
Washington, CT 06793-0260
(203) 868-0518

Museum of Connecticut History
Connecticut State Library
231 Capitol Ave.
Hartford, CT 06115

Tantaquidgeon Indian Museum
Route 32, Norwich–New London
Turnpike
Uncasville, CT 06382
(203) 848-9145

Maine

Central Maine Indian Association
P.O. Box 2280
Bangor, ME 04401
(207) 942-2926

Maine Indian Affairs Commission
State Health Station No. 38
Augusta, ME 04333

Massachusetts

Boston Indian Council, Inc
105 South Huntington
Jamaica Plain, MA 02130
(617) 232-0343

Children's Museum
Museum Wharf, 300 Congress St.
Boston, MA 02210
(617) 426-6500

Indian Meeting House
Rt. 28
Mashpee, MA 06249
(508) 428-6133

Mashpee Wampanoag Indian Museum
Rt. 130
Mashpee, MA
(508) 477-1536

Massachusetts Commission on Indian
  Affairs
One Ashburton Place, Room 1004
Boston, MA 02108
(617) 727-6394/6966

Peabody Museum of Archaeology and
  Ethnology
Harvard University
11 Divinity Ave.
Cambridge, MA 02138
(617) 495-2248

Plimoth Plantation
Wampanoag Indian Program
Plymouth, MA 02362
P.O. Box 1620
(617) 746-1622

Robert S. Peabody Foundation for Archaeology
Phillips Academy
Andover, MA 01810
(508) 475-0248

Rhode Island

Haffenreffer Museum of Anthropology
Brown University, Mt. Hope Grant
Bristol, RI 02809
(401) 253-8388

Museum of Primitive Art and Culture
Peace Dale, RI
(401) 783-5711

Rhode Island Historical Society
  Museum
52 Power St.
Providence, RI 02906
(401) 331-8575

Rhode Island Indian Council
444 Friendship St.
Providence, RI 02907
(401) 331-4440

Museum of Natural History
Roger Williams Park
Providence, RI 02906
(401) 785 9450 Ext. 225

Tomaquag Indian Memorial Museum
Arcadia Village
Summit Rd.
Exeter, RI 02822
(401) 539-7213

Index

About the Editor and Contributors

LAURIE WEINSTEIN is Assistant Professor of Social Science at Western Connecticut State University. She is author of numerous articles and one book (*The Wampanoag*, 1989) on the southern New England Indians. She is currently launching WCSU's first summer archaeology field school and research center.

KENNETH L. FEDER is Professor of Anthropology at Central Connecticut State University. He is the Founder and Director of the Farmington Valley Archaeological Project. Dr. Feder has published numerous books, including *A Village of Outcasts: Historical Archaeology and Documentary Research at the Lighthouse Site* (1994); *Frauds, Myths, and Mysteries: Science and Pseudoscience in Archaeology* (1990); and *Human Antiquity: An Introduction to Physical Anthropology and Archaeology* (1989) (with Michael Park).

BARRIE KAVASCH is an author, illustrator, and ethnobotanist who contributes her expertise to the Institute for American Indian Studies and the Institute for Ecosystem Studies. She is the author of *Native Harvests: Recipes and Botanicals of the American Indians* (1979). She is of mixed Cherokee, Creek, Powhatan, and European descent. She has traveled extensively and has studied with many natives whose works and contributions she honors.

JOAN LESTER is Native American Curator at the Boston Children's Museum. She is also Adjunct Lecturer in Native American Studies in the American Studies Program at Tufts University. She recently completed a National Endowment for the Humanities exhibit on Tomah Joseph. She is devoted to making clear the connections between past and present lives and art, the vitality of native culture, and artistic expression today, as is evident in her book, *We're Still Here: Art of Indian New England* (1987).

KEVIN A. MCBRIDE is Associate Professor of Anthropology at the University of Connecticut. He is also the Director of the Mashantucket Pequot Ethnohistory Project. Dr. McBride has authored numerous publications on the archaeology of southern New England Indians, including "The Historical Archaeology of the Mashantucket Pequot" (in *The Pequots: The Fall and Rise of an American Indian Nation*, 1990), and "Ancient and Crazie: Pequot Lifeways during the Historic Period" (*Dublin Seminar for New England FolkLife Annual Proceedings* 1991)

ANN MCMULLEN is Curator of North American Ethnology at the Milwaukee Public Museum and a doctoral candidate in the Department of Anthropology, Brown University. Formerly Curator of the American Indian Archaeological Institute, she has guest-curated a number of exhibitions for New England museums, including "Entering the Circle: Native Traditions in Southeastern New England" (1992) at the Haffenreffer Museum of Anthropology, Brown University. She is the author of numerous articles on woodsplint basketery of the Native Northeast, and co-editor (with Russell G. Handsman) of *A Key into the Language of Woodsplint Baskets* (1987).

ANABELA MARQUES is a graduate of the Department of Social Sciences at Western Connecticut State University. She is currently studying in Paris for her Master's in Business Administration through the University of Hartford extension program.

DELINDA PASSAS is a graduate of the Department of Social Sciences at Western Connecticut State University, where she received the Anthropology award for her scholastic achievement. She is planning a career in law.

RUSSELL PETERS is the President of the Mashpee Tribal Council. He is the author of *Clambake: A Wampanoag Tradition* (1992) and *The Wampanoag of Mashpee* (1987).

TRUDIE LAMB RICHMOND is a Schaghticoke Tribal Elder and Storyteller. She is also Assistant Director for Public Programs at the Institute for American Indian Studies. She has published numerous articles on the Schaghticoke in *Artifacts* (a publication of the IAIS), *Rooted Like the Ash Tree: New England Indians and the Land* (1987), and *A Key into the Language of Woodsplint Basketry* (1987). She lectures throughout New England, and she is widely respected for her native insights.

PAUL A. ROBINSON is the State Archaeologist at the Rhode Island His-torical Preservation Commission. Since becoming State Archaeologist in 1982, he has worked to promote a collaborative relationship between Rhode Island archaeologists and the Narragansett Indian tribe.